The
'6Os Report

BOOKS BY TOBY THOMPSON

Positively Main Street—An Unorthodox View of Bob Dylan
Saloon
The '60s Report

The '60s Report

Toby Thompson

RAWSON, WADE PUBLISHERS, INC.   New York

Library of Congress Cataloging in Publication Data
Thompson, Toby.
  The '60s report.
    1. United States—Popular culture. 2. United
States—Civilization—1945-   I. Title.
E169.12.T53 1979   973.92   78-64810
ISBN 0-89256-072-X
ISBN 0-89256-112-2 pbk.

Published simultaneously in Canada by McClelland and Stewart, Ltd.
Manufactured in the United States of America
Designed by A. Christopher Simon
First Edition

Contents

Preface   *vii*

Introduction: Elvis to Dylan to Root Boy Slim   *3*

Sex: Patricia Alston to Kathy MacDonald to Jane Ed-
monds to Michael Lally   *16*

Speed: Dennis Durbin to Michael Collins   *68*

Sport: Joe Don Looney   *101*

War: Henry Di Giacinto   *133*

Dissent: Corinne Collins to Kevin Walsh to Thiên-Kim
to Sandy Rock   *157*

Art: Thomas McGuane to Jimmy Buffett to Hunter S.
Thompson   *196*

Futures: Ed Guinan to Matt Koehl to Sam Love   *257*

Preface

That a book completed during the centenary of Einstein's birth should find as its focus a preoccupation with energy is no doubt fitting. Born during World War II, we are a generation reared on apocalypse, weaned on geysers of energy released with the advent of an atomic age. Technology, corporations, Wall Street—each bridled postwar energy to its best use, an energy malevolent and benign. That energy trotted despair in tandem with hope. It altered the physiognomy of a culture, and we rode it instead of tricycles.

We might not remember Hiroshima, but we recall fallout shelters. Civil Defense. Air raid sirens. We hid beneath school desks, stored contingency rations. We set our dials on Conelrad. We lived in the backwash of nuclear holocaust without thinking such a condition absurd. We confronted annihilation the way other generations confronted the moon and stars.

A nightmare was eternity spent underground, in a concrete bunker, alone. Not so different from childhoods spent in the concrete blockhouses of suburbia. Also alone. Nestled a millimeter from that Conelrad pyramid on our radio dial was the galaxy of rock 'n' roll. Barbarism had long placated the children of Armageddon. We proved no exception. Alone, we found solace in radio waves, communion in primitive rhythms conveyed electronically. It seemed we'd never escape suburbia. But if so there was a world of hip waiting.

Hip was nonchalance in the face of disaster. It presumed an inner-city primitive (classically black) whose familiarity with the uncertain raised him as paradigm. His grace before the entropic sketched him as heroic. Suburbia knew this hipster through his art: rhythm and blues, jazz. He was not isolated. He called his neighbor "brother." We rarely knew our neighbor's name. He was sexual, lithe, a verbal acrobat. We sat bludgeoned by TV. The street-corner hipster embodied life apart from suburbia and the attrition of bomb-shelter purgatories. That view was romantic and racist, but it was what we held.

Hip, as ethos, was the first ionization of rebellion for the white middle class. We learned it most forcefully through rock 'n' roll, but insistently through horse opera TV, cowboy and war films. Outlaw savants and war heroes stood stoically in the face of danger as did street-corner hipsters. Their music was hip language, a defiant reserve.

Music would bind us together—through record hops, rock concerts, rock extravaganzas—but not without a battle. Community, or communism, was an idea our parents disparaged. Their ethic was self-aggrandizement to the detriment of blacks, orientals, other "primitives." Their tool was the pesticide of technology. They had fought Japan, would fight Korea. They would ship us to Vietnam. They resisted a future of community, having been raised on individuality: that nineteenth-century mandate of expansionism. Our parents were racist. So were we. They were isolationist, culturally, but the culture was splitting apart. Blacks moved north, crowded the cities; one could not escape black influence. Blacks shared in community, if a community of oppression. Communism fostered complacency, our parents felt. Men should suffer alone.

Suburbia was their escape from inner city. A separation from blacks. Technology made that division easier, for servants could be dismissed. We grew up knowing no one but peers. Vietnam aligned us with blacks after years of encountering them only through music. Our parents may have orchestrated Vietnam, but we played it, taking a curious dividend from that horror. We shook hands with black language, marijuana, G.I. hip. We swung through the jungle. Vietnam assuaged some instinct for the primitive, set at arm's length by the technology of suburbia. The war to erase communism created a fresh sense of community. We had faced absurdity together. We stepped back. If Vietnam represented the furthest reach of nineteenth-century expansionism, a retreat to the twentieth had been instigated.

That retreat carried us home through an underworld of psychic archetypes. Most notably, cowboy and redneck "chic": a sense of Western and rural utopias, engendered by film and folk music. If Vietnam was the apogee of that search for the East inaugurated by Columbus, we found ourselves winding home through the Wild West and small-town America, to a reassessment of neighborhood. And the inner-city hipster who'd godfathered our solidarity.

Hip lent us purpose, but by its nature decried community. It was the ethos of a loner. A tension between community and individuality, in hip, was old as the division between beatnik and hipster, hippie and punk. The primogeniture of hip demanded solitude, but that solitude bred consanguinity. An irony deserving of hip.

These pages celebrate those who followed that essential paradox. From hundreds tapped these nineteen were culled: a rock star, a prostitute, a Playmate, a computer person, a radical priest, a poet, a drag racer, an astronaut, a punk rocker, a pro footballer, a Green Beret, a female Vietnam vet, a Saigon bar girl, a rural physician, a Gonzo journalist, a street sleeper, a film maker/novelist, a futurist, an American Nazi, each with something to tell of where we've been. How these people belayed sixties energy and yoked it to their ends is the stuff of this book.

Toby Thompson

Cabin John, 1977

The
'60s Report

Introduction

The day after Elvis Presley's death, I met Root Boy Slim for beers at a little redneck bar in Glen Echo, Maryland. I arrived five minutes late, wearing a twenty-year-old I LIKE ELVIS button and toting a calfskin attaché case. Root Boy was nursing a Pabst. He was seated in a far booth directly under the television set and affected that freshly showered glow of "just up" which wears so poorly on the truly dissipated. He also looked frightened; not at the metaphysical implications of Presley's death, it appeared, but at the bedrock of his surroundings.

Trav's Inn—yet another victim of Redneck Chic and that excess of brother Billyisms so thoroughly publicized during the Carter campaign—had, in recent years, acquired a patina of suburban hip. Yes, at certain hours, Trav's was all khakis and leather Topsiders. But at two o'clock on a Wednesday afternoon, one barmaid, Root Boy Slim and a couple of short-haul truckers from Cabin John were Trav's only occupants.

"Caught you on TV," a trucker said as I placed my order. "Last night, from the Red Fox." Then he laughed.

I shrugged, embarrassed. I had indeed been on TV the previous evening, cornered by an ABC team and probed as a "typical Elvis fan" for my reaction to Presley's death. The interview was phony, but had been set up at a bluegrass bar in Bethesda to look spontaneous. I'd spoken from a welter of shock and had rambled on, spouting inanities about Presley's contribution some five minutes. The quote ABC had clipped to lead its report was: "I'm depressed. Possibly more depressed than at the death of President Kennedy." Which was true.

"Checked this morning's listings," my trucker friend said, twisting the barb. "Ain't got you scheduled for tonight."

I mumbled something and shuffled back toward where Root Boy was caressing his fear.

The man was a star. A new wave, the toast of the town. By August of 1977, Root Boy Slim and the Sex Change Band (featuring the Rootettes) was the hottest cabaret act in Washington. I'd first experienced Root Boy one sweltering July evening at a club called the Childe Harold, just north of Dupont Circle. I'd thought to plunge into Childe Harold's air conditioning, step up to the bar and unwind to a bit of easy listening. Small chance. I did not know Root Boy was booked that night. Billows of steam presaged the inevitable. A crowd of several hundred spilled from Childe Harold's front room to the sidewalk, battered by the sounds of driven rock 'n' roll. I fought my way inside, to discover Root Boy slithering across the stage with his head in the bass drum, blowing harmonica and growling lyrics to a tune called "You Broke My Mood Ring."

> *When I first saw you tonight, could not believe my eyes*
> *Had my mood ring steamin' twice normal size*
> *Drank three tequilas just to calm me down*
> *Damn thing explode, spread my mood around.**

He was stripped to the waist and drenched in perspiration; there was nothing slim about Root Boy. He was tall, perhaps six-two, and weighed at least two hundred and thirty pounds. An enormous beer belly preceded him about the stage, shuddering and rippling as he minced through the abbreviated soul strut of James Brown. Eyebrows thick as tar, a Cro-Magnon forehead, Root Boy's face shone purple with exertion. He looked about ready to die. "You're sixteen, I'm thirty-two, I'm not too old for

---

* "Mood Ring," Greenlee-Mackenzie-Lancaster. Courtesy of Root Boy Music, Inc. (BMI).

you," he moaned, as two sleazo backup singers—the Rootettes—bumped their hips and whined, "He's not too old for you." Between numbers, the audience chanted "Root! Root! Root!" Root Boy sweated his way through "The Heartbreak of Psoriasis," "Bride of the Burro," "Jail in Jacksonville," "Too Sick to Reggae," and the penultimate "Boogie 'Til You Puke" (*form a big boss line, it's pukin' time*), before relinquishing stage-front to a pair of ladies from the audience who writhed bare-breasted to "Christmas at K-Mart." It was a class performance. I had not seen a crowd come alive with such enthusiasm since the turn of the decade. It seemed the seventies had finally arrived.

Two weeks later, Root Boy reappeared at Childe Harold for the Root Boy Slim All Nite Bathing Suit Party. He wore "swim goggles, blue trunks, a beach towel about his neck, plastic inner tube on his head, and played the bass with his teeth," the Washington *Post** reported. "They were turning people away at the door."

Root Boy's face, an amalgam of Lee Marvin's and Charles Bukowski's, if that can be envisioned, provided a key to his appeal. It was an alarming face. Captivating onstage, here at Trav's Inn it was supremely disquieting.

"Yeah, the fifties are dead," Root Boy said, eyeing my Elvis button cautiously. "I was more into Bo Diddley, but no question about it, Elvis was the king of rock 'n' roll."

To encounter Root Boy's speaking voice was an equally disturbing experience. It was deep, lugubrious, vaguely Southern: a Smokey Robinson falsetto, recorded at 45 and played back at 33⅓.

I could heartily attest to Root Boy's fascination with black music. Several nights previous, I had spent time at Root Boy's apartment, in the company of a local politician's son—Root Boy's manager and proprietor of an oldies' bin in Saverna Park—two questionable groupies, a brace of pharmacists from upstairs, and Root Boy himself. The pharmacists were possessed of extraordinary pharmaceuticals. Over the evening's course, Root Boy, these two pharmacists, two groupies, the politician's

* Stephanie Mansfield.

son and I smoked or snorted our way through a multiformity of chemicals, swilling beer, perspiring in the hundred-degree heat, and staggering beneath a panoply of recorded sounds which ran the gamut from Bill Doggett, Chuck Berry, Howlin' Wolf, Reverend Gary Davis, the Meters and assorted African chants, to Muddy Waters' band. Root Boy's lone concessions to white culture were the selected *Recollections of Edward R. Murrow* and a *Bozo Under the Sea* album.

"Forbidden to play *Bozo* unless we break out that laughing gas," Root Boy had chortled.

Root Boy, of course, was white.

Born Foster MacKenzie III—elder son of a golf course architect—Root Boy had attended private schools, played football at Yale and taken his B.A. in American Studies ("the Cadillac of majors") before descending into psychedelics, a life of blunted psychosis and exacerbating psychiatric lockups. While at Yale, he had fronted a band known as Prince La La, Percy Uptight and the Midnight Creepers, "featuring Baby Dynamite and Count Body," a mock soul review which included Yale's football captain on bass, Bob Greenlee of the Greenlee tool fortune, still with Root Boy—"my musical director for over thirteen years; an All American who used to do acid before the games"—plus several other wastrels from the jock fraternity.

"We had James Brown's show down to the last drop of sweat," Root Boy bragged. "I wore a leopard-skin cape, leopard-skin gold-lamé tuxedo, and the processed hair which I wrapped in a rag and used about half a can of hair spray on to keep up, a lot of Brylcreem to grease it down . . . and little Italian shoes with quarter-inch soles so I could slide across the floor like James."

Root Boy's major within American Studies was black history. From his fantasies to what passed for real life, Root Boy had immersed himself in black culture. For all intents and purposes, Root Boy *was* black.

Except, like me, his roots were the whitest of vanilla white. Raised in Spring Valley—Washington's most exclusive white neighborhood—Root Boy had cultivated an interest in black music first through AM radio and available soul stations, later through adventurous trips to the old Howard Theater in the heart of black Washington . . . for classic Lloyd Price, Otis Redding, Wilson Pickett reviews, ripples of fast talk, an emcee with that hip walk, sharkskin suits, microphone which emerged proboscis-like from the stage floor; chorus girls, long-legged chocolates draped in satin loincloths, next to nothing, who ground through stupefying routines, eight or ten of them backing soul man number one: Wilson, Otis, James . . . James Brown! as he dropped to his knees and cried, "Baybee-ay!" Soul sisters fibrillating the breadth of the auditorium. By 1965 at Yale, Root Boy would consider rhythm and blues his roots, recalling summers spent in high school carrying bricks with blacks, "where I got my soul." During the '68 riots—black riots in furious response to Martin Luther King's assassination—Root Boy would freak, suffering a full fledged, lock-me-up, nervous breakdown.

"I should have been out stealing color TVs," Root Boy reflected. "Alongside my friends. I'd liked to have gone down and burned, but I didn't have the guts."

The contradiction sounds forced: a white man from polite circumstances, boozing like a wino, popping pills, eating Wyamine, dropping acid, living like a derelict in dilapidated urban housing; obsessed with black art, black talk, black music, black history, a black future . . . to the extent that he would invest a year at George Washington University studying urban planning that he might help rebuild the city; proselytizing loudly for Methadone clinics in Washington years before that treatment became available so that inner-city blacks might have an advantage. A contradiction—funny, absurd? A miscegenation of the spirit? But how different in its commitment from that of countless other sixties deviationists?

Used to be a radical,

Root Boy would sing.

Pissed on the Pentagon.
Didn't have no values,
*Didn't know what was goin' on.**

* "I Used to Be a Radical," Greenlee-Mackenzie-Lancaster. Courtesy of Root Boy Music, Inc. (BMI).

And the satire would ring false, bittersweet; like a crowbar skirling off a sidewalk.

My involvement with black culture was less direct. Like Root Boy and a majority of young Americans, my appreciation of black art derived principally from music. Country blues, rhythm and blues, and progressive jazz were the main conduits of black style for that white middle class which came to adolescence in the nineteen-fifties. Style was the bottom line, for few white "superkids" of those prosperous postwar years had the guts or inclination to brave inner-city reviews. Black music sifted across suburban airwaves, mostly rhythm and blues. Who could forget Fats Domino, Little Richard, or the Platters? Who would diminish their influence, wish to recall those years without fealty to "Blueberry Hill," "Lucille," or "The Great Pretender"? Who could remember a party which had not culminated in hot musky gropings to the strains of "Smoke Gets in Your Eyes" or "Sixteen Candles"? Black r&b musicians slashed more color, bright, primary colors, across fifties America than any cadre of white novelists, composers or abstract impressionists. For the white adolescent, already muddled by years of TV—alienated from literature, too lazy for jazz—rhythm and blues provided a sole introduction to hip. Hip *was* black style, a style bred in nihilism, born of rebellion and bathed in sex. Music was its medium. But until one man hit the scene in 1954 and cut a hillbilly version of a Big Boy Crudup blues, "That's All Right," total identification was privy to the few.

"A black sound inside a white body," was what Sam Phillips had been looking for that year he signed Elvis Presley to a contract at Sun Records. A Memphis trucker with sideburns, long hair, inordinately long for '54, and androgynous good looks, nineteen-year-old Elvis Presley was the missing link. By taking a raucous black sound, spitting it through a white voice, curing it, translating black expressiveness into white sex, humping it, grinding it, shaking his ass from backwater fairs to Main Street movie houses, Louisiana Hayrides to the Steve Allen Show, Ed Sullivan to Hollywood, Hollywood to Las Vegas . . . Elvis, within ten years of his first record would be the highest-paid performer in the world; within twenty would have starred in a satellite TV special watched by more people than had watched Neil Armstrong step across the moon.

Elvis's first nickname as a performer was "the Hillbilly Cat," and that pinpointed it. He was white, he was hip, he talked that talk, he walked that walk, he rode Harley-Davidsons, bought pink Cadillacs, dressed outrageously and drove audiences wild. He was everything a white adolescent with an ounce of spirit might wish to emulate. I recall crouching before my record player for hours in 1956—an entire summer, spinning "Hound Dog" and "Don't Be Cruel," hear one side then flip it over, reach for "Heartbreak Hotel"—studying obsessively that photo on "Hound Dog" 's dust cover: Elvis's pompadour, Elvis's hip grin, Elvis's white leather motorcycle jacket which sprang from the photo like a cougar. What was his secret? How best to imitate him? A fifteen-dollar guitar lurked around the bend. There were Mickey Mantles in my life, Marilyn Monroes; but I had not felt such total identification with a hero since my cowboy crush on Hopalong Cassidy.

The first conversation I overheard a friend's parents having about Elvis concerned a photo spread they'd seen in *Life* of the man with his shirt off. "Pimples down his back," they'd smirked. As if that was the flaw which could dissuade us. We weren't so removed from pimples ourselves. Our elders hated Elvis—not with the hatred they'd reserve, say, for George Lincoln Rockwell, but with a stultifying derision. A bemused tolerance. Elvis was less the palpable threat than an exercise in bad taste. Most parents had grown up with black music or its white variants: swing, boogie-woogie, New Orleans jazz. It wasn't the beat which bugged them. It was Elvis's low rent, rockabilly, white Southern, zoot-suited, blue-suede, Total Assault on propriety.

Suburban propriety. That same propriety which isolated itself from class incursion with a fifty-thousand-dollar mortgage; from miscegenation with proper schools and a segregated country club; from bigotry with a liberal's tolerance for blacks; from sex with clothes that fit like garbage sacks; and from illiteracy with books that would not print "shit." Suburban propriety, which isolated everyone—most especially children, who car-pooled from school to neighborhood to club to first date without ever transgressing ethnic boundaries or encountering a different class. Not only had most middle-class kids failed to experience black culture, or blacks, but few had been exposed to what later they'd embrace as Redneck Chic. Elvis Presley was the first man to fill that spotlight. He proved more powerful as a threat to suburban propriety than a thousand blacks, because he lobbied from a posture of class, not race. Low class. He represented everything in America most suburbanites had labored to erase from their backgrounds, no matter the generations removed; he would take your proper fork and stick it up your ass, then he would take your daughter. Not just into sex, that would be painful enough. But toward a refutation of all that was genteel.

Elvis brought us together. We had no idea we weren't alone until Elvis. Those odd stirrings even boys felt riveted there to the Victrola were magnified a thousandfold once the man was encountered live. We'd sensed a modicum of Elvis's strength home by the record bin, we knew he was cutting number-one discs, we'd heard our friends express a certain interest . . . but had no *idea* until we caught that first concert live: the screaming, the hysteria, the bludgeoned beat, Elvis twisting and thrusting like a Port Said floozy—male performers weren't sexual in the fifties, not that way—Elvis with his mojo out, sucking us closer, until the whole crowd was his, he ours, we . . . us! For the first time we had broken through suburban isolation and absorbed—the spirit. Jesus, here were five hundred kids in this dilapidated concert hall who felt *like me*. Five hundred maniacs hopping and jelly-bopping who felt *something* passionately enough to shed those staid rules of decorum for an oracle tough, crude, blatantly sexual, more than a touch effeminate, and so low rent he'd never have made it past the parents' front door. Gene Vincent, Carl Perkins, the Everlys, Buddy Holly, Eddy Cochran—they were cut from the same cloth, each following Elvis's lead toward hip with calculated determination. But Elvis remained king. He was shaman, witch doctor, psychic therapist, social prophet. If the subtlest hints of future dissent were dropped (slow dancing to "Don't," "Loving You," or "That's When Your Heartaches Begin") in those agonizing skirmishes with parents over who would control party lighting, the seeds of open revolt were sown in those first experiences of Elvis Presley live.

Elvis gave us back our bodies, no question: blue jeans, long hair, tight motorcycle jackets, fitted shirts. Men weren't supposed to radiate sex in the nineteen-fifties ... their demeanor reflected that fact: bloated figures, soft from excess, symmetrical as fire plugs and draped in monochromatic garb which censored every movement. Men weren't supposed to move; they'd spent long war years busting ass, cars were supposed to move. Cars provided the primary outlet for sexual expression during the fifties: horsepower, length, breadth, *size,* shazam, *style* with all those ... niggery extras like military spots, fender skirts, tailfins, chrome trim. Even in the most sedate suburban neighborhood these monsters would be lined up along the driveways, hubcapped libidos for the world to fondle, pastel boudoirs of the soul. Not for nothing would fifties adolescents prefer the quick hunch across a naugahyde back seat to any number of blanket bingos. Sex was inextricably tied to the automobile, and the automobile hid the body. One's car was one's second skin, cleated firmer to the psyche than any suit of clothing. Elvis helped us shed that neurosis, striding onstage before God and Ed Sullivan, openly, joyously shaking that thing until it dawned on us that, hot damn, we had one too.

If Elvis Presley liberated our bodies, he also lubricated our minds. He lent us an eye for color, an ear for music, and an openness to multifarious vistas of expression: in fashion, dance, sound, and social protest. It was not such a quantum leap from that first gut reaction to rock 'n' roll to a curiosity about Negro blues; from the blues to what blues were about—Negro problems and the people themselves. The prediction in Bob Dylan's high school yearbook read: "To join Little Richard," and that was not far off the mark. Bob Dylan, a middle-class Jew growing up in Hibbing, Minnesota, *believed* he was Little Richard. At least while pounding the piano in his high school band. He would keep late hours digging Gatemouth Page's r&b broadcasts to the north country from Little Rock, Arkansas, all those proscribed tunes—"Maybelline," "I'm Walkin'," "Lawdy, Miss Clawdy."

Rock 'n' roll remained Dylan's path of expression until he dug a little deeper; then from "John Henry" on a coffee house stage in Minneapolis, to "Medgar Evers" at a civil rights rally in Greenville, Mississippi was not such a fierce step.

Dylan, like the rest of the country, would circle back toward rock 'n' roll. By his fifth album, Dylan had shucked all the Peter, Paul and Maryisms, the Tom Paxton and Pete Seegerisms, for hard-driving rock. *Bringing It All Back Home* was a prophetic disc, not just for its embracement of electronic America, but for its exclusion of "folk"—that non-hip, grad school, Jewish activist, namby-pamby, "Barbary Allen" blow-by which had been threatening to strangle . . . the Movement. The Movement at this hour was more feeling than commitment. That feeling, Dylan sought to rescue; that crazed, early sixties, nightmarish fix of energy run amok, which had been infuriating so many, engulfing the few; the saved, the attuned, the ready, the hip. Hip was the commitment Dylan embraced, not as salvation, nor as panacea, nor prophylaxis. That would contradict the very notion of hip. Readiness was all, wariness the defense, cool that no man's land between vulnerability and strength. Dylan took his intellectual's predilection for polemics and flung it against hip; clothed it in black language, black rhythm, black innuendo, black beat. He understood what sixties politicos rarely could—that verbal grace was essential, physical grace important, that intellectualism could antagonize, that a movement was permanent as its art, and that this movement—The Sixties—held its roots firmly in Black, saw its flowering in rock 'n' roll. Half a generation fell into step.

And Dylan never forgot Elvis. In his 1969 *Rolling Stone* interview, Dylan stated for posterity: "Elvis Presley recorded a song of mine. That's the one recording I treasure most . . . it was called 'Tomorrow Is a Long Time' . . . He did it with just guitar."

How terrible to contemplate Presley dead at forty-two. Elvis obese, wasted from drugs, addicted to junk food, paranoid, reclusive, a virtual Howard Hughes in his reliance on functionaries, angry, vindictive—and most awful, contemptuous of fans, to a degree that he had not poured his soul into a recording since 1969's "Suspicious Minds" . . . its title prophetic of a burgeoning disaffection, its mood repetitive and implosive, circling *in* astride that awesome Presley energy instead of out, toward release. Chronically constipated since the turn of the decade, it was nearly fitting that Presley's heart had burst on the throne, in his bathroom, straining at stool.

"Where were *you* New Year's Eve, 1969?" I said, startling Root Boy Slim. He set down his Pabst.

"I was busting out of the puzzle house. I'd tried to hang myself but my belt'd snapped. It was one of those thin, cheap ones, you know—and anyhow, I was much too fat."

If Root Boy Slim foreboded the apocalypse of rock 'n' roll, as critics were asserting, what strange times lay ahead. Root Boy had yet to land his recording contract at Warner Brothers, but that deal was less than a month away. Root Boy had been subsisting off the family trust fund. That and what he earned three nights a week at local clubs. The past twenty years had broken strange for Root Boy Slim. Expelled from Sidwell Friends for "reaching puberty," he had endured five long years in the boarding department at St. James; had played football, basketball, track, and had earned high marks: "I cheated a bit, but they never knew." He'd graduated third in his class, with an early acceptance at Yale—having composed his writing sample on the decline of morality in America. He went out for freshman football at New Haven but quit after two weeks: "People *hurt* me there. I was too light for tackle. They wanted me to play end but I had hands like ping-pong paddles." What he wanted to do was shoot pool and get drunk. At DKE, he was elected social chairman. In 1964 he encountered LSD, spending weeks hallucinating in and out of paintings at the Yale art gallery. He became Prince La La, formed his first band. Graduating from Yale in 1967, he moved home to Washington, to 1741 F. Street, across from the Selective Service. There he lived with a mélange of freaks, dropping acid, smoking grass, snorting speed. Manic about a Methadone program for D.C. addicts, he attempted to join VISTA. He landed a job at the Washington architecture firm of Perkins and Will. "I was trying to stay straight, wearing a blue suit every morning, but I'd come home in the evening and do acid. It flipped me out." He'd been reviewing a hospital design manual, analyzing layouts of psychiatric units, when he was admitted to one. He'd eaten too much LSD, abhorred his life; was confused by Vietnam, having pleaded everything from heroin to lace panties to avoid induction; by SDSers he'd been hanging with, by radical blacks, by junkies who were his friends. The '68 riots tipped the balance. He was committed to George Washington University Medical Center for three months' observation, "their maximum stay." Released from G. W.'s psych ward, "still crazy as a loon," he bummed around with an SDS crowd, hippies, winos, before entering the University of Southern California's architecture school. In Los Angeles he fell in with the Nicherin Shoshu people, shakubukuing novices, chanting *nam-myoho-renge-kyo* until it pushed him over the psychic red-line. The night of 1969's Rolling Stones concert in Washington, he took a walk up Ninth Street with a Bible, chanting his way to the White House fence, where he was arrested shouting: "I want to die, I want to see Nixon. I'm looking for the center of the earth." After a breather at St. Elizabeth's Hospital, he flunked out of U.S.C., got into urban planning at George Washington. Took LSD the day before his graduate record exams, nailed down a 740 and a 710. He quit after a year, drove a cab. Vegetated around Takoma Park for a couple of seasons, courting Alcoholics Anonymous, munching tranquilizers, contemplating songs such as "Graveyard Losers," "Thorazine Queen," "Too Many Brain Cells Gone," and "My Love Is Real—Look at It Running Down Your Leg," which would lay the groundwork for his act with the Sex Change Band.

Root Boy the prepster, Root Boy the all-conference footballer, Root Boy the dabbler in Eastern thought, Root Boy the Negrophile, Root Boy the Al Jolson of American Studies, Root Boy the draft evader, Root Boy the speed freak, alcoholic, avatar and aggregate of the most privileged generation in the history of the world.

"I can't even go downtown any more," Root Boy was saying. "I'm afraid. Last time I saw James Brown, two niggers tried to rape my date and I caught a brick in the face protecting her."

Absorbing Root Boy Slim and Sex Change that first night at Childe Harold, I'd thought to categorize their sound. It was not

exactly punk rock, not exactly swamp rock, not
blues. The only tag I could come up with was glandu

"I'm ready to talk about the sixties," Root Boy said, fi
his Pabst. "We'll tape about half your book. But why not s
someplace where I can smoke this herb."

The khakis and leather Topsiders had failed to show. A hard-
core of olive drab and crepe-soled Red Wings held Trav's fort.
As we were leaving, a sheet metal worker I'd known since childhood staggered up—a fellow who'd regaled me with more hilari-
ous tales, engaged friends in more unspeakable pranks than any
man I knew. I had not seen him in years. He was drinking and
his hair had grayed. He wore a beard. He looked to be about
Elvis's age. He still carried himself with wit, élan, but one sensed
a gearing down.

I spotted a tattoo on his forearm I did not recognize.

"When'd you pick up that fresh one?" I asked. The tattoo was
of a mouse in a cocktail glass, the legend TRAV'S INN just
beneath.

"I got that one week before Trav flagged me," he said.
"Flagged me for *two years*. Ain't that some luck?"

I laughed, but the irony cut deep. It seemed the irony of an ultimate loss ... that tattoo a metaphor for an entire decade: A
pledging of allegiance fogged in alienation, the recitation of vows
in an empty church. It was worse than someone handing back
your I.D. bracelet. I collected Root Boy and let him pay our bill.
Fingering my Elvis button tentatively, I headed for the door beside the future of rock 'n' roll.

The summer of 1960 proved a watershed season. It was the summer I got my license to drive and it was the summer I finally got laid. I'd been driving for years, of course, borrowing family cars, friends', friends of friends' too wasted to navigate ... an extended spate of vehicular derring-do from which I feel lucky to have survived. I say "finally" about the sex with a blush, for I was fifteen when the deed was accomplished, but it had been a long time coming. It had seemed like forever. The sixties had found me a rather dissolute sophomore in prep school, guitarist for a rock group called the Corpse Combo, and a student of jazz. The winter of 1960 was a dark time, shaded by academic failure and sexual duress. I flunked two courses that winter, flogged my dummy until I thought I'd go blind, and retreated into the guitar. The guitar provided my surest release; I beat it vengefully from CYO teenhalls to Chevy Chase deb parties, playing for drinks and the odd twenty or thirty bucks. Winter equalled school and school was imprisonment. How I endured until summer I'll never know; but I'm glad I held out. It would be the summer which saved my life.

When I think of sixties beginnings, I envision that summer. It was the first of the decade, a season which defined my passions for the next fifteen years: sex, cars, music, beer. A prescription for freedom. Elvis had been discharged from the army, "It's Now or Never" his big hit, one which saturated the airwaves as thoroughly as french fries at a drive-in. Mountains of french fries were consumed that summer, a glacier of beer; countless hours were spent cruising the Hot Shoppes, drag racing in a '54 Olds ... and chasing women. Public school women I was just getting to know, after seven years in an all-boys' school. Seven years of forgetting what women even smelled like.

I had a friend in 1960, a bricklayer's son from Cabin John, who introduced me to a wealth of public school girls. That he was a bricklayer's son from Cabin John is hardly incidental. It underscores a dichotomy in my rearing. Having attended private schools since third grade, really the classiest private schools in Washington, I knew no one from my academic life who was not urban middle class at least. But I had grown up in a uniquely rural neighborhood—Cabin John, Maryland—barely five miles from the District line, where my good friends were blue-collar aristocrats: sons of printers, bus drivers, house painters, West Virginian emigrants or descendants of frontiersmen who had worked the Chesapeake and Ohio Canal. It was a schizophrenic upbringing for which I am grateful. On one hand, I was barraged by nervous rock, bluegrass, fast cars, an entire hot-rod milieu, gang fights, soda fountain Saturday nights, coon hunting, fishing from john boats poled by oldtimers who wove endless tales, transmitting a vanishing frontier heritage . . . . On the other, I was upbraided by an Episcopal boys' school regimen, coat and tie every morning and dancing class one night each weekend to blow off steam. Not hard to imagine which extreme I preferred.

The choice was actually less precise. I had always been susceptible to style. Not in a bogus fashion, but appreciatively, recognizing style as the cutting edge of a culture's self-esteem: the cowboy's Stetson, the musician's hip walk, the executive's briefcase. This sensitivity lent me cachet with a variety of groups; it meant I could travel as comfortably with my Cabin John neighbors as with my prep school peers, and it graced me with a certain individuality. I was a half-breed culturally. I could drift either way, never accepting an extreme in its totality.

My Cabin John friend worked part-time in a garage that winter, and one evening when I stopped by to see him, he asked if I'd like to meet his new girlfriend, at home with a cold. I said sure. A third friend drove us to the girl's house, where we sat watching television abstractly, until somebody suggested going for a six-pack. It was snowing hard and I had no desire to move; the girl couldn't leave, so my friend and our driver undertook this project with the fervor of expeditionists. They were gone quite a while. The first half hour this girl and I talked about school, music, books, all the time glued to the tube. Gradually our conversation shifted toward sex—she was scarcely fourteen, I fifteen—and before long she had enticed me into an embrace; we were kissing ardently, rather intricately as I recall, when she began pulling me down. I was terrified. She gripped me fiercely, digging her heels into the small of my back. It was an impossible situation. There in her parents' den, her father upstairs, my good pals returning any moment . . . there was opportunity for nothing. I was rescued by the doorbell, my Cabin John friends standing cold and markedly dour. Apparently they had witnessed much from a ground-level window. I did not realize this until weeks later; I was simply relieved at their interruption. Why they did not kick the shit out of me I'll never know. Possibly because I was such a faithful companion.

My friend's romance with this young lady blossomed despite my indiscretion. I let the affair alone, feeling remorse but not forgetting one minute what had been my most passionate entanglement to date. All that winter I would nurture the recollection, but I would stay aloof. I owed my friend that much. It was the summer of 1960 before I recanted, inaugurating a series of encounters which would stand as the most recklessly sensual of my adolescence.

Seventeen summers later I met the same girl for lunch at a seafood restaurant in Philadelphia. She drove up in a blue 1956 Corvette, greeting me with waves and a kiss on the cheek. She was elegantly dressed in a white blouse and black silk slacks. She looked quite the young executive. She was five months pregnant and did not look that. Her name was Patricia Alston now;* she had a good job at COMSAT. If anything, she was more attractive than I recalled. Her auburn hair framed her face prettily, she'd kept that same mischievous smile, and her figure was slim. She still moved like a cat, aggressive yet tentative, and that's what I remembered best.

We caught up over drinks. She'd been married six or seven years, separated a short time, and had weathered one serious affair. A fact which she confessed flirtatiously. It was startling how easily our conversation turned toward sex. Pat remained a desirable woman. At thirty-two, much of her youthful energy had survived, that nervous enthusiasm which, as an adolescent, had left her open to any new experience. We talked at length about marriage—Pat felt the institution fulfilled only certain of her needs: dependence, stability. She did not regard extramarital sex as reprehensible; in fact, she saw it as no more than the natural expression of friendship. In past years she had found illicit sex erotic and mysterious, admitting that "nothing is more exciting than an affair. I mean, Jesus, that kind of clandestine motel-room sex where you're there for one purpose, and you're going to make the most of it. And you give it all you've got. God, that's super. That's a hell of a way to spend an afternoon." Pat had no open marriage in the conventional sense, and described her husband as conservative, straight. But devoted. Despite their differences.

Listening to Pat describe her marriage, it was not difficult to recall 1960. I'd been in similar straits. Not married, but dating a girl to whom I might as well have been married, for the excitement our romance afforded. She was the first girl with whom I'd made love; I the first boy for her, and we'd guided each other through those adventures with concern. But it had come to resemble family, and at fifteen I was too restless for that. Too crazed, energetic and impetuous for a one-on-one relationship, yet too insecure to cut completely loose. The dealing with par-

---

* This person's name, and some identifying characteristics, have been altered to protect her privacy.

ents, the bickering over sex, the weeping about right and wrong ... this girlfriend was sensitive and a dear, but much too staid for my bawdier sensibility.

She was a public school girl, part of that crowd introduced to me by my Cabin John friend; one of her classmates was Patricia Alston. I would see Pat at parties, I'd admire the way she handled herself, with cockiness, careless abandon. Pat dressed a bit sexier than her friends, she danced a good bit sexier, and she already had a reputation with boys. You could score with Pat Alston, went the rumors: Pat Alston was a whore.

"That's what they branded you then," Pat reflected. "It was crass and hypocritical, but that's what they called you if you liked sex. My parents got a note in the mail which said as much. That's a nice experience, I can tell you. Real nice.

"The word was out on me, and part of it was grounded in fact. I'd been fascinated with sex since elementary school. We'd started makeout parties and 'dating' about sixth grade. It was a precocious group of kids I got in with. By the time I was twelve or thirteen I had a reputation, and when I was thirteen I actually made love. These kids were precocious, but I was way ahead of the group. I had terribly mixed feelings about that first encounter. On one hand, I liked it. And was very excited and aroused by that fact. I liked it from the beginning. But I also felt, wow, you know ... none of my girlfriends had heavy petted."

That dark winter I cared nothing for the word, nor Pat's reputation; what I remembered was the sex. That throaty moaning in her parents' den, the croaking and bleating so competently doused by exigencies of the evening. I forget where we completed that arc, finished what we'd begun, but I suspect that same den—a musty couch, mom and dad upstairs, TV for light and a rutting from which memories were made. The exact place does not matter, for quickly there were many places: parties, cars, playgrounds, parks. I don't think ever a bed. The intensity was what impressed. That and the sophistication. We fell toward a multitude of positions that first encounter, a touch of slap, more than a hint of lick, all at fifteen years old, mind you, she fourteen.

"That was the fun of it," Pat agreed. "Guys weren't so experienced they'd acquired that jaded disconcern you get as an adult.

Everybody was hot . . . I certainly was. Those sexual experiences were incredibly exciting . . . that kind of experimenting the result of being so terribly aroused that you wanted it all. You wanted to do everything there was to do. And it was so much fun."

Fun more than for sex. Both of us were involved, I with my girl, Pat with whatever jock of the hour—she was always in love with some monstrous athlete—so that a typical evening would begin on the sly, promising other activities. I'd call for Pat in the family car. We'd be dressed neatly if headed downtown, she in lacy gown, I in coat and tie . . . . I seemed to impress her parents; such a nice lad from such a polite background, right school, right family, so much the young gentleman . . . . And we'd roar toward a bout of jazz clubs: the Bohemian Caverns, Showboat, Mayfair, for sounds, drinks on the fake I.D., a giggle, a feel, and early retirement to the gymnasium of mutual consent. There our evening would conclude, not in simple affection, not in approximated desire, but calculated lust. Lust which commenced with tantalizing kisses, kisses so deep the very soul was touched; licking of face, licking of neck, a tickling of ear, sighs, moans, an unleashing of emotions which dismissed all tenets of "civilized" behavior.

On more casual evenings, we'd meet exclusively for sex, she in jeans, I in grass-stained chinos, and we'd drive straight for the trysting ground—a meadow by the canal, moonglow and blankets, a flashlight and hurried stripping to dainties. Pat curled in black underthings reading from Henry Miller. Reciting the poses, then acting them out. Pat reading aloud there in her underwear, twenty minutes of breathy mutterings delineating a scenario. Me barking like a puppy in distended undershorts. Lights, action, and an appreciation of English literature more firmly instilled than by a hundred classroom show and tells. "Go deep," Pat would cry, embellishing her part, or "stab me." Stab I would, it is my recollection, stab, spill, and stab again.

"I've always been more stimulated by reading something sexy than almost any other thing," Pat reflected. "Skin flicks or sometimes real life won't live up to what you read."

This was a world of uncontested romance, of imagination and invention—at fifteen, sixteen, seventeen, nothing conventional about it.

Our hunger manifested itself in more than sex; there was a constant awareness of style, of the hip life as it reached toward suburbia, of black music, rock, jazz. I was a dedicated student of jazz guitar now; of literature and literate modes of expression. So was Pat. Later we would explore a succession of white-booted, low rent, hillbilly bars, dancing under blue lights, swilling cough syrup, our evening capped by an oral fantasia or two in the parking lot. It always came back to sex; but there was an intellectual underpinning to much of our exploration which undercut the dross. A sign of the times.

"I went into sex very well prepared," Pat said, "because I was a reader. I knew clinically exactly what the process was about. I suppose I'd read five or six rather technical books on sex, which talked about positions and things, before I started junior high. Reading had always been a primary interest. I'd gone to a school in New York, a school for . . . well, gifted children, and that early experience, coupled with my mother's encouragement as a reader, had got me so channeled that I was absorbed by reading—to the point that my parents couldn't get me outside to play. I'd come home and read *Nancy Drew*, you know. I mean I was narrow. Well suddenly it was a pendulum swing. It was—eureka, boys! That was fourth grade. It was like I had discovered candy or something. I couldn't believe there were boys in this world and how cute they were. I was tremendously interested. We had these makeout parties very young, and when my first sexual experience came along I was ready; ready biologically and intellectually, from the reading.

"That first boy was so sweet. He was my boyfriend, the boy I was seeing. Of course at that age, thirteen, your boyfriend lasts for maybe a month, it's no long-term relationship. I remember I'd had a party that night, had a bunch of kids over, and we'd been dancing. He'd left some records and he came back after dark, after everybody had gone to bed, and threw stones at my window. I sneaked down and let him in the back door. We went into the den and started to talk, whispered little voices. We talked about doing it. He discussed a lot of the clinical aspects with me, birth control, pregnancy; then he was very gentle, and really quite good for a fifteen-year-old.

"I had no regrets. A prelude, though, was that there was this other boy with whom I'd rolled around one night, who'd failed to score but who had told everyone he'd succeeded. I got that reputation then. So when my boyfriend persisted, there didn't seem any reason not to. Everybody thought I had anyway. And then," Pat laughed, "it went from bad to worse."

Pat could not guess how many boys she slept with during that period. Practically every boy she dated engaged her in some form of sexual activity, Pat was bad at saying no ... why say no when she liked it so much, why pretend when the world thought otherwise? "I remember one girlfriend coming up on the playground after it got to be general knowledge that I had done it, and saying something like: You actually let a man put his hand between your legs? And I said: You shouldn't knock it 'til you've tried it. I was thirteen and already I had that attitude. It was her narrow-mindedness which pissed me off. I remember thinking: You prude! If there wasn't something good to it, why is the whole world absolutely transfixed by the subject?"

This was the tail-end of the nineteen-fifties, by many accounts the most sexually repressed decade of the twentieth century. Elvis's magic was cutting through, but the lethargy of fifties recidivism ... all that post-holocaust stoking up on vittles and virtue ... would fence most people away from arbitrary sack-hopping until 1965. Pat Alston was ahead of her time, but she was not atypical. If a Pat Alston knew thirty lovers her sixteenth year, another girl might know three. That was three more than the average had known ten years previous. Sexual experimentation, which would explode with '67's summer of love, started for post-war baby boomers about the turn of the decade. You could not drive those cars, dance those dances, dig that music, or live that drive-in, Saturday-night-drag, chug-a-gallon existence and dismiss sex. That same imperviousness to danger which allowed kids to race a hundred miles an hour down a crowded boulevard, drink until blind puking drunk, later trip until permanently zonked, found its adjunct in nondiscriminate fucking. Those early years we were a generation beyond catastrophe, beyond responsibility. There was nothing worth answering to but our own tortured libidos.

If you were to look right, to swing, to radiate sex, you needed things. Material things. Nineteen-sixty was eons removed from unisex, from prole-wear of any thread. A girl had to resemble a girl; if she were sexy she wanted to advertise sexiness. Pat began shoplifting. For about six months, she and a group of girls from school ransacked local department stores. Shoplifting new outfits for parties. Wanting to look their best, wanting to be liked, to be dated, but more mysteriously . . . wanting that thrill. Same thrill as that first feel on the parents' couch, same thrill as stealing the old man's car. Until they got caught.

"That was a bad scene. And another incident which was real good for my reputation."

Pat was on the edge, she remembered. With nothing to live up to, her promiscuity intensified . . . what the hell, it was always summer, ever a soft July evening, tennis-court dancing to pirated 45s, a kiss in the backseat with hot fudge lips, hot fudge ice-cream cake her favorite take-out from the Hot Shoppes, lick again, feel again, jive up jelly tight, until her seventeenth year . . . and pregnancy.

She was in love, ironically; had settled into a steady relationship. He was a basketball guard with a reputation for violence and a short temper. This was one period when Pat and I fooled around very little. I was at college when I heard the news. By then Pat had dropped out of high school and faced her parents.

"They were super," Pat said, "but extremely upset. As you can imagine. There were many tears and awful nights of lying in bed listening to my father cry. Very upsetting stuff. Of course I had tried everything on my own rather than tell—all kinds of crazy things to abort it. By the time my parents found out, I was a good five-and-a-half months pregnant. Too far along for them to do anything other than make arrangements for me to have it. I went into a work home first, where I had to scrub floors and do laundry for my room and board. I did that for a couple of months. God, it was depressing. From there I went to a home for unwed mothers. To complicate matters I was a month overdue. Which meant that my boyfriend Jake had to take on an extra job to pay for that extra month. And it meant kids at school really did know, I was gone so long.

"And then giving it up. All intentional punishment. You go to the hospital by yourself, nobody there to ease you through labor or be with you. You wake up and ... I'd had the baby so fast I'd spilled blood all over my tennis shoes, where they hadn't had the chance to get them off. You wake up in a delivery room and you climb down off a table and there's blood all over your shoes. They put you in a wheelchair and hand you the baby, and back you go to the home. It's two weeks, maybe three, that you stay there with your baby before it's adopted. That's all intentional. That's so you'll feed it and love it and clothe it and change it, and so you'll hurt real bad. Then it's adopted.

"The only thing my parents asked of me was that I break up with Jake. They'd let him stay by my side through the whole ordeal. But afterwards ... they wanted us to split. My parents had been so decent that this was something I felt I truly owed them. So the day I gave my baby for adoption, Jake was there with me. We took it out wrapped in its little blanket and handed it to this woman. And I put my face down in the blanket and kissed it goodbye, and then Jake and I walked inside. I sat down in a chair and he said: Okay, I'm going—I want you to close your eyes and I'll be holding your hand and then ... all of a sudden I won't be there any more. And absolutely, Toby, when he walked off and left me, after everything I'd been through, I think it was worse than giving up the baby.

"Jake and I really loved each other. I don't discount that kind of love because we were young. We loved each other for years following that experience. I remember after he let go of my hand they had to keep me sedated for a couple of days. But then I came home and really tried to be good. I promised my parents I wasn't going to see him. About six months went by where I stuck to that. Then he called me and said: Will you meet me? I have something for you. We met. He'd saved all his money and bought me a gold bracelet. I brought it home and showed it to my parents and said: I'm not going to lie to you, I can't do without him. And they said: Fine. He has represented himself with such dignity and responsibility through this whole matter that we believe he loves you. If you want to start seeing each other again, all right, we think you've proven yourselves and your relationship. They had done what they'd thought was right, trying to break us up, but when they saw the evidence that this was not fly-by-night material, they stood by me, as they have with everything."

Pat was the youngest of four children, born to a mother thirty-five years old when she had Pat ... her menopause coinciding awkwardly with her daughter's adolescence. Pat's father sold new cars when Pat was growing up. Both parents had attended college but had dropped out, second semester senior year, to marry. During the years I knew Pat, her mother was always home, most often stretched out on the sofa reading a book.

"Mother read constantly," Pat said, as we drove south from Philadelphia toward the Pennsylvania countryside. "Which rubbed off on me, that interest in reading. She had a fantastic vocabulary. She'd majored in Russian literature in college and was a brilliant woman. I think it irked her never to have done anything with that part of her life. In their relationship Daddy was definitely the less capable. She was in charge, and he needed her."

Pat's mother had been sick a great deal when Pat was an adolescent. She'd had a nervous breakdown and was an alcoholic. She shared none of her husband's preference for the physical, and communicated her distaste for sex to her daughters: "Mother was strange about that side of life. She was quite earthy about nudity and body functions, to a point where it embarrassed me. I'd had my period three years before my parents knew because I was afraid my mother would insist on showing me how to insert a Tampax. But mother was uptight about sex. There was a delineation in her mind between things that were body functions and things that were sexual. Daddy had an obvious lustiness about him—he'd been a studly-type guy, physically oriented, and I'm certain he'd lost his virginity quite young. Mother was exactly the opposite. She thought sex was disgusting, a necessary act that one performed for procreation, and to satisfy one's husband.

"She could barely stand to discuss it. One day she was in the kitchen and I came in, sat down and said : Mother, what does fellatio mean? It startled her so that she dropped the pan she was holding. She said: Where did you hear that word? Why are you asking me that? It embarrassed her to have me even ask such a question.

"I've often wondered what part Mother's attitude played in my sexual looseness. Normally it would seem that if your mother has a Victorian attitude and tells you the whole thing's kind of messy and not quite nice, you would carry that into your life. I seem to've had the opposite reaction.

"Except that I did feel guilt. I had this reputation of being the town pump, of being a shoplifter, and later an unwed mother . . . yet I had wonderful parents who loved me dearly and who didn't deserve to have a daughter who would get herself into this kind of trouble.

"And I was such a ninny. They couldn't figure me out. Here I was so timid that I couldn't return a package to a store alone, wouldn't unless my father came and stood in line with me . . . still, I was constantly in trouble. Part of that trouble was a result of the timidity. Of wanting to be liked. On one hand I did not care what other kids thought, the prudish kids, about sex and stuff, but on the other I wanted to be liked. That's what so much promiscuity is. In my case, it was complicated by a difficulty at saying no and a real biological need. I could do without it, but I didn't *want* to do without it. And I didn't feel I had the right to say no."

The biological need I'd been aware of, but this professed timidity was a shocker. I looked hard at Pat Alston behind the wheel of her 1956 Corvette and tried to recall one instance of timidity. There were times when we'd attended a prep school or country club function where she may have felt ill at ease, and there had always been a formality to Pat's manner, a Victorian precision of self-expression which complemented the bump and whine of her more relaxed moments. But never could I recall a second of intimidation. It seemed that Pat may have fogged this aspect of her past, tinged it with an overdose of vulnerability which may not have been valid. Like many physically centered, sexually oriented people, she had grown conservative in her middle years. Like many an aging hipster, she had shifted her politics toward the right—as she'd shifted the focus of her morality. She admitted to being a materialist, appeared to glory in that fact. But then she had always gloried in the material world; she was a carnal being no matter how precise her intellect. I stared at Pat's face, at her hands as she maneuvered the little car through traffic, at her feet and legs adeptly manipulating clutch and brake, and thought no, I remember too much.

By the time late sixties free sex and attendant horseplay had been accepted pervasively, Pat had sloughed through it all. There was no need to hop aboard a conformist's bandwagon ten years after hitting the trenches. That railing against suburbia's confines had played too many theaters. We had smoked grass in 1963, balling with friends in a deserted woodlot, and had thought nothing of it. We had made the hip jazz, black night spot, rhythm and blues scene years previous, why orgasm to the Beatles? Pat's primary response to late-sixties activism had been a continued sexual experimentation (more carefully, more responsibly after her pregnancy) and some college legwork for a civil rights activist.

"I was very liberal about blacks and civil rights during the sixties," Pat said. "But I think my political awareness has gotten stronger in the seventies because I see things like the energy crisis affecting *me*. As a result I'm more concerned. In the sixties life was just . . . fun. It was more partying and screwing around than developing a social conscience. I lacked a social consciousness at that time, which was the primary ingredient to being part of the protest movement. But then Vietnam never touched me. I wasn't close to anyone who went. I didn't know anyone who was killed. Looking back now, I think I was awfully shallow.

"But then my experiences with men are terribly important to me. Having known so many men, and having known them that way, I find enriching. I don't feel that I've wasted my time. I'm glad I didn't get married a virgin. You grow from every relationship you have and every type of person you deal with . . . . I feel like I've tasted life a bit more than a lot of women."

We stopped at a tavern in Chadds Ford, Pennsylvania. It was an old spot, attractive and well-run, so we stood up to the bar. We resuscitated beneath paddled ceiling fans, sipping cold beers. Pat spoke again of her marriage.

"I married in 1971 and remained faithful for over two years

... I thought that was pretty good," Pat grinned. "But then for a while there it was: break the chains, maniac unleashed." This was a period when her husband, a businessman whom Pat describes as quite straight, quite conservative, was having personal problems. Pat's mother was dying of cancer. It was a tumultuous time. Pat and her husband separated, and she took up with an associate at COMSAT, a fellow much laxer in his attitude toward drugs, spacey music, clothes ... the entire seventies middle-class hip trip. Pat started smoking grass regularly and on one occasion dropped LSD.

"That was a a terrible experience for me. You cannot perceive the horror of it. I was so concerned with my mother's illness that all I saw were visions of her physical deterioration. Mother had lost her hair by that time, and her face got very skeletal, like King Tut's, and there was no flesh, just teeth that jutted out, eye sockets, and skin. Her belly got distended as if she were eight months pregnant. She was hallucinating toward the last seven months of it. She hallucinated badly. She'd wake Daddy up in the middle of the night screaming. It was horrible. She died at home, with Daddy sleeping in bed beside her—and it was horrible. I feel that I have probably grown somehow from having suffered through that."

It appeared to me that Pat had grown a great deal. From her ingenuous flaunting of sexuality against the disapproval of peers to her thorough experimentation; from her reckless promiscuity, beyond catastrophe, to the responsibility of childbirth; from small rebellions like shoplifting to an acceptance of parental love and the horrors of disease; from an instinctual affection for sexual drives to a dutiful concern about motherhood ... Pat Alston had grown immeasureably. Of the women I'd known during the nineteen-sixties, Pat Alston remained truest to character. Her maturity was personal rather than generational, yet she could stand for the best of her generation.

"Do you gratify yourself or do you do right by your children?" Pat conjectured. "That's the sort of question I've been asking. Or by your husband? Our relationship has been idyllic for the last couple of years, but relationships are so cyclical. You know ... you're mean to me, I'm going to be mean to you back. When

Ben was having difficulties, the nastier he acted toward me, the nastier I acted toward him; and the more indifferent. One thing breeds another. Miraculously, we got out of that cycle. We started another, which is: You be nice to me and I'll be nice to you. Now we try to outdo each other in how nice we can be.

"So I'm not doing anything extramaritally, because I would feel a tremendous amount of guilt. I have too much to lose to make it worth the excitement. Not to say I don't miss the excitement, and that I don't salivate once in a while at the thought.

"I'm quite interested in sex. Ben and I have a good sex life; we maintain a lot of experimentation. But any kind of marital relationship is bound to be less thrilling than variety. Which is the whole reason people seek variety. But with Ben I really have to choose.

"My sexual fantasies currently are two: Two lovers, both men, making love to me, offering some supreme pleasure. I'd be uncomfortable in the presence of another woman. And making love to a young boy: taking him through all the steps I've learned, giving him a kind of ultimate satisfaction and providing an initiation so erotic he would cherish it always. I think that would be wonderful," Pat laughed. "I really have learned quite a lot."

———

Dear Kathy, P.F.C. Alan S. Bersinski of Marine City, Michigan had written: *You don't probably remember me but I was one of the guys you talked to in Vietnam. You did me the favor of calling my uncle and aunt for me. So I am writing you to thank you for doing me the favor. I am doing fine. I made it home for Christmas. I would like to know what size panty hose you wear, so I could hang them up over the fireplace and hope Santa Claus brings you for Christmas. I hope in the near future I will be able to see you. I can't guarantee anything, but I sure will try. This from a poor lonely G.I. you visited in Vietnam—*

I carefully refolded P.F.C. Alan S. Bersinski's letter and handed it back across the table to Kathy MacDonald.

"Received over two thousand like that last year," Kathy said.

"Not all of them from G.I.s, but a majority I guess. Even before I went to Vietnam."

Kathy slipped the letter into its envelope, back under the pink, yellow and blue spruce branches of an enclosed Christmas card, and dropped it in her purse. She came up with several others, plus a simulated leather notebook.

"They're all pretty much like that," she said. "Most guys seem a little embarrassed. In a whole year I've gotten one dirty letter." Kathy MacDonald smiled, the same smile you could see so well in any March, 1969 *Playboy*, on the centerfold, just above the shoulders. There in Chicago at Hef's Playboy Mansion, she was stretched out like a vanilla eclair on somebody's yellow silk sheets. Here in College Park, at the University of Maryland's Varsity Grill, she sat straight up on the crumby brown neo-Capote ice cream chairs like everyone else. And drank draft beer. She even sampled free peanuts. The Varsity Grill was not the Pump Room.

"Here," Kathy said, sliding the notebook toward me, "take a look at this. It's silly I suppose. But maybe it can give you some idea of what I meant when I said going to Vietnam changed my life."

There was free music at the Varsity Grill in 1970, as well as free peanuts, and the three of us—Kathy, me, and Sam, the fellow Kathy lived with—were seated at a table about five feet from two of the hugest speaker rigs imaginable. Kathy MacDonald leaned closer. The faded jeans and pullover sweater she was wearing lent her a weird off-duty air. Her hair was pulled back in pigtails, and as the fluorescent lights shifted I was surprised to see that her complexion was not bunny soft.

"Just don't laugh," Kathy said. I took the little black-and-red notebook and began leafing through it. *Started September 22, 1969*, the notebook said.

"Why don't you tell me what it was like," I suggested. "Being a Playmate of the Month." Kathy smiled again. "I mean I've never met a Playmate before. How did you start? And what are you doing in College Park?" I glanced over at Sam, who was a black belt in karate and the fastest man I had ever known, but he didn't seem to have heard. He was watching some fat guy making a fool of himself. When I'd first known Sam in 1968, he'd had every *Playboy* magazine there was stacked up in his room. He'd had the centerfolds tacked over his bed. When I'd asked Sam yesterday if he had a spare March, 1969 issue I could borrow, he'd said naw, threw that stuff away.

"I studied nursing here at Maryland," Kathy said. "And I suppose I still have some friends around. I'm from Glen Burnie ... between here and Baltimore ... so when I left my husband I just came back. That was after Vietnam, too."

"You're married now?" I asked, glancing at Sam.

"Yeah. But he's out in Hollywood." Sam stared back at me and grinned. "He's the executive producer of *Playboy after Dark*. The TV show. You know, it's supposed to be a party."

Heard first artillery ... the ground shakes and so do your insides, the notebook said.

I didn't know what Sam did for a living. He'd been a student, then he'd taught karate, then he'd wheeler-dealed second-hand sports cars; lately he'd been talking of rigging up an old bus as a camper, to ferry Kathy and him into the wilds for a season. Sam had done a lot of that.

"I was a Bunny at the club in Baltimore for two years. That's where I started. Then when the new Montreal club was opening and they needed Bunnies with experience to train younger Bunnies, I decided to go up there. I was a Bunny mother for a while. That's hard work; don't let anybody tell you different. I wouldn't want the job full-time."

Walked on a dead man, the notebook said. *Flood lights on rice paddies.*

"Then this funny little Chinaman, David Chan, came around. He was scouting for possible Playmates, and asked me if I'd like to try some test shots. We had a session, and about a week later I heard from *Playboy* that I'd gotten the spot. They set up a date for the shooting and sent me a first-class plane ticket. Plus fifteen hundred dollars. That's what they pay.

"So I left quaint Montreal and hopped on this jet for Chicago. Champagne, all you could eat, the works. By the time I got to Chicago I was smashed. But that didn't matter. There was this

man in a dark suit to meet me at the airport, who informed me he
was Hugh Hefner's personal chauffeur and that I could wait in
the car if I liked. He took my baggage check and left me in this
limousine—with bar, TV, stereo, everything. From there we
went straight to the House, the Mansion, whatever you want to
call it, and I was given the most incredible guest room. Monstrous . . . shared an adjoining bath with Shel Silverstein."

*Our helicopter almost crashed at Hawk's Nest. Hair curler
broke.*

"I met my husband at the house. He lived there then; he's one
of Hef's best friends. Anyway, we hit it off from the start—or
thought we did. I stuck around for a week or so while David
Chan posed me . . . You'd never believe how many shots it takes
to get that one centerfold. Fifty for each position, and they're all
unnatural. Uncomfortable, I mean."

"What kind of make-up do they slap on you for that?" I
asked. There were so many questions. Talking with a Playmate,
actually *drinking* with one. Sam excused himself with a grunt and
got up to buy another beer.

"Only make-up is on the face," Kathy answered. I stared, then
looked away.

"The rest is done with an air brush," Kathy laughed. "Few
girls can look good enough without that. Ursula Andress—that
spread her husband did of her a number of years back—she's the
kind of exception you're up against. I can't imagine they used an
air brush on her."

*He had my picture on his wall and I promised to sign it. Got Sil-
ver Star from a fellow.*

"That's when my life became really complicated," Kathy continued. "I had it all, the whole bit—a house in Beverly Hills, Hollywood husband, money, clothes. But . . . well, it's all such a
cliché. Gradually the whole business meant less and less. I found
myself walking around town and doing stupid things like going
into a shop to spend a fortune just because the saleslady had
given my blue jeans a dirty look. Imagine caring enough about
what a saleslady thinks to go in and spend a couple of hundred
dollars on stupid clothes you don't need. My whole life revolved
around parties and Beverly Hills society and wondering whether

I'd be able to get my Pucci cleaned before Friday night. I wasn't getting along with my husband. So when this chance to go to Vietnam came up, I jumped at it."

Gave us scarfs taken off dead gooks.

"Did *Playboy* organize the tour for you?"

"No. *Playboy* had nothing to do with it. The USO contacted me, and I arranged for the entire thing myself. I was proud of that. There's only one other Playmate who's been to Vietnam— Jo Collins. I was proud of that distinction, too."

The Marines are truly great. Rowdy, but great ... no one grossed us out, which was fine, because Captain would have gotten uptight.

"It was what they call a handshake tour. Nothing glamorous, just traveling around to various bases. I went with two other people, Dixie Clegg, a dancer on the Dean Martin show, and Tom Tully, the actor. He was in *The Caine Mutiny*, I think. The tour lasted twenty-two days. That's not a long time, but it would be impossible for me to explain how much it changed my life. I can tell you stories, or you could read my notebook...."

"I'm reading your notebook," I confessed. The notebook had been propped up on my knee and balanced against a pitcher of beer. *Most of the men had been there for eight days*, it said. *Saw body in field on the way in.*

"Oh."

"But why don't you try to tell me."

Kathy MacDonald again leaned closer, and I caught the smooth outline of a denim-clad thigh as she crossed her legs. *Some of the guys wanted Dix and me to dance up on stage.*

"I suppose the principal lesson I've learned is that ... life is very short. And that it doesn't take much to end it. You have so little time, and there is so much you have to go through. Things that seemed important before now seem meaningless. Hollywood, my being somewhat famous. I think I've learned something of the value of life."

Kathy sipped from her beer and started to crack a peanut. "But these letters," she said, reaching for her purse. "So many try to justify our being there in some way or another. Then again, others seem to have no idea. It's a hard war to understand. I used to think being there was right ... but no, not anymore." Kathy plucked a bunch of unopened letters from her purse and held them gently to the fluorescents. "It's hard to expect people to understand something they can't explain."

Sam got up again and walked toward the pinball machines. Suddenly I felt very close to Kathy MacDonald. It was like a rush of pillow feathers the way it came over me. Kathy MacDonald tossed her hair and took another slug of beer. *Got under my bed*, the notebook said. I wanted to put my arm around Kathy and lead her home. Fix things. Give her a room of her own where she could be safe, tack her upstairs in my house where she wouldn't have to worry.

"It's funny," Kathy said. "The first time I saw my picture on somebody's wall, I was shocked."

I glanced down my list of prepared questions. None of them seemed right. "What are your plans?" I settled for.

"Sam and I are splitting," Kathy said. "We're getting together enough money to buy land in southern California. Several other people will be in on it. There's nothing else I want to do right now. I'm still employed by *Playboy* ... they send me around to auto shows and stuff—promotional work. That's fun, actually. I meet a type of person I've never associated with, the custom car freak. They all want me to pose in front of their machines. *Went down into the pits and had our pictures taken with fellows next to their guns.* Sometimes they're kind of shocked to see a Playmate dressed in jeans, with pimples on her face. You hear a lot of 'I liked her better with her clothes off' commentary. But most of those guys are friendly. I'll probably drop *Playboy* completely once Sam and I get settled."

Sam finished his pinball game and sauntered back to our table. He made restless noises at Kathy. They got up to leave.

"You can borrow my notebook if you like," Kathy said.

"Thanks, I'd like that." She looked good as she walked out. She was pretty. But too many goons were making eyes, that ruined it.

A friend slapped his sixteen-óunce Black Label into the peanut shells and shook his head. "You think that chick's for real?" he asked. I glanced back at Kathy's Vietnam notebook, flipping through to the last page.

Desire to be alone, it said. That was the whole entry.

POSTSCRIPT: As of 1979, Kathy MacDonald was living on a farm in Nebraska and completing her degree in nursing.

———————

Jane Edmonds* sat facing the sun on a bench in Jackson Square, her head propped against an uppermost slat. It was lunchtime in New Orleans. All around, people picked at sandwiches, nipped from paper bags or shifted self-consciously toward the sunshine. It had been cold in New Orleans. A black guitarist strummed the wino blues on numbed fingers as a clutch of brethren tapped empty cans, saying yeah. Tourists drifted by. Someone called to a child in German. A horse along St. Ann whinnied in its traces. Jane Edmonds drew a sweater tight across her chest and slipped further down, heels braced solidly against the pavement.

"I did it for the money," she said. "And it was no little money involved. One hundred to one hundred-fifty bucks a throw, all night much more than that. My regular customers were dropping six hundred bucks a week, not counting what they spent on booze, flowers, gifts. Most were big-time businessmen or politicians, so they could afford it. I kept my straight job the whole time. The hustling money was gravy. I wanted that money. I was partying hard and there were things I needed.

"I hustled from '64 to '66, when I was set up by the F.B.I. and busted. All those years I kept a secretarial job. Previously, I had worked the tourist joints along Bourbon Street, as a waitress. I made a lot of money at that. But nothing like I made from hustling. As I said, we were partying hard. I'd get off work and there

———————

* This person's name, and some identifying characteristics, have been altered to protect her privacy.

was no going home, I'd meet friends and we'd hit every bar in the Quarter—listen to music, dance, drink all night every night. I prided myself one year in having seen three-hundred-sixty-five sunrises and sunsets. Even if you were a good-looking broad you needed money to party like that. You wanted nice clothes and you wanted nice places to live. Waitressing couldn't cut it.

"I was waiting tables at Pat Obrien's when I started. I'd been stealing from customers, pocketing change from checks, ripping off the register. It's simple to steal from a bar. I had no qualms about it. A fellow I met at Obrien's, a customer, got me into hustling. His name was Ed and he was something of a dude. He set up the deals, and for that he took forty percent. Didn't take me long to realize I'd do better on my own. He squawked, but I knew enough people around town that he was afraid to strong-arm me.

"I quit Obrien's and took this straight job as a secretary. It was at the same hospital where I'm working now. I was living with a black man then, he wasn't working, so I had two party styles to support. He knew about the hustling. He was all for it.

"The hustling never was for sex. On the contrary. Most hustlers build a hostility toward men. The sex was no more than a mechanical feat for me. I got no charge from it. Many of my customers came to depend emotionally on me, let it develop into a relationship. I was in it for the cash. I never worked the streets. I was a call girl. I'd meet a man at his hotel. Or at a restaurant, or one of the nicer bars. I wouldn't go with anyone I didn't know about. A lot of them were politicians, like I say, senators, congressmen, city people. They had clout and they tipped big.

"I didn't realize the F.B.I. had me pegged until they'd tapped my phone, staked out my apartment, followed and photographed me with my hottest clients. They weren't after me particularly, they were after this fellow Ed who'd started me hustling. He'd been bouncing bad checks, that sort of thing. He was into some fairly complicated deals around New Orleans. The F.B.I. wanted him and they stumbled onto my political friends by mistake. They stumbled onto a bit more than they could handle. I was being threatened by the F.B.I. because I had nothing to say about Ed, really knew very little about him. They were ready to throw me in jail when the word came down to lighten up. Apparently they had photographs and tape recordings of the wrong politicians in the wrong situations. Charges were dropped against me, and I quit hustling.

"I'd been ready to quit. The life was grinding me down. I hadn't been aware of it consciously. But I'd developed a case of hives and couldn't figure why. The doctor I consulted asked what I did for a living, and I saw no reason to lie. He was tough and sized me up fairly quickly. He saw I had psychological problems. 'You may have everybody elses's balls on the mantelpiece,' he said, 'but you won't get mine.' He talked me into seeing a psychiatrist. I won't bore you with a case history of that, but it's a fact that psychotherapy changed my life."

Jane Edmonds hiked out of her slouch and shivered. She was slim, her blonde hair clipped short, and wore a lightweight dress. She wore no makeup. The sun had dropped behind a Pontalba. "Let's get some coffee," she said.

At Tujague's I had the Sazerac, she had brandy and a demitasse. "I married fairly young," Jane said. "I was still in college. I got pregnant by the guy I was going with and insisted on getting married. My first mistake. I had the kid, who is twenty now. Then I had two others. My husband was resentful and insisted on an open marriage. I didn't want that. When he started screwing around, so did I. That finished the relationship. I left the kids with him in Ohio and split for Miami. I needed to get away. Miami Beach was a ball. I got a job waiting tables at a bar called the Seagull, which was an underworld hangout. It was also a fight bar, Dundee's crowd hung out there. Patterson, Clay, whoever big was in town sooner or later would hit the Seagull. It was a big Seven-Up bar. That was funny. A crowd of the meanest-looking dudes you ever saw would sidle in, tip big for a table, then order twenty Seven-Ups. I met Sonny Liston there. We had a thing for a while. He considered me his Miami girlfriend, though he never laid a hand on me. I was making a fortune in tips. A number of characters who I figured to be Mafia sort of took me under their wing. One guy in particular the F.B.I. later grilled me about. They were quite interested in him. He flew me all over the country, chauffeured me around in his limousine.

That was the beginning of my party life, 1960, 1961; I was letting a lot of stuff loose. Those people took good care of me. Showed me some fine times, and stuck by me when I was down. This one Mafioso chauffered me to the hospital when I caught pneumonia, bought me a private room and the best doctors. They seemed to care.

"In New Orleans I stepped up the party life, but on a more sophisticated level. I fell in with this black fellow and we lived together for about seven years, until 1970. He loved to party. We partied all through the sixties. That's what led to our break-up. He wanted to continue that sixties existence, the drugs, the staying up forty-eight hours straight, the irresponsible, owe-nothing life that ... to me, epitomized the 1960s. By 1970, I was interested in other things. I'd had enough. I was feeling responsibility. Psychotherapy had turned me around. I wanted my kids back and I wanted a different life.

"I started a counseling service for prostitutes at the hospital where I work. That's been successful. I got into politics. On a community level. I'm on a number of city commissions, I've run for office once or twice. I know a good deal about New Orleans from my underworld connections, I'm a natural for city politics. I know how to get things done.

"I got my kids back several years ago," Jane said, "That's rewarding. I haven't had a steady relationship with a man since 1970, when that affair broke up. I'm forty years old, and I don't see a lasting relationship in the future. The easiest thing in the world, though, in this town, is to get laid. You walk into a bar, let someone buy you a drink, and hit the sack. You might not know the guy's name. There's satisfaction in that. It takes so little time. And it's really all you need."

---

from 5 to 30 it was
only women, then
for almost one year
it was only men
now it's like the first

5 years and back
to everyone again*

Michael Lally, poet, editor and publisher, inhabits a lower Manhattan loft not far from old Washington Market. The apartment he keeps was once a sweatshop. It is a duplex affair, chopped into cubbyholes, lately encrusted with industrial carbon. Lally shares the loft with his eight-year-old son, Miles, and a friend, Rain Worthington. Rain is a photographic technician employed by *Saturday Night Live.* Her darkroom occupies the apartment's upper level, in tandem with Miles' bedroom. She is a composer/pianist, and her weathered upright faces the north wall of what might be called a living room and flanks Michael Lally's work area: a desk, typewriter, several cabinets. It is a modest work space. The apartment is modest, but not without a gracious air. There is the kitchen, comfortably large, and a long, narrow bathroom with a toilet that juts out like a prop. There is a tight, constricted hall, packed with books. There is the front room with its day bed and wide, industrial windows. But the dominant feature of the apartment, around which every other radiates, is Michael and Rain's bedroom.

It is the building's abandoned lift shaft. The lift has been secured at the second landing, a double bed inserted; the heavy doors opening to the apartment's living space stand closed or ajar, depending upon whim. A tall window braced with iron bars left draped or undraped, dependent upon the same, illuminates the shaft completely. So that one may shut its doors tight and feel dissevered from the world. There is the bed, its colorful spread, three scarred wooden walls, iron bars and the window facing Church Street. During daylight hours it is a child's dreamed of hiding place. After dark it is something extraterrestial, a sleeping chamber suspended above the city, floating, its window open on summer nights to flickering traffic and soft breezes from New Jersey.

One warm day in September, I hiked down to Washington

* Michael Lally, "Now I'm Only Thirty-two," *Rocky Dies Yellow* (Berkeley: Blue Wind Press, 1975), p. 10.

Market and shouted for Lally from the street. He was expecting
me. What I knew of Lally was this: He had been born in New
Jersey, raised in South Orange, had been a hipster, street punk,
greaser, gangster, jazz musician, white Negro, dope dealer,
doper, alcoholic, Iowa Writers' Workshop graduate, radical
anti-war activist, SDS sympathizer, communist, candidate for
sheriff of Johnson County, Iowa, college instructor, father, husband, bisexual, gay proselytizer, literary critic, pamphleteer and
poet. He was thirty-five years old. Most of this I'd learned from a
long poem he'd written called *My Life*—a remarkable confes-
sional. I had met Lally once, at a poetry reading in Washington.
That was '71 or '72. What I recalled about our first meeting was
that our styles had clashed. I had been encased in the woodsy
brogans of Redneck Chic, Lally in the sharp black Beatle boots
of New Jersey street punk.

Lally greeted me on the stairs with a firm handshake. His hair
had grayed. He hadn't shaved. He was dressed in loose-fitting
denims which moved easily over his body. He was thin. His
manner had changed, his style was softer, less abrasive. He led
me to the kitchen and introduced me to Miles and Rain, both attractive in an unassuming way. We conversed awkwardly for
several minutes over iced tea.

"What impressed me most about *My Life*," I said, "were those
lines about hip—where you wrote, *'I love the hipness in me I
thought was black back in the fifties, the vulnerability I took for
feminine in the seventies.'* "

Lally brightened.

"That pinpoints a dichotomy about the sixties," I continued.
"One I've been toying with. Seems like that old conflict between
hipster and beat—the rightist, violent reactionary and the leftist,
nonviolent intellectual—remains constant. That conflict may be
a key to sixties divisionism. Politically and socially. A conflict
which comes back to style, basically."

Lally relaxed. "Yeah, that's something I was constantly confronted with in Movement people. That conflict of styles."

Stylistic, indeed substantive, differences between hipster and
beat had been apparent at last since 1959, when Norman Mailer
delineated them in *Advertisements for Myself.* Mailer had been

describing the fifties, but he might have been cataloguing the sixties, when "hip" became ethos to millions of white middle class.

Hip meant to be aware, on top of things, to be malleable, capable of flow. A hipster was sensitive to change. He could fluctuate to fit needs of any given situation, where the beat was stolid, beaten, jelled in a turgid mold. That mold was traditional bohemianism. It was European. It relied on discourse, logical thought patterns, small movement, and a physical slovenliness which was anathema to proprieties of the middle class. The beat's background was middle class, he was most often white, classically Jewish. His hip counterpart was lower class, Third World, he was black or black in spirit, and he dressed with hints of chic. The hipster was conscious of his body, how he walked, his sexuality; he carried himself with restrained machismo. The beat was more feminine, less physical. Less sexy. The hipster was a loner; the beat communal, seeking comfort in crash pads of his peers. The hipster was an American existentialist, searching kicks in solitude, violence and the unpredictable. The beat had a social conscience; occasionally he might exercise it. In the sixties, he could be found organizing moratoriums or marching to the Capitol encircled by thousands of his ilk. The hipster would remain alone, as rock star, technocrat, or Green Beret. Often he aligned with the right. If he worked within the antiwar movement, it was as point man. More likely he would stand apart, hitting off sixties energy—at home or in Vietnam—with no regard for which side produced the current. If the beat's psychological profile was depressive, the hipster's reached toward the psychopathic.

We finished our drinks, then moved to the front room, where, over truck horns and shrill whistles, blunted voices and screaming brakes, Lally began to tell me of his life.

"I didn't know what the hell I was," he said. "I was born in '42 to Irish American parents who were pretty old when they had me. I was the youngest of seven children. One brother was a cop, one a teacher, the oldest a priest, one sister studied to be a nun, another married a cop. A typical Irish American family, really, a stereotype in literature."

Lally's father had run a hardware store, later a home maintenance business from the back of a truck. But his art had been politics. He'd been the Democratic chairman for his district in New Jersey, and his specialty was getting out the vote. "He was so good at it, he could call the county chairman and tell him which way the election was going to go, within fifty or a hundred votes. It was all based on favors and payoffs. My father was very honest about that. I got an inside perception, from being involved with this giant Democratic machine in New Jersey, quite young ... as to American politics and how things got accomplished. That perception stuck with me through a lot of what I got involved with later in the sixties."

South Orange was a suburb of Newark which included two wealthy neighborhoods, one Waspish, established, older, with some Irish Catholics, the other Jewish, parvenu, and modern. "That was Newstead," Lally said. "We called it Jewstead. We'd go over there and do terrible anti-Semitic things, like drawing swastikas on their streets. Jews were seen as invaders. The area where I lived was distinctly working class, a mixture of Italians, Eastern European ethnics like Germans, and some blacks. Though the blacks were highly segregated from us, they were accepted as our blacks. It was a working-class neighborhood with working-class standards ... but I didn't feel particularly working class. My father usually had a job where he was his own boss, and because of politics and the people he associated with, we were looked on as being a little better off than everyone else."

Lally had smarts, he was the bishop's favorite altar boy, so it was arranged for him to attend St. Benedict's, a prep school in Newark for upper-middle-class Catholic kids, mostly bad kids who required some discipline. The bishop would pay Lally's tuition. "So I had this confusing background. I came from a neighborhood with strict working-class standards; then I was thrown in with these kids who were completely different, who had standards which made fun of mine. I wore pointy-toed shoes and owned one sport jacket. And greased my hair back a little bit. I had more of the style of working-class kids in the fifties. Going to a prep school made me an object for the wit of richer kids, who certainly knew how to make you feel self-conscious about that shit."

Although St. Benedict's was a prep school for "bad" kids, Lally did not really fit that mold. He was sent there because he was bright. But he did need discipline, it was felt. He was constantly being suspended from school and never conformed to any of the institutions of which he was a part. "I saw myself as a thug," Lally said. "I was a skinny kid and I was always trying to overcome that by being so stupidly courageous that people would think I was great." He'd take any dare, had a reputation *for always getting my ass kicked so bad neighborhood kids would ask to see the marks.* *

"The first people I really got close to, who I didn't feel were taking advantage of my craziness and making fun of me," Lally reflected, "were blacks. There seemed to be much more tolerance among blacks. So I got in with them at a very early age. And I got into their music."

Lally's brothers were musicians. The two oldest had served in World War Two and played swing, were in bands, had made records. Lally'd been engulfed with that kind of music. One day he heard Johnny Ace, a black r&b star, singing "Pledging My Love" and that turned his head. " 'Pledging My Love' happened to be Elvis Presley's last recording, which is ironic, because it was Johnny Ace's last recording before he killed himself." Lally got thoroughly into black music, moving quickly through rock 'n' roll to jazz, and by playing it, digging it, he got into black women. "That helped me see how much bullshit there was around me," Lally said, "because in those days there was no room for mixed couples, especially teenagers; especially among thugs who were totally racist. So that put me in a unique position to see a lot of jive for what it was . . . . I mean everything I'd been taught about society seemed to be a lot of crap."

Lally had joined a couple of white gangs, but dropped them once he became fascinated with blacks. He adopted black styles and black manners to the extent that, by the time he graduated from St. Benedict's, he had no white friends. He hung out in New York or he hung out with blacks in other towns in New Jersey. He was into being hip and into hip music, listening to jazz,

* Michael Lally, *My Life* (New York: Wyrd Press, 1975), p. 2.

smoking grass, dressing hip—Miles Davis was his model—and
he was encountering violence. People were always saying things
to him. He was dating black girls, on the sly, but everyone knew.
He accepted the consequences, realizing quickly that no front
was worth the bullshit. He was bluntly honest. The consequences
were unpredictable and, in some ways, shattering.

"By 1961 there were already a lot of freedom riders around,
but among my black friends that stuff was considered dumb . . .
to sit in a place where nobody wanted you and get your ass
kicked and thrown in jail was considered unhip. The hip thing
was to do what you did. I went out with my girlfriend and if anyone gave me grief I smacked him in the mouth. If they were bigger than me, maybe they beat me up. That's the way we handled
it. We didn't want to carry placards."

I interrupted Lally to ask how bad the fights had been. His
face was unmarked. He had all his teeth. He didn't look kicked
around.

"I was. That's one of the things black dudes in bars always
said to me: You must have something going, brother, you a real
thoroughbred the way you look. I always protected my face. I
knew it was my ticket. I had kind of a sweet, innocent face which
got me through a lot of things.

"I also thought I was alone . . . that was a characteristic of the
fifties, right? I figured there was nobody like me. Friends
couldn't understand what I saw in black girls. They could understand how I might want to fuck one, but not the other."

Lally became engaged to a black girl. He was eighteen, had
been living mostly in New York, hanging out, sleeping in Washington Square Park. The girl was from Atlantic City and beautiful; she was also Catholic, which made a difference to Lally. "I
figured my family would have to accept whoever I wanted to
marry if she was Catholic, wouldn't matter that she was black—
which of course was ridiculous." They were too young to marry
without parental consent, except in Southern states—where miscegenation laws cancelled that option. Confusion resulted, Lally
didn't know what to do, so in 1962 he joined the Air Force—
"because this hip recruiter convinced me the Air Force was full
of mixed couples and that was the place to be." Lally had been

about to be drafted, so what the hell. Needless to say, mixed couples in the Air Force were a rarity.

Lally quickly was in trouble. Shipped to Lackland, Texas, for training, with a group from Newark and New York, he was greeted as a hoodlum and began acting like one. "First day, this sergeant hits me in the stomach with a clipboard and says: Whose knife are you running from, stud?" Lally's friends were black or Puerto Rican; he could barely talk English, muttering a street-black dialect. Hip airmen in the barracks nicknamed him Bebop. Every hipster but him was bounced out of training. Lally made it through but stayed restricted to base, assigned extra duty and knocked around by sergeants. Eventually, he was sent to a tech school in Illinois, from which he went AWOL, and got court-martialed.

"A couple of black guys I knew got arrested for grand larceny; I mean they robbed a TV set. They were being held in jail about fifty miles from base. This was July and the grand jury wasn't scheduled to meet until September, so they were really stuck. I was going out with this black girl from East Orange and she'd gone to school with one of these guys. I wanted to see them. A guy from the base was going AWOL in that direction and I hitched a ride. I stayed a while, then rode a little further, going as far as San Francisco. We ended up staying there about three weeks. Funny thing was I immediately ran into this black guy I'd known from New York. I walked into a spot in North Beach and I had like a quarter. I couldn't figure whether to spend it on chocolate cake or the jukebox, 'cause both things were really seductive after being in the service. I ended up putting it in the jukebox. I pulled this chair over to the speaker, had my ear right there, was being a real character with this little no-brim cap like we used to wear, an action-back coat, the whole number, and was sitting there when this black junkie from New York taps me on the shoulder, says, You got a car, man, 'cause there's this party in Berkeley. Didn't ask me where I'd been or how I got to California; nothing. I stayed out there a few weeks then I came back. And I got court-martialed. One of the political lessons from that was: the guy I went with was rich, from Darien, Connecticut; he'd packed all his personal belongings, left a note—

and he got off lighter than me. They'd had to arrest him and I'd turned myself in. I got thirty days in the stockade, busted to Airman Basic, a fine. That sentence was suspended though because I said at the court-martial I had gone home to visit this black woman I was engaged to who was pregnant, and because both my first sergeant and his assistant were white and from Mississippi, was no way they were going to let me. Which was true, except that I'd headed in the other direction."

Lally was reassigned to Greenville, South Carolina, where he acquired a reputation, becoming the first white man to do this, first white man to do that. Greenville in 1962 was totally segregated. The base social club alternated dances, two a week, one white, one black. The white a drag: bright lights, lame music, people staring, no booze, everyone straight. Check the black: lights way down, people lit out of their minds, dynamite band— but a modicum of trouble. *What you doin' chasin' Sapphire, white boy? Who you think.... Listen,* Lally said, *jus' 'cause you see some foxy white lady and you too scared to do somethin' 'bout it— I see somethin' I like don' care what color it is, I go after it.* Which worked. "I used to tell people I was one-eighth black, and they dug it. I had the right clothes, the right talk. I was accepted into that community immediately. When they found out I played music—piano because I couldn't carry my bass in the service—I played with some black bands. One band worked this motel called the Ghana, which billed itself as the largest colored resort in the United States. They had a grove, a giant dance hall, dining rooms, outdoor pool, it was an incredible place. Was run by a small effete gay black doctor who owned most black real estate in Greenville, and who controlled all the drug traffic. Whenever any big names came through that part of the South, they played the Ghana 'cause Doc had the drugs. Little Willy John, Clyde McPhatter ... I played behind those dudes. Was this group called Little Julius and the Swinging Shepherds, some name like that, and I fell for one of their dancers. They asked me to play with them, which turned into sort of a gimmick. They started their act by running through a side door, up this alley and onto the stage, screaming. They wore short jackets, big cummerbunds, glitter, tight pants. They'd come screaming onstage and in the middle would be this skinny white dude, me, banging on the piano. It was a great drawing card. People loved it and I became incredibly popular, made a lot of friends, had a good time."

But things were happening in Greenville, South Carolina, racial things that authorities felt determined to keep the lid on. James Meredith was active in Mississippi, civil rights had become a national bugaboo. Greenville was more segregated than most places but few people knew about it. Greenville's sheriff heard of Lally and came in to reprimand his commander. Lally was asked where he'd like to be transferred. Fort Monmouth, Lally said, close to New York. Where there were six airmen stationed. Lally's orders were cut for June one. It was the end of March but his commander said go. "I came home and fucked around for two months. They wanted me out of their hair, they wanted me out of Greenville, which was nice. I got my ass kicked a few times there, too."

Lally stayed in Jersey a while, then was shipped to Spokane, Washington. He spent his last two years in the Air Force at Spokane, playing music in a beat coffee house, drinking heavily, hanging out in black bars, encouraging fights, getting stomped, passing out on duty, tasting group sex, smoking dope, garnering a reputation as the local hipster. His heart was continually being broken by his black girlfriend in New York. One night on impulse he telephoned a series of black women, asking them to come live with him. "They all dug it, thought I was crazy, crazy Michael doing his number. But none of them came. Then I called this white girl in Buffalo I had met years before and she agreed to come live with me. She was hip. We'd corresponded. A few weeks later I took leave and married her."

She couldn't accept Lally's scene. "First time we went out in Spokane, two black guys got into a razor fight, knocking over tables, smashing chairs, and she didn't sleep all night she was so upset. So I eventually quit drinking. I quit hanging out, and met some more white people through her. One was this intellectual dude who talked me into going to Iowa."

Lally's intellectual background was spotty at best. What literary interests he possessed centered around jazz and the hip scene.

He'd met beat poet Bob Kaufman in the Village when he was sixteen, Jack Kerouac, Ginsberg, Dylan in his folk stage, others, and he'd hung out some in beat bars. "But those beatniks weren't ever nice to me. They weren't nice to hipsters. To teenaged be-boppin' jitterbugs. It was that clash of styles." Still, Lally read. If he saw a literary reference in some article or liner note, he'd check it. He'd read Krim's anthology, Kerouac, Holmes, that ilk. Kaufman's *Does the Secret Mind Whisper* was particularly impressive. He'd wrestled through Heidegger. Lally's wife, Lee, had attended college, so she pointed him toward her New Directions shelf, more Rimbaud than Leonard Feather. Lally subscribed to the *Village Voice;* one day he ran across an ad for a new magazine soliciting submissions. Lally wrote two poems and a short prose piece about the Village which were accepted. "They sent me a check for twenty-five dollars, which brought tears to my eyes."

Discharged from the Air Force in '66, Lally nurtured vague intentions of returning to New York. To play music, write and earn a living. He and Lee loaded everything into a '56 Pontiac, took off, sliding south through San Francisco where, in February, 1966, something new was occurring. Lally had encountered LSD several years before, psychedelics had eased up the coast, but this burgeoning Haight-Ashbury . . . style, proved antithetical to Lally's sensibility. He couldn't get with it. Kids would straggle up, fix him in the eye and say, Wow. Lally'd say, Later. He was still very much the hipster. They split San Francisco, traveling cross-country, stopping with friends here, check a scene there, and miraculously the car survived. Back in New York the Village apartment black friends of Lally's were saving had sprouted dog shit in the halls, junkies on the stairs, shattered door jambs. Lee sat down and cried. Most of Lally's haunts in the Village were gone and a lot of people hanging around were hippies. "Hippy was a pejorative term used on me when I was younger," Lally said. "When you came over from Jersey for the weekend, you were a weekend hipster; they called you a hippy and it was meant to be an insult. I associated it with college kids whom I didn't feel that sympathetic toward. And I felt out of place, didn't know who the fuck I was, what I was doing. Seemed like the scene I knew had gone. So I let this guy talk me into coming to Iowa."

Lally worked for several months as a recreational therapist at a mental institute in New Jersey before making that commitment. His mother had died; he and Lee had moved back to South Orange to live with his father. But it drove Lally bananas. He was miserable. The hip scene had died, hippy was nascent. Lee, once hip herself, had mellowed. Lally felt haunted by his Irish American sense of family; he wanted to do right by his father, by his wife. Iowa seemed the happiest compromise. Lally longed to write and this friend, Roy Harvey, had convinced him he already wrote better than most kids in Iowa's workshop. Lally rented a van, arriving one week before the semester. He discovered he couldn't enroll in the Writers' Workshop without an undergraduate degree. So he applied for the G.I. bill, took several part-time jobs and entered Iowa University as a freshman.

"Of course I was what I was: Twenty-four years old, a hipster who wore skinny black pants, Beatle boots, collarless sports jackets and shades to class with these Iowa kids straight out of high school. Again, I was the local character."

Lee had been politically active, that was another facet of university life she'd exposed Lally to. He still thought politics foolish, especially demonstration politics where you wore your heart on a sign. He remembered how things had gotten done in New Jersey, the old way, through payoffs and favors. Nobody could seduce him into that. Lee attended demonstrations, though; Lally would go along to make sure no one gave her shit, but he refused to participate. Friends at Iowa were calling themselves communists, which was difficult for Lally to accept. He felt America's involvement in Vietnam to be stupid, but he still thought my country right or wrong. Early that fall Lally attended a demonstration against the war in his customary role as protector. Lee was carrying a sign. Hecklers started throwing rocks, tearing up banners, shoving people around. Lally waded in, protecting his wife, and confronted a squad car leading the march. "Why don't you defend these kids?" he shouted. The squad car rolled up its windows. Lally waded back, kicking and punching;

by the time the demonstration circled around he was in the march.

"That was my political initiation into radical politics," Lally reflected.

Shortly thereafter, at a soapbox sound-off in the student union, he made his first speech. A conservative had railed against the demonstrators, calling them cowards and peaceniks. Lally couldn't take it. He got up, identifying himself as a veteran who had witnessed the march—witnessed anti-demonstrators chanting *Kill, Kill, Kill*—a veteran who had served his country, taken all the shit it could shovel because he thought that had been his duty. He was married, paid taxes, but didn't see how a system could work which treated its citizens thusly. . . . Campus radicals embraced him. He was the first veteran at Iowa to speak out against the war. They were ecstatic.

Lally was fingered by the F.B.I. for this modest declaration, a fact which further disillusioned him. "I had seen that Democratic Party at work, but I had this naive concept that at higher levels it didn't go like that." Lally moved quickly from having his doubts about radicalism to believing the Left was correct. He became a popular speaker. His years of street experience gave him a touch with ordinary people that most middle-class radicals couldn't emulate. He sidled naturally toward communism, "with a lower-case c," feeling that ordinary people possessed the wit and compassion to look out for themselves. He sensed that the antagonism most moderates felt toward the Movement was a re-action to its style, not its ideas. "I cared deeply about the Movement's ideals, but I never could get into its style. It was that same split. Their thinking was dry, formal, derived from systematic analysis, and so was their manner. It was very unhip, uptight and unsexy. The black style which I carried to my politics was much looser, more reliant on intuitive intellect, sexier. People related to it."

1968 when John Sinclair said read Mao because it PISSES THEM OFF! & I said Clifford Brown/Johnny Ace/ Frankie Lyman/d.a. levy *

* Michael Lally, *Charisma* (New York, O Press, 1976), p. 9.

By 1968, Lally had won a good bit of national attention for his radical posture and was active in numerous political groups, notably SDS and Progressive Labor, though he refused to join either. The Peace and Freedom Party had planned to run Eldridge Cleaver for President that year; it wanted as much state support as it could get. Lally was encouraged to run for sheriff of Johnson County, Iowa, on the Peace and Freedom ticket, which he did, winning twelve percent of the vote. It came back to that common touch. Lally would debate reactionary candidates in Methodist churches in rural parts of the county and coax voters to his corner. This was a full year before Hunter Thompson's and George Kimball's more celebrated candidacies for sheriff. Lally was self-effacing about the endeavor, shunning interviews from national publications, shucking the Yippie image so popular with media. "I wanted to win people to my ideals," Lally said. "That's what I cared about. I felt guilty about being well-known. I believed in communism with a small c and thought personal aggrandizement to be wrong. It was uncool. So much of that Movement trip was uncool. The nonviolence, getting arrested. I was arrested once, nonviolently, then never let it happen again. You didn't get arrested where I came from. Like those old black dudes'd told me, *Hey: The cat who's pulled time he may be bad, but he ain't that bad, he got caught. You be bad, you do the same thing and get away with it.* Demonstrations released a lot of excess energy in me. The rush they provided was nearly sexual. Running from police, taking care of business, not getting busted, saying what you had to say. I loved that part. But most Movement folks . . . their hearts were okay but they weren't very reliable, weren't real good at getting things done."

By the time Lally ran for sheriff, he had a baby daughter who'd been tear-gassed; his wife, daughter and himself had had their lives threatened. It had reached the point where Lally thought twice every time he switched on the ignition of his car. A friend who'd been a red-diaper baby in the forties talked Lally into backing off after the election, for his family's sake and for his sanity. "I was incredibly tense. I was paying my way through school, supporting a wife and kid, holding down three part-time jobs, taking extra credit, working on graduate and undergraduate degrees simultaneously, doing my writing and beginning to publish. It was all catching up with me. I still had a tremendous love for the country, its basic principles and the people in it. I'd lived in a lot of cities and hung out in a lot of places with a lot of different folks, from hillbillies to spades. Those people were my source of inspiration and creative energy. I couldn't share the same attitude most radicals had toward them."

The last straw for Lally was 1969's SDS split at Chicago: Internecine squabbling between Progressive Labor and the Weather faction. Lally had been working with Rising Up Angry, the white greaser organization led by SDS's Mike James, who was more or less sympathetic to the Weather people. Lally attended the conference with James's group—dressed in three-quarter-length black jackets, hair greased, their thug style rooted firmly in the fifties. Lally had cut his hair for the trip, first time in years: "It was that street thing—what am I going to do, *ask* for trouble? We get to Chicago and this little SDS hippy's not going to let me in. He was convinced I was a cop. I grabbed him and started choking him, I was so furious. Here I'd traveled all this way, gone through all this shit, my wife and kid getting death threats, and this dork's not going to let me into . . . a convention which meant a hell of a lot." Lally finally watched the proceedings from a balcony with Mike James and his greasers. The result was disappointing to say the least.

"Progressive Labor I found totally offensive in their self-righteousness, the Weather people equally offensive in their obeisance to the Black Panthers. I could see through that black shit, you know . . . something most Movement people couldn't. This Panther gets up at Chicago and starts rapping about pussy power and how you wimps in SDS might take shit from PL but we don't, and you ain't gonna have no more to do with Panthers if you keep on. I wanted to refute him, but they wouldn't let me speak. I was so pissed off. Movement people were constantly putting themselves down for being students; any spade could give them shit and they'd cave in to it. I wanted to say to this dude, hey: You Panthers're getting your asses killed all over town, but you still murder-mouth. When's the last time you killed a cop who killed a Panther? You ain't even done it yet, so don't be up here talking bad and doing this number on these kids, when they're achieving a whole lot too. It was a tremendously frustrating experience. I went back to Iowa City and gave a report to the SDS chapter there, recommending they maintain their own organization and not affiliate with either PL or the Weather people. On grounds that the so-called leaders of SDS were no more above the petty, jive, self-righteous shit than the people we'd been fighting. That was the culmination of my disaffection with Movement politics. Though I still shared their ideals, their tactics and their style had finally put me off."

From then on it was pretty much a free fall. Mike James needed Lally in Chicago to continue with Rising Up Angry. "I'd liked to have worked with those greasers, but I'd been offered a job teaching in Washington, D.C., my wife was pregnant again, and I knew she couldn't take James's scene. I figured it was my duty to make her happy, and I figured I could do what I had to do in Washington as well as anywhere else."

What Lally had been doing most seriously, most intensely, was composing poems. "That saved me during those years. While I tried hard to be self-effacing in politics, in my writing I was digging more into my past, into a personal mythology . . . . I wrote a piece called *The South Orange Sonnets* in '68, published as a small chapbook which sold out several editions. It consisted of twenty poems on growing up in New Jersey in the fifties. I'd heard somebody read a series called *The Paris Sonnets,* which I thought fairly pretentious; since I'd never been anywhere like that, I decided to write these South Orange sonnets. I was also publishing academic-type poems in academic-type quarterlies, just to prove I could do it, and even they were reflections of my emotional life—which was confused. I discovered so much about myself through writing that by the time the seventies hit, with feminism and the gay revolution, I was ready for the personal revelations and explorations demanded by those tendencies in the Movement."

> *I never made it to Morocco, Paris, Tangiers,*
> *Tokyo, Madrid. I just live here, in Newark*

> *& wait, for Morocco, Paris, Tangiers, Tokyo*
> *& Madrid to make it to me, here in Newark.* *

The South Orange Sonnets are a precise evocation of neighborhood, Irish in their sentimentality, controlled, tough like an American street-tough, bitter . . . yet interlaced with vulnerability. In other poems of the same period Lally's vulnerability fairly courses. Courses along the Jersey shore of the nineteen-fifties, with its boardwalks, hot cars, mugging greasers, smarmy nights, jukebox cantatas; its stylized clothing, hysterical clubhouses, teen canteens, dulling work, ward politics, racial hatred, cherished relatives, black girlfriends, drunken parties, jazz, Catholicism, sex . . . always sex, most eloquently sex . . . sex, sex, most vulnerably sex.

As an Irish Catholic kid in the fifties, Lally's sexuality had overflowed. He could not keep his hands off himself—he was chasing skirts from age five. His earliest activities were typical: playing doctor with neighborhood kids, necking, masturbating. Always swathed in guilt. Lally dismissed sex with other children at his first communion, confronted with the inevitability of confession. But he could not stop masturbating. At age twelve Lally had his first conclusive sexual experiences, with a nineteen-year-old girl, and with a boy. The girl Lally'd met at a New Jersey beach; it was his first sexual intercourse and an intricately disturbing encounter.

"My grandmother had a house at Belmar, on the Jersey shore, and I used to hang out there during summers. That was a whole other fantasy life—kids could be much thuggier at Belmar, more exaggerated in their dress and mannerisms, because nobody knew what their lives were like at home. I fell into that, and ran around one summer with two guys from New York, both older, one Italian and one Jewish, who were pretty tough. And tremendously slick. They were groovy people. One night they picked up a couple of girls, and couldn't find one for me. We met this woman's bathroom attendant on the boardwalk. They talked her

* Michael Lally, "Newark Poem—June, 1968," *Stupid Rabbits* (1971), p. 14.

into coming out to the beach. Everybody was fucking around.
All of a sudden I found myself in this position—I was totally
frightened, felt overwhelmed and disappointed, awed by her wo-
manness, the actual genitalia . . . all kinds of things. I don't know
if I came fucking her or not, it's an unclear memory. I just know I
came. It scared me. I'd only been coming by myself a short time;
I hadn't even mastered masturbation. To have somebody else do
something was totally awe-inspiring. On one hand, I was overwhelmed with respect and gratitude that this existed, could be
done for me; on the other hand I felt like a little baby . . . . I was
frightened by the fact that here was this grownup who was being
very callous, and who didn't sense what the experience meant to
me. I felt vulnerable in that regard. I mean I was twelve years
old. But vulnerability's the point. I'd developed those macho,
thug defenses to protect me from being hurt. That was one of the
few instances of my vulnerability having been touched. Me being
hurt, and learning a lesson about that stuff."

About the same time, back in South Orange, Lally had a ho-
mosexual encounter with a neighborhood boy who'd acquired a
certain notoriety for jerking off his friends. The boy was younger,
so Lally cornered him, playing protector, and warned that he'd
kick the kid's ass if he heard any more of such activities. The kid
didn't want to become queer, did he? And what the hell did
queers *do*, anyway? Lally got a demonstration. Then he grabbed
the boy and told him he'd break his arm if he ever ratted.

*"I waited nineteen years to try it again with a male and was sorry
I waited so long,"* Lally would write, *"I waited two weeks to try it
again with a woman and was sorry I waited so long."** Lally did a
whole lot of fucking, all of it straight, from that year on. "I came
off as a real madman, scaring women, crazy . . . I had a terrible
reputation. When I was in that prep school I'd call girls from
three towns away and they'd say no, un'unh, I ain't going to the
dance with you. It was a drag. Mostly because I was overcom-
pensating to protect myself. I was getting laid, I knew what sex
was about and wanted it. Deep in my heart I loved it and felt
awed and inspired by it. But every time I let that show, some girl

* *My Life,* p. 1.

would cut off my balls. I was being hurt and made a fool of by girls, regularly. In ways that only I could see. By the time I got married I was in a shell. I didn't let anything out. I never said I love you. Even to that black girl I was engaged to. I couldn't show an emotion."

Lally had gotten into black women because they were looser sexually than white women, in a fundamental way. If a black girl showed interest in Lally, and he in her, they were prepared to act on that fact, there was no point in bullshitting around. There were no amenities to observe. As a mixed couple they existed apart from any social stratum. They weren't going to be coy about it. There were no rewards to the experience except what they derived personally. So they got down to sex fast.

Ironically, what impressed Lally about the black girl he became engaged to was that she resisted making love with him for nearly two months. That and the fact that she was hip, beautiful, intelligent and remarkably sensual. She was Catholic and an only daughter. Her mother'd brought her up "seditty," she had social sophistication; she also had a father who hated whites and swore he'd shoot Lally if he didn't leave his daughter alone.

"She'd gotten pregnant by another guy while I was away in the Air Force. I'd come back to be with her in the hospital when she had the baby. We had our wedding set, I was going to marry her, but the monsignor backed out at the last minute—actually left town. He was scared to touch it 'cause it was a mixed marriage. After she had the baby, I brought her to Fort Monmouth ... it was about the eighth time we were going to get married .... We went to Asbury Park, and by then she was into a hippy number. I'd been away in the service doing my thing and she had made the transformation with the times. She was walking around in bare feet, wearing print dresses and sleeping in the park ... she'd been through a bunch of drugs. We got into a fight basically over style. I was still an uptight dude in a lot of ways. My feeling was that because we were mixed and drew so much attention, we should be cool. Walking around in bare feet and funky old dresses wasn't my idea of being cool. She looked like somebody off a goddam plantation. I got mean. I said that's it, gimme the ring back. She pretended she couldn't get it off her finger. Afterwards I met her in New York, we went to bed and talked about how the affair was over and how we'd always be friends, but it wasn't over for me. I was still madly in love with her. I was just too proud and adamant in my macho thing to give in. I got married to Lee about six months later."

Lally's attraction to Lee had been primarily through letters. He'd begun writing her shortly after they'd met in 1961, when he was stationed in Spokane. Because he had met her only once, because she was two thousand miles away, he let out little things about himself he could admit to no one else. He discussed his problems with women, particularly his black girlfriend. Lee seemed to understand. The letters got quite sexy. At the very least they were passionate.

Lee was white, more intellectual than Lally, sensual, and hip in her way—she'd been running with a friend who belonged to the Road Vultures, Buffalo's version of the Hell's Angels. She hung out in a bar which catered to Buffalo's subterraneans: gay, beat-intellectual, hipster, black. The classic recipe. She understood much of what Lally was into, but on a more cerebral level. She was more experienced sexually than Lally—had explored a wider variety of sex. But she was running.

She moved two thousand miles with a stranger, a most difficult stranger. She got married to escape—something. She reacted to Lally's eccentricities with corsetted disdain. Except in the bedroom. There she coaxed Lally toward a more relaxed, more sensual mode of behavior.

"It was thought of where I grew up that if you went down on a woman that was queer. I'd tried it a few times but I didn't really understand it. A lot of those things I experimented with in my marriage. The sex I'd had up to that point was very fifties-oriented, very make-out and fuck, me always on top. I'd fucked a bunch of different women, from blacks to rednecks to artists to strippers, but it had all been pretty straight. I'd never had much fun in sex. I thought to get ladies, and to survive, you had to be aloof. But I didn't really feel that way. The more women I fucked, the more confused I became. So getting married was a tremendous relief. It was a very rich time for me, sexually and sensually. It was woodshedding—taking myself out of the scene until I figured things out, and practicing. But I was hungry. I wanted more than just my wife."

It was 1972 before Lally slept with anyone but Lee; he'd held out seven years. Seven years of Irish Catholic resolve. He'd traveled to the Midwest for a dope deal, met a girl and made love to her. And brought home a horrendous case of clap. Which was bad enough, but Lee had evolved into a serious feminist. Lally's dalliance was far from the last straw, but it was a step toward a new kind of sexual awakening.

In Washington, D.C., Lally had spirited his excess energy in numerous directions. He was teaching full-time at a Catholic women's college; he had effected a poetry renaissance in Washington—the poets were there, but Lally had brought them together—he'd founded a small press, a magazine, helped organize the Community Bookshop, a series of readings, related events; helped run a film project called D.C. Newsreel, another called the Washington Film Classroom; was working with "blocks," D.C.'s version of Rising Up Angry; writing articles, books, poems . . . was, in short, a dynamo of creative activity. He'd been getting his picture in the paper again; that bugaboo of self-effacement was haunting him. And the feminist/gay element in Movement politics had gotten under his skin.

"With the black thing I'd been able to say, shit, I paid more dues than you, I've had my ass kicked up and down the street. But with the women and gay thing I had no credentials. I'd been reading articles and I thought they were right. So I started washing dishes and diapers, cleaning house. Once I brought home the clap, though, none of that seemed enough. It was getting down to more basic shit: My sexuality and how I acted it out in my life."

The whole time Lally'd been active in Movement politics, Lee had been the person who'd served coffee. Though she'd initiated Lally's fascination with politics, nothing really had captured her attention until the women's movement. She was an avid feminist now, a lesbian, and all Lally's macho defenses were being threatened.

At a Community Bookshop meeting, Lally was confronted directly. He'd been chairing this meeting, which concerned an exclusion of gays from a sugar-cutting delegation to Cuba, and considerable hostility had been expressed. A tough working-class gay from Chicago stood up and screamed at Lally. "Goddam it, man," Lally exploded. "I'm trying to give you people a chance to state your case. Give *me* some credit, I used to *roll* gay guys." The fellow looked at Lally and said, "Motherfucker, I was who you rolled."

Despite Lally's hipness, having accepted homosexuals as part of the subculture, he still thought homosexuality weird. And politically a sign of capitalist decadence. But things kept happening in meetings around D.C. which impressed him. At one, in a gay commune, Lally glanced around, realized no one was present but men, all of whom were gay. For the first time in a public situation he was removed from competition with men for women's attention. He was overwhelmed with relief. He felt none of the old fears; this was a new environment. At another, a gay poetry reading, Lally sensed people had begun to think him gay, and was astonished to discover he didn't care.

The gays Lally could admire, from his macho posture, were heavy revolutionaries, people with pseudonyms like Total Assault, who "came at you like a motherfucker." Gay revolutionaries who had done time, who'd trashed public accommodations when refused admittance. Gays who thought the Weatherman, straight-left, macho trip nothing but bullshit. Gays who were so into homosexuality they considered bisexuality a cop-out; a liberal position, where one could reap benefits of the straight world while enjoying pleasures of the gay. Of course, the worst thing on the left in those days was to be called a liberal.

Lally brought a couple of these gays home one evening, was sitting around rapping, drinking coffee, taking shots on what were left of his macho defenses—when he hit a point where he would normally withdraw. Lally's house was a collective by then, several gays were living in. As Lally began to withdraw, this gay leaned over and touched him. Touched that vulnerability and made it stay. Lee said, "Jesus Christ. I've been trying to do that for eight years." And walked out of the room.

Lally started crying. He hadn't cried hard since he was a kid. The gay comforted him. "Real nice, real nice," Lally remembered. "When he finished comforting me, he suggested we go in to bed. At first I resisted, saying hey, man, no, I'm into Lee. But somehow Lee goes up to bed by herself and I join this guy downstairs. Soon as we get in bed I look at him. He's got a beard and a hairy chest. I think, what the fuck am I up against? So I turn and say: What do you guys do, anyway? He says: What do you *want* to do? And I started laughing."

Lally got loose. He had fun. The restrictions he'd imposed upon himself melted away. Next morning he thought, okay, I've been to bed with a man, what do I call myself? Not bisexual, that's a cop-out, that's liberalism. I obviously dig women, that's my number—but I can't present myself to the world as bisexual. Fuck it, I'm a faggot. He walked out the door, confronted the world, said here I am, a brand-new faggot.

He lost his job at the college. Lost most of his friends. "I went out with about eight billion gay men those first months. Hung out in gay bars, danced for the first time since I was fifteen—realizing all those years I hadn't danced I'd been embarrassed of my physical being, with spades and with women. But with gay men it didn't matter. People were looking me over and saying, God, you're handsome. What lady had done that? Where I'd grown up it was considered animalistic, very *Italian* to look at yourself in the mirror and like comb your hair. I'd grown up with this modest sense of physical presence ... though relatives had always pinched my cheeks and told me what a cute boy I was, sexually I'd experienced none of that. Suddenly it was gratification up the ass. I was overwhelmed by my own sensuality. The more I got into it, the more it showed. I became a much looser and more beautiful person. It changed my whole style. I was walking around D.C. in necklaces, long hair, colorful shirts tied at the waist, platform shoes, pink pants. I pushed it to the hilt."

The apotheosis of Lally's affection for his feminine half occurred at 1972's Republican National Convention. A major political event which Lally'd planned to attend, in consort with legions of old Movement friends and a contingent of D.C. gays. He drove to Miami with two gay men, one black, both fairly outrageous, not stopping except for gas and food from machines, for fear of attracting attention in the South. Neither of Lally's passengers could drive, so Lally pushed through the twenty hours himself. Got to Miami at five A.M. after driving all day and night. Located headquarters for the afternoon's demonstration and immediately crashed. Except, Lally couldn't sleep. He was too wired; anxious because he couldn't find his current lover, he sat around waiting for people to awaken. Finally made contact just as everybody was getting up; made love, picked a crab off himself and went out to get something to eat. It was time for the day's first demonstration, which commenced with hostile vibrations. A motorcycle cop fixed Lally, drawled from behind aviator shades: "We're going to get you bastards." To encounter that behind no sleep, total exhaustion, wiped Lally out. He retreated to the motel and proceeded to get wasted.

"I joined some guys in the gay wing that we'd rented, I was getting loaded on dope when they started fucking around with dresses. Putting them on. I didn't want to act like I wasn't into this, or that I hadn't done it before—that's not hip, right? Someone said, oh this'll look nice on you, so I slipped it on. Wearing nothing underneath. And I got to admit, first thing happened was I got an erection. To feel that silk after wearing men's underwear—I got no shoes on, this long hair, and I'm in this sort of formal. These dresses have stiff things in them even makes you look like you got breasts. Somebody zipped it up, somebody else painted my nails. Suddenly I realized I was alone. I'm a heavy doper so I'm doping up. They'd closed the door to do some recording in another room. I can hear noise from the straight wing, I know the kitchen's there so I decide to change clothes, head over, get something to eat, join the fun. But I can't get the zipper down on this dress. I open the door, thinking some gay will unzip me . . . and there's this room full of straight Movement people having a party. Not everybody, but one or two turned and looked at me. That was enough. These were people I'd trashed the streets with. To have them see me in a dress . . . I felt so vulnerable. It took me ten minutes to turn around and walk out. I couldn't even ask anyone to unzip me. I go back to my room, smoke some more dope. Then my friend Total Assault sends in some straight married dude he's decided's the next guy he'll bring out, to talk to me, 'cause I'm married. Here I'm going through this major personal crisis of my life—how will I over-

eome this fear, how can I be cool and get my courage back to
face people in this dress?—and this motherfucker's rapping.
Every time I try to talk, he cuts me off. I'm thinking, what the
fuck's he cutting me off for? He's cutting me off like I'm a *sissy* or
a *woman*. He's not respecting me in a way I'm used to getting respect. I look down, the moonlight's shining through the window,
and I see these ... knees crossed under my dress, this hand on
them with painted nails. I'm thinking how attractive they are.
I'm floating a million feet above it when I realize, goddam, that's
me. I turned to this motherfucker, feeling an incredible well-
spring of strength—he gets up and splits. I don't know what I did
or said. I was in touch with some big thing, a power. I felt attracted to this person, who was me, but a whole *other* person.
And I dug it.

"Suddenly I'm ready to go back in that room. Ask somebody
to undo my dress, 'cause I'm *in* this dress now, I don't give a fuck.
I was feeling the power. I felt magic. This guy heading out had
closed the door. On its back was a full-length mirror. In the
moonlight here's this creature crossing the room, and it's me.
Wonderful. I had this indescribable rush, this intuitive understanding of how the universe worked. I walked back to the party,
in my dress, and sat around; got high with this woman I'd been
attracted to in her work boots and dungarees .... We started
rapping about how great we looked, me in my dress, she in her
men's clothes, and things turned out okay.

"That night, I took the dress off, got into my pants and went
out to do the duty. I been in a lot of demonstrations. This was
one of the heaviest. Over a thousand people arrested. They had
these helicopters like they used in Vietnam, with lights that could
illuminate a football field and rockets which would fire tear gas
bombs overhead, exploding and injuring people with fragments.
There was a lot of panic. It was a very, very spooky night. I was
in the middle of this, and for the first time my fear came out in
my head. I'd always been able to suppress my fear through righteous anger and macho defenses. But this time I broke up. I was
so scared I was going to wet my pants. Who wouldn't be? The
problem, I realized, was being in touch with this feminine, gay
side. I got down in my car where no one could see me and waited

the thing out. It was a moment of hysteria like I'd never encountered. It was a turning point for me. After that, I began less and less to make myself vulnerable to the world's abuse, to the possibility of being turned into a bowl of jelly. It gave me tremendous insight into what I'd been able to overcome as a man, but it also gave me a glimpse of what I'd been letting myself in for—as a revolutionary."

What persisted in confusing Lally was his attraction to women. All the technique he knew about approaching ladies was from the nineteen-fifties. How do you treat a woman like an equal and still pick her up and go to bed? Lally reacted by going to extremes as a gay, at one period seeing sixteen regular lovers, plus anyone who wanted to stop off on his lunch break. He caught all the diseases, played most of the roles. A dilemma over alternative role-playing bothered Lally most. He thought sexual roles should be spur-of-the-moment. But according to revolutionary gays Lally hung around with, role playing was sick behavior. It was reactionary. If somebody does this for you, in sex, you should do it for them, they felt. Self-conscious stuff which repeatedly got in Lally's way. He began shying away from revolutionaries, picking up nonpolitical strangers. A nice thing about the gay world was that it blurred social categories . . . because of its secrecy, its illegitimacy. Gays from different cultural and economic backgrounds mixed with ease. Lally met upper-class people he found he liked—that chip slid off his shoulder. The scene opened him up immeasurably. He became intrigued with food for the first time, his taste buds flowered. He attended concerts, the ballet, opera. Politically, though, he remained in an awkward position. He still believed in communism, an American brand of socialism. Also a sexual communism. But he wasn't really gay, there were many things in the gay world he couldn't identify with. Violence, though largely verbal, worked on as devastating a level among gays as among straights. Lally found himself alienated, reliving his old life as a white-black, where no one existed to whom he could say, hey man, you know what I mean? Because nobody knew what he meant.

Lee was living her own life as a lesbian feminist. She and Lally were sleeping in separate bedrooms, though still in the collective they'd formed at the turn of the decade. What had started with a stimulating diversity of types—a Jewish woman Trotskyite from London, a gay male poet from Washington, a feminist lesbian from Trinity College, Lally, his kids, Lee—had evolved into all lesbian feminists, the kids and Lally. He became victim of the house, his sexuality constantly up for discussion. If he went out with another woman, the house exploded, accusing Lally of abusive sexual politics. His son was walking around saying, It'd be easier if I was a girl. Lally left for a year, lived in an apartment by himself, exploring his new gay identity. As well as indulging his attraction for women, in a less macho, less straight way. Eventually the pressure from several relatively steady lovers of different sexual persuasions, plus the judgments and constant criticism of feminist and gay revolutionary communities, as well as the demands to be publicly accountable for his private behavior, became too great and he fled to New York. He brought Miles to live with him. He moved in with an upper-class Latin American woman—very tough, independent, but the epitome of everything the women's movement hated. In terms of style. Lally was living off a couple of poetry grants, was writing book reviews for the *Washington Post*. He and the Latin American woman broke up over money, largely. That and the responsibility of raising a child. She missed the excitement of Lally's more sexually adventurous period. And she missed the cash. Lally lived alone with Miles for a year, seeing both men and women. But too much sexual experimentation he decided was harmful to Miles' best interests.

"The confusion of the sort of life I was living—numerous bed partners, alternate role-playing—which was invigorating and which taught me a lot, seemed a bit much to lay on a kid. He was starting to become like a parent, worrying about me and my love life and lifestyle. And it wasn't all that satisfying, or as exciting as it had been when I first rediscovered my dormant sensuality and androgyny and all that. So I was just beginning to accept the idea that my life would be resigned to some quiet affairs and relatively normal relationships, with no big passion, when I met Rain—she crashed one of my annual birthday parties, my thirty-fifth. I fell totally and passionately in love with her. She somehow brought back the romanticism I had dreamt of as early as my first sexual experiences but had been missing in my recent experimentation and encounters. And she seemed to understand and accept all my crazy selves."

Lally had moved in with Rain one week before our conversation. As Lally and I relaxed in his big front room, the sound of jackhammers and traffic heavier now as the afternoon lengthened, I asked whether he'd drawn matters toward any sort of intellectual conclusion.

"Nothing finally conclusive," Lally said. "The easy distinctions between black and white, gay and straight, don't seem to apply to my existence. The pleasure I derive from sexuality is a wide spectrum, a conglomeration of feminine qualities and masculine qualities, straight and gay. I'm in the process of getting divorced from my wife. I have no moral nor political restrictions on my sexuality. I can still be as gay as I want. Go to bed with whomever I want. I see nothing wrong in that. But right now I'm happily involved with Rain. And Miles has improved so dramatically that I tend not to overextend things in my sexual style. Whenever he has any questions about sex or sexual identity or anything for that matter, I answer him as honestly as I can, often using myself and my experiences to illustrate. And the same goes for his sister, Caitlin, whom we see every holiday and summer."

Rain slipped past as I reached to shut off the tape recorder. She eased toward the center of the lift-bed, busying herself with prints. Lally and I conversed a few minutes longer. I inquired about O Press, his current job, and how the writing was going.

"Fine. I'm publishing a number of poets; David Drum, Terence Winch, Tim Dlugos, Phyllis Rosensweig included. It's a lot of work and the money's scarce, but publishing people's work you admire is rewarding. My job is at The Franklin Library. I edit, rewrite, and write reader's guides to leatherbound reprints of classics and contemporary bestsellers they publish. It's nine to five, my first job like that, and I don't know how much longer I'll keep it. I have a book of love poems coming out this winter called *Just Let Me Do It* plus an overdue collection of mostly prose from the 1960s called *Catch My Breath.* I'm excited about

both. Rain's giving concerts, she's ᵥ
photography. Miles is doing good,

There was a tattoo on Lally's f(
about. It was the black figure of a
suit of cards.

Lally flinched. "For years I ke
was embarrassed to show anyon
figure what the hell."

> When the back of my swan
> divides your body with feathers
> it doesn't matter that they are
> white or black
> only that they are soft*

POSTSCRIPT: In August, 1978, Michael Lally quit his nine-to-five
job; thereafter, he began supplementing his art and income with
a career in acting.

* Michael Lally, "Revolution," *Dues* (The Stone Wall Press, 1975), p. 18.

Speed

Before Interstate 495 there was Route 240, heading north. A calm road—linear, minus a circle to confuse—240 ran from Washington to Frederick above restful pastureland, placid Guernseys and a dotting of red barns to an actual Midwest beyond. The Midwest was presumed actual, though never perceived, for Frederick was the finish line . . . a spot for negotiating U-turns. Archaic automobiles bobbed atop 240's macadam: sleek plesiosauri with undulating fins, subcaudal blinker lights in teardrop or mortar-point trim; boxy pickups and tractor-trailers after the old style, scuttling northward with deliberate gustiness, as if self-propelled from weed patch to bridge piling, ever thankful to make cover. There was a 1959 Bonneville with the 300-horsepower engine, 389 cubic inches nestled into the widest, longest passenger frame Detroit produced. There were white vinyl seats with aqua trim, a bright chromium instrument panel canopied like an F-series jet's, and more interior space than six hysterical teenagers could fill. It was a car built for the open road, and 240 was that. A cooler of beer, hamburger wrappers from the Bethesda Hot Shoppes, damp loafers or discarded tennis sweaters, wet bathing suits, rhythm and blues from WDON and the cruise control set at one hundred twenty. Route 240 catapulted that Bonneville to Frederick in less time than it took to chugalug a six-pack of malt liquor. One hundred twenty miles per hour with the

radio up loud and the air conditioner on high. Weaving through
a wagon train of lesser vehicles traveling half one's speed—like
negotiating a lotful of parked cars at sixty.

The road was straight and faraway, the activity ecstatic. There
was a circle at the Hot Shoppes, where one made his play, and
there was the U-turn at Frederick. Often one sat at the Bethesda
Shoppes and allowed himself to be circled. A 1949 Jeepster was
prime for that, the piss-yellow Willys, good to whip up on an occasional Falcon or Corvair along Rockville Pike, but inadequate
for 240. Zero to 50 she was quick, but much over that and you
risked throwing a rod. Perfect for the Shoppes, though, top
down, summertime music, seeing and being seen as a caravan of
outrageous vehicles lapped the premises.

Street racing predominated. One sped south along 211 to
Charlottesville and university parties never to be forgotten, to
Richmond, east on Highway 60 to Williamsburg and a half-hour
of one-hundred-miles-per-hour cruising through pine forests so
sparse they threatened to hypnotize with ten thousand flickers of
sunlight. One knew the wind, the blackest rural night and a kin-
ship to speed which approached the elemental. We sensed what
Einstein had discovered of matter, that through velocity mass
might be ineluctably altered had long been considered old news
by every farm boy who had pushed a modified stocker to its
limits along a deserted country road. Rumors of a new road—to
be opened soon, in a few years—that would encircle Washington
D.C. Sixty-odd miles of high-speed interstate which would ...
circle the city. Could one comprehend? A natural Le Mans there
in the night; sixty-odd miles of Le Mans being constructed *legally*
by the state for our delectation. We awaited not so frantically the
date, August 17, 1964, when the Capitol Beltway would open,
but an evening sometime before: the monster asleep without a
truck on its back, lying there like a serpent enveloping the city,
burning no light, macadam as yet unlined, exits blocked, no police, an open road to nowhere, an invitation to emptiness. And
speed.

* * *

The Bethesda Hot Shoppes stood as base camp to that perimeter. Like many another post-World War II drive-in, it flanked a high school. A Shell station marked its north side, a funeral home just down the block. The Shell station salvaged wrecks, displaying their crushed and mangled forms in didactic view. A lighted sign above Pumphrey's funeral home oversaw the cavalcade. Police were omnipresent. On weekend nights you could not find a slot—traffic would be stalled for blocks. During summer hours the Hot Shoppes would be packed from late to early morning, all day every day. Cars circled endlessly. Cars seeking challenges, cars courting sex, cars obsessed with their own peculiar vibrancy, ceaselessly twirling.

A black '57 Chevy stalked the teletrays in 1960, a Bel Air coupe with oversized tires and traction bars jacking up the rear. Several other '57s prowled the Bethesda Shoppes that year, but none so special as this. It had '57 Corvair bucket seats, a modified dash and four-speed floor shift. It pulled 270 horsepower out of a 283-cubic-inch engine, stock, with two four-barrel carburetors and an 097 cam. It belonged to a boy named Dennis Durbin and it was fast: 13.9 seconds for the quarter mile, at 102.2 miles per hour. It was a car with which Durbin would win two hundred fifty first place trophies in drag racing and set two national records.

All that had little to do with the Hot Shoppes. Track racing occupied one afternoon a week. Drivers could race legally on Sunday, which left the other six nights restricted to improvisation. Durbin cruised. Usually late, usually alone. The black '57 would materialize in one's rear-view mirror, turn at a far pole and circle. Durbin's pipes would throb. His rear end, set up for racing, would pitch out from low gear and whine. He'd be slouched toward the door, expressionless, appraising talent. You'd never catch him looking. Hair greased back, he seemed small, defined by what you saw framed in the window. Saturday night nobody missed at the teletrays, but any night was open to action. The revving of an engine. A challenge presented by functionaries. Conditions of the duel, a time fixed, then a somber retreat to the purlieus of hip. On a hot Saturday there'd be fifty to a hundred cars lined up on either side of Route 240, awaiting the principals. Kids sprawled along the banks on blankets, drink, beer, juking to the radio, wolfing cheeseburgers, throwin, punches. A guard would be set at either remove. The race would commence. Police could do nothing. They never caught anybody. It got so good they started patrolling with helicopters. Durbin rarely lost. His driving was infamous. His '57 a legend.

There was something anointed about the 1957 Chevrolet. Durbin's was special, though representative of a genus which had fascinated teenagers since its inception. The '57 Chevrolet epitomized teenage culture during the nineteen-fifties. It was a Del Vikings song. It was black slacks. It was Brenda Lee. "Aerodynamically stable," with outsized fins and a bull-nozed hood, it was light, which meant fast, and with the 283-cubic-inch V-8, possessed of a formidable power-to-weight ratio. V-8s were hitting their stride about 1957, and Chevrolet was the first company to offer a booming teen culture what it wanted in an automotive product, speed. Fuel injection had become available in passenger cars by 1957. Engines were bigger, options more baroque. You could order a car from Chevrolet in '57 set up for racing in a manner previously available only from speed shops. But speed was half the story. Style carried equal weight—there was something spacey about those fins arching out, that side panel of chrome licking the fender, those cartoon colors. Fifty-seven was the year of Sputnik, and cars thrust toward space with bright indulgences of alloy and horsepower. Tailfins were pervasive by 1957. They had been introduced with the 1949 Cadillac (modeled after World War II's P-38 fighter, revered stylistically for its dual propellers and tailfins),* but '57 was the year fins became standard equipment. It would be four years before John Kennedy inaugurated the decade of Space, but Detroit was already reaching past airplanes in styling toward rockets and the inevitability of space consciousness.

Nineteen-fifty-seven saw fifties culture peak along a broader spectrum.** Economically, it proved the last year of America's postwar boom—1958 would bottom out in recession, cars re-

* Sam Love, "Visions of Tomorrow" (see *Futures* chapter).

** It was the year of Norman Mailer's *The White Negro,* a primary exegesis of hip. It was the year of Kerouac's *On the Road.*

flecting the new despondency with heavier, boxier shapes. Already teen culture had entered its mannerist phase: music, clothes, cars, each was changing. Elvis's sound had evolved in one year from the leather-jacketed defiance of "Hound Dog" and "Blue Suede Shoes" to the angora complaisance of "Teddy Bear." By 1958, clothing styles were more reserved, shifting toward the Ivy League camouflage of a pre-Camelot best and the brightest. Cars became outwardly more familial: huge, "elegant," limousine-like ... while hiding violent masses of cast iron and steel beneath their hoods, the most brutishly powerful engines Detroit had yet produced. The horsepower race during those years paralleled the arms race with some terrible proclivity for irony. The new respectability of fashion styles closeted a similar cauldron of explosive sexual energy. The whole culture was sublimated in technique. Rock 'n' roll would move toward an era of self-parody before rejuvenating itself in the revisionist waters of rock. By 1960 innocence had fled, but even that fact remained hidden. Camelot was what politics had learned from ad men during the fifties, hope with a capital H had already burned itself out.

If the '57 Chevrolet survived among sixties Quixotes as a symbol of deflected innocence, drag racing flowered as the paradigm of its self-assertiveness. Drag racing—that psychopathic, omnisexual, onanistic spurt toward metamorphosis; that quarter-mile come in the palm, circle back and come again, which had been draining teens since the nineteen-forties, since the adolescence of suburbia. During the thirties they were called hot rodders. First noted in California, at the finish of pioneer trails the length of that coast, they were everywhere the automobile had extended boundaries of speed. Man now was less reliant on the capriciousness of animals to satisfy his craving for velocity than on the ingenuity of machinery and mind ... a thirties notion, born of Depression, nurtured in scientific method. Hot rodders gathered at trail's end for the variegated reasons California had always spawned supernovas of the pioneer spirit. They congregated in gangs. Hot rodding was begotten as outlaw behavior, centered around speed shops west of Los Angeles, which sprang up like frontier saloons, like outfitting posts of the new dynamism, in

protest of societal ills, of an encroaching federal totalitarianism
... but most dramatically in defiance of that terrifying homogeneity of culture which sloughed at the next crossroads.

From the start hot rodders built their own cars out of bits and pieces of the available. Fords were a favorite—stripped model T's or '32 roadsters—because they were cheap, because they were the many. Because they were landaus of the common order. Hot rodders could race along wide boulevards surrounding Los Angeles in those years, because suburbia had yet to choke them off. Street racing was cathartic, but it was not drag racing. Drag racing would evolve as compromise, in the wake of stoplights at each corner and constricted street grids. The pinched rapaciousness of suburbia. Hot rodders raced out of drive-ins, out of roadhouses and speed shops, but their Mecca was the desert. Dry lakes northeast of Los Angeles were the promised land. Great prehistoric lake beds of the Mojave, crossed less than a century before by pioneer ancestors, sucked hot rodders from the city in droves. Lake Muroc proved the most satisfying, twenty-five miles of slick alkali, wide open to sun and wind. Hot rodders flooded Lake Muroc by the thousand on weekends; they raced haphazardly, hysterically—no pissy quarter-mile ejaculata at Muroc, but unfrustrated strivings toward flight. There was something atavistically sexual about defiling a lake bed. Hot rodders would keep Muroc for their own until bumped off by Uncle Sam; Uncle Sam's technology in the guise of Edwards Air Force Base and experimental rockets tested there.

It is no psychic accident that aviation developed concomitantly with automotive racing. The only comparable sensation of dragging from a dead stop to a hundred miles per hour plus, in a quarter mile, was the take-off of a big jet. Once lake beds around Muroc had been secured by the Air Force, hot rodders turned toward deactivated air strips as an alternative to street racing. The first Santa Ana drags were held in 1950 at an abandoned blimp base. In the July, 1950 issue of then nascent *Hot Rod* magazine, an editorial called for "the need to build an all-weather racing facility for hot rodders by hot rodders."* Those dry lakes not se-

---

* Gray Baskerville, "The Hot Rod Story," *Hot Rod,* January, 1978, p. 37.

questered by the Air Force had been decimated by ten years of rodders' antics. And kids all over America were feeling the push to race legally, without fear of stiffening traffic citations.

A quarter mile was the margin for safety at most air strips; stoplights were the go with which most rodders were familiar. Details of the sport simply evolved. But ranks of outlaw hot rodders were dwindling. Even in California's vastness, suburbs pulsed across boulevards like amoebae ... not surprisingly the favorite monster of fifties horror movies was a shapeless, all-smothering blob. Development was envelopment. Suburbia, which owed its existence to the automobile, would do more to discourage ecstasis of driving than any factor short of the seventies' oil crunch. Lake beds, but for Bonneville and the occupied Muroc, lay ruined, ravaged, parched as crones. Gone were the days of unrestricted speeding, the mile after mile of flat-out cruising. Mojave's open range had been fenced, Philistines held the promised land. A famine of prophylaxis—the nineteen-sixties—soon commenced. A decade which would see drag racing develop as a national pastime, horsepower consciousness a disease, in terrifying affinity to professional football, the velocity of rock, and war.

Dennis Durbin interested me. He'd been through the changes as a drag racer, having raced both professionally and as an amateur. He held several national records. He had raced straight through the nineteen-sixties, to abandon the sport at decade's turn. He ran his own trucking business now. He owned a fencing company. He had been nearly impossible to contact. Once cornered, he proved affable in an interview but difficult to pin down. The man seemed to possess no free time. He was his own boss, and like many such professionals, spared few minutes of the day to nonessentials.

Durbin's house, in a suburb of Washington, was brick, tract, and unoffensive to the camouflage of its block. His yard was trimmed. A station wagon blocked his drive. For me to find Durbin living in suburbia after what I knew he'd accomplished as a racer was disconcerting. But Durbin had grown up in suburbia, he was typically post-Muroc in that regard. A disenfranchised hot rodder, laboring under the roughest handicap:

suburbia as clonedom, sterilized launch pad and top eliminator, rolled into one. Durbin's wife, Joan, ushered me into a living room so typical as to discourage description. It held a deep shag rug, glass and steel coffee table, one or two easy chairs and a hanging lamp of glittery design. A small desk, from which Durbin ran his businesses, stood crowded with files and billing material—the work desk an anomaly in this family-oriented room. Children lolled about.

Dennis Durbin greeted me wearing Levis, blue Topsiders and a white T-shirt, each immaculately clean. A Kenworth buckle set off his leather belt. He was tanned and wore his hair blown-dry. He looked supremely out of place, as if he'd stepped from the pits at Indianapolis, or from Tom Wolfe's *Last American Hero*— movie paean to southern stock car racing and the cult of the sixties' Good Old Boy. Durbin moved gracefully but with a calculated unease ... as if, traversing this suburban living room, he might wreck or inadvertently soil something. He carried himself like a man who had spent his life coated in engine grease— usually out of doors, always at some terrifying rate of speed.

"What do you do now that you've given up racing," I asked— "to satisfy that longing for horsepower and velocity?"

"I fix trucks," Durbin said. He laughed.

It would not be painless interviewing Dennis Durbin. He promised to be as awkward expressing his affection for automobiles as he appeared in this deep-pile and stainless-steel setting. The air conditioner sobbed. Durbin, with his tanned face, white skivvy and deck shoes, might have strolled from a skiff at Islamorada to the formica chill of a tourist lounge. His trophies were on the dock but there wasn't any way he was going to tell you about them.

"Dennis has been mechanically inclined from the day he's been born," Joan said. "Because his mother has said how, when he was nine years old, he used to take clocks and things apart to see how they worked. And he'd put them back together. We've got two of our kids do that. Plus the fooling with go-karts." Joan Durbin was an ebullient woman, cheerful, with the recollection of wilder times in her smile. She proferred this information easily.

"Horsepower has always fascinated me," Durbin interjected. Then he was silent. "We'll go to the races today and watch those fuelers and funny cars make a couple of passes, and those cars are producing 1,400 or 1,500 horsepower." Another pause. "It's the sound of speed, you know."

"The combination of an actual *feel* of it, with the abstract fascination for the mechanics of it?" I asked.

"Right."

"Was there an earlier sense of speed, other than from automobiles, that affected you?"

"There were these go-karts," Durbin said. "We'd go out on Friday nights to a construction job and steal a five-horsepower motor off a cement mixer. Then mount it on a piece of plywood with four wheels. I was probably eleven, twelve. Seven or eight of us in the neighborhood had go-karts, and mine was the fastest. We were clocked at fifty-five miles an hour on the street one day by Montgomery County police and had to push that thing all the way home."

He'd bought his first car in 1957, when he was fifteen years old. It was a '47 Ford coupe, for which he paid one hundred fifty dollars, money earned cutting grass. He worked on that Ford a year until he was old enough, legally, to drive. He got it tagged and drove straight to Aquasco Speedway, where he won his first trophy. His parents gave him hell. They said he was crazy. Durbin's Ford had turned the quarter in sixty-three m.p.h. He came up with another, a '51 Ford Gladiator, which turned seventy m.p.h. Then he bought his '57 Chevy. He was racing every weekend by then. Durbin's parents were predictably incensed. His father—Washington branch manager for Ditto Incorporated, a duplicating machine company—envisioned soberer goals. Durbin was working odd jobs as a mechanic, house painter, maintenance foreman, to support his habit. "Hear my dad talk nowadays, though," Durbin reflected, "something goes wrong with his car, him being retired ... first place he brings it is my house."

Durbin neglected his schooling. "Seemed like at one time there was nothing else but cars. I got so involved I started skipping school just to work on 'em. Engines—the way they operate,

the way they sound. Most guys would be out Friday night partying or down at Arthur Murray learning to dance, and I'd be in
the garage laying underneath the car, covered with grease."

"How about girls?" I asked.

"We sat and watched everything that went on," Joan said.

"Sat and watched, and pulled on your arm to go to the
movies," Durbin added. "We didn't have time to fool with any
women."

Things could get hairy. "Was this wild gal from Virginia,"
Durbin recalled. "Came by the garage one night and wanted to
party. We said no, so she came by and threw eggs at us. Was
driving a Chrysler Imperial or something. She threw eggs and
they came in the garage and hit me and my buddy. So I grabbed
a tire iron and ran through the back yard. As she swung around I
cut loose and stuck that iron right in the door of her car."

Women like Joan Durbin, sympathetic to automobiles, were
treated more kindly. Joan and Dennis had gone to junior high
school together, but they met, courted and married out of the
Bethesda Hot Shoppes.

"Nobody ever planned anything for those weekends," Joan
said. "You'd go up and sit at the teletrays and wait for your
friends to come by. The boys would pick races—or wait for the
rescue squad to go out, to follow them, for entertainment. One
Saturday night we did that. I parked right behind Dennis and
when we walked back from this accident, my car had a flat.
Dennis held the flashlight while somebody else changed my tire.
That's how we met. He had his '57 Chevy. We didn't quit hanging around the Hot Shoppes until '62 or '63, when they closed the
teletrays down. We were married by then. Married with that '57
and took it on our honeymoon. It was set up for racing and I remember Dennis had to change the rear end so we could travel.
My mother used to laugh because on our honeymoon I told her
Dennis had borrowed Mickey Cling's rear end. She said, well,
that's pretty bad."

"I'd been caught speeding several times, had my license re-
voked for raising hell," Durbin said. "Way that '57 looked didn't
help me none. I'd get stopped as a whiskey runner if nothing else.
The car looked like it was carrying a tank. We had traction bars

and big tires in the back ... in those days only ones that had them were race cars and whiskey runners. So that was another thing pushed us toward the track."

I'd noticed that whenever Durbin spoke of cars or his involvement in racing, he'd slip toward the editorial we. Or was it the sovereign we? In any case, he felt most comfortable with the altruistic parlance of statesmen, astronauts and team-based professional athletes. There could be no more egotistical sport than drag racing.

Durbin recounted some of his bigger wins for me. Of the four hundred plus trophies minting tarnish in his basement, the two most cherished were his first, won at Aquasco Speedway when he was sixteen; and one of his last, a record-winner at Indianapolis in a 1968 Z-28 Camaro, with which Durbin set three different national records. The final record, set in 1969, he held for a year and a half. "I'd say that was my most exciting win, because some of the cars there at Indianapolis were running quicker than we were. But I was able to outdrive them. It was a shock to everybody that we did win. I would say that was my biggest."

By 1967, with the acquisition of that Z-28 Camaro, things had started to change for Durbin. His '57 Chevrolet, raced since 1960 and with which he'd won two hundred fifty first place trophies—including the super stock nationals at York, various IHRA and NASCAR records—had been let out to pasture. Durbin went into partnership with another racer on the '68 Camaro, foreshadowing professionalism. He kept that car until 1970; during those years, demands on his attention approached that of a job. After the Camaro's big win at Indianapolis, more and more meets wanted to see the car. Promoters would telephone. Durbin's entry fees were being waived in deference to his national records. He was being sponsored by both a local Chevrolet dealership and an independent speed shop. Chevrolet provided him with parts at cost, plus a new pickup and camper for Indianapolis in '69; the speed shop offered speed parts at cost, free oil, free spark plugs, and about two thousand dollars in cash. At meets like Indianapolis you won cash as well as a trophy. By 1970 Durbin was driving a '70½ Camaro with the 427 rat motor, which advanced him to a pro-stock class. This Camaro belonged to an investor;

Durbin merely drove and maintained it. The earlier innocence of street and Sunday racing seemed a thing of the past. Durbin was a professional.

"Once we bought that '70½ Camaro we went on a local circuit here. We were obligated to run all their meets. Which were in South Carolina, Georgia, North Carolina, Pennsylvania, Ohio . . . . We'd leave here Friday nights and wouldn't get back until Monday mornings. It was professional racing. Your big-name drivers who had been around. You had to know what you were doing, you had to have a lot of money and a lot of time."

In 1971 Durbin decided to build his own car, also pro-stock, a '71 Vega. The car was reworked from the ground up. Durbin bought it as a standard passenger car but stripped it completely, shipping the body to San Diego for acid dipping. This cut down on weight. From San Diego it went to Spring City, Pennsylvania, where a tube chassis was installed. The Vega was what would be called a funny car on the circuit, except that Durbin was required to keep its metal body, from the cowl back, intact. Durbin dropped a junk motor in it for testing. The car turned a 9.98 quarter at 130 m.p.h.

"We were getting ready to put in a good engine for competition, 'cause I had all the bugs worked out and the handling problems solved, when I got more involved in my trucking business, the family got bigger . . . so on and so forth."

That Vega was the last race-car Durbin owned. He sold it to an investor for ten thousand dollars, minus an engine.

About the time Volkswagens were becoming a cliché in America, Durbin loaded his onto the camper/trailer rig he'd designed to haul his dragsters and headed for Ocean City. It was personal reassessment time. Like many Americans, Durbin had reacted to the nineteen-seventies with a mature conservatism. The pressure to dig in financially, to create a more secure foothold for one's family, had touched even a roughed-up old speed freak like Durbin. The camper and Volkswagen rig, so emblematic of seventies practicality, exhibited Durbin's genius for automotive self-expression nearly in spite of itself. It was a '63 GMC flatbed with a camper mounted forward and a ramp for the race-car aft. Parked beside Durbin that week in Ocean City was a representative from Winnebago, the great recreational vehicle conglomerate of the early seventies. A whole herd of Winnebago's thirty-thousand-dollar dinosaurs hunkered across the camp ground. Each time their owners wished to drive to the beach or go for dinner they'd have to pull in TV antennas, disconnect water, electricity, haul in their cords and fire the mother up. Durbin would merely hop in his Volkswagen and roll off the rear of his truck. The man from Winnebago told Durbin he ought to consider taking out a patent on his design. Durbin laughed, came home and sold the rig to the investor who'd bought his Vega. If you wanted to dry out you had to shake all the water off your back.

The fate of recreational vehicles in the nineteen seventies oddly paralleled that of race cars Detroit had been producing, pellmell, since the mid-fifties. Both eventually fell prey to spiraling fuel costs, exorbitant insurance rates, and restrictions levied by the Environmental Protection Agency. But not before they effected a vehicular consciousness-raising unprecedented since World War II. World War II pigeonholes the essence of the story. WW II and those interruptions in corporate strategy it wrought—a strategy epitomized by exhibitions pervasive at New York's 1939 World's Fair.*

The theme of the '39 World's Fair was "Building the World of Tomorrow." Its principal motif was a future as implemented by corporate America, Detroit being the largest corporate body represented. The fair was an ad man's holiday. Concepts such as streamlining . . . of toothbrushes to automobiles . . . were introduced, plus culture-permeating slogans such as, "There's a Ford in Your Future." GM boasted a Futurama ride; RCA exhibited television sets; AT&T offered free long-distance telephone calls. Everywhere industrial designers sought to convince manufacturers that the clean, uncluttered lines of Art Deco or Bauhaus could best sell their products. Tailfins were demonstrated in "cars of the future," and "self-sufficient" modular living units, suggestive of recreational vehicles or their tract-based counterparts, were envisioned. The future was now, according to ad

* Sam Love, "Visions of Tomorrow" (see "Futures" chapter).

men; but the payoff was to be delayed six years while the last vestiges of an old world, in Europe and Asia, ripped themselves apart.

World War II—technological harbinger of the age to come— introduced both the army's four-wheel-drive jeep, or General Purpose Vehicle, and the navy's "lettered" vessels, the LSDs, LSTs and LCIs: amphibious landing craft which lumbered from surf to beach like antediluvian polliwogs. They didn't belong in water and they didn't belong on land; they were transmogrifications of function ... grandfathers of intention, if not design, to seventies' RVs. Four-wheel-drive jeeps and "amphibious" vehicles would reincarnate in civilian life as pleasure craft—technological interlopers on wilderness no matter how assessed. For twenty-five years after World War II, though, the big sell in Detroit would remain the Road. A road truncated by suburbia and geared to the short haul—no less ecstatic, if infinitely more complex, for its quarter-mile limits.

Previous to World War II, Detroit had designed cars principally for the long haul; that open road with its coast-to-coast possibilities. Cars such as the Pierce Arrow, the Cord or Packard were sturdy transcontinental vehicles. They suggested, in design, great transcontinental trains of their day: the Super Chief or Twentieth Century Limited. They were expensive; during Depression years available to the few. After World War II, everyone wanted an automobile and most people had the means to afford one. Detroit stood ill-advised to design cars of prewar endurance for this postwar glut. There wasn't time; besides, planned obsolescence would assure future indebtedness, perpetuating a market. The short haul insinuated itself into quality as surely as design, and for a while both parties to the automotive contract were happy.

By 1957 Detroit had proved to its satisfaction that fins and firepower were what Americans wanted in their cars—thus streamlining of models such as the '57 Chevrolet, design mandates which concealed awesomely powerful one-horse-percubic-inch V-8s. Except for Corvette and Thunderbird "sports" models, production cars continued to pose as family sedans until 1964 when Pontiac introduced the Tempest LeMans. By grafting a mammoth engine to a minuscule frame, Detroit cloned the muscle-car era, making accessible, even obligatory, exorbitant power-to-weight ratios for the general public. No longer was America's passion for automotive violence hidden behind the guise of suburban practicality. Cars came out of the closet about the same time as did sex, fashion, and the Vietnam war. An unprecedented decade of carnage ensued on the nation's highways. Drag racing progressed concomitantly, if not so carnivorously. The key item there, as with Vietnam and rock 'n' roll, was technology. A behind-the-scenes involvement with space-age technique and corporate deceit which infiltrated every layer of the market.

If Detroit's thrust had remained subtly paramilitary since World War II, drag racing's parry slashed out blatantly. Hot rodders had been imitating aircraft since their eviction from Lake Muroc by Edwards' test pilots. Those early drags along abandoned air strips had evolved to experimentation with nitromethane fuel and "aviation" designs. By 1965, slingshot dragsters, complete with jet engines, aerodynamic stabilizers and parachute braking systems, had revolutionized the sport. Drivers wore fireproof suits, oxygen masks and intergalactic crash helmets. They resembled astronauts more than hot rodders, their rails accelerating from standstill to two hundred m.p.h. in less than ten seconds, straining toward orbit. It was a complex time for racing; a man nearly had to possess an engineering degree to compete, the courage of a Lindbergh to test a strip. That casualness, looseness and freedom of fifties street racing seemed light years removed.

As did asphalt chivalry. Races were being fixed. What had begun at local tracks as hometown favoritism—a late starting light here, a garbled elapsed time there—snowballed toward corporate fraud.

"Drag racing got like everything else," Durbin recalled. "Serious. There was a lot of politics. A lot of hanky panky which involved big corporations on a national level. Races were rigged. People would be paid under the table. It had to do with reputations and selling products. We lost races several times we thought we shouldn't have. The spectators would see something phony and the competitors would see something, but you never could prove it. Was a lot of fights because of that."

Corporate fraud in cahoots with technological mania erased all vestiges of fun from the sport. No sense of the looser side of American life was evident in drag racing during the sixties; like long hair, drugs, free sex.

"People that wanted to race came to the track," Durbin noted. "People that wanted to smoke and do things like this went somewhere else. Never the two mixed. Even today there's none of it going on at race tracks. Except for the spectators."

The technological orgy in drag racing burned itself out about 1973—the year of armistice in Vietnam and the most devastating fuel shortages at home. Monster rails still rocketed down the track, but spectator interest shifted toward the less arcane. Vans became a major item for Detroit in the mid-seventies. Dowdy old delivery trucks cheaply customized and hopped up as miniature RVs, modular living (and bed) rooms on wheels. "Come love me in my Chevey van," a pop song pleaded. Come love me, stone me, fuck me, hide me, its message. Four-wheel-drive vehicles of every make and design invaded America's beaches, her forests. They were sexy like vans. Tractor pulls—the biggest innovation in drag racing during the seventies—evolved from one of its most primitive antecedents, dray horse competition at county fairs. Tractors, pickups and four-wheel-drives were being outfitted with supercharged engines, transformed into funnies and fuelers as maniacally as their asphalt counterparts. They hauled weighted sleds upwards of forty thousand pounds across a dirt-filled arena, defying mass and gravity. The sport was insanely dangerous, vehicles disintegrating from strain, yet undeniably sensual. It was feminine, smacked of tilling the earth, of a sexy incursion upon soil ... reminiscent of those lost hot rod days rutting across Lake Muroc. It was anti-asphalt and non-stratospheric; that in itself seemed an improvement. Yet it was drag racing—by nature onanistic, ejaculatory, wedded to the short haul. A further manifestation of Redneck Chic, tractor pulling proved sentimental and incipiently suicidal. Its fantasies remained harnessed to the WW II programming of a four-wheel-drive invasion force and the postwar promise of a Ford in every future. Like rural utopians nearly everywhere, tractor pullers missed the kharmic boat. Life outside urban centers still kowtowed to Detroit, and Detroit promised death. Cars could not save us.

Durbin had been reflecting on his earliest years, pre-suburbia, living in the horse country of Potomac: "We had some wrecks on those horses," Durbin mused. "But I had to leave them alone. They didn't have a motor."

Then Durbin made a startling statement.

"I want my kids to have the experiences I had as a youngster. I've bought about seven hundred acres in Howard County, nice piece of land with a couple of springs. I'm going to get my kids into 4-H, buy them each a steer, let them raise it. I can't stand living in the city like this. No wonder a kid starts smoking dope. Nothing for him to do but go out on the sidewalk and ride his bicycle."

Where Durbin lived in Wheaton, Maryland, was as removed from "city life" as the Sea of Tranquility was from downtown Manhattan. It was the pits of suburbia, isolated and removed from all but the automobile. Not a store within walking distance, not a convenience for miles—Durbin was more at odds with the support system of city life than if he'd been living nomadically in New Mexico. That he planned to relocate suggested an improvement. But like many sixties refugees, Durbin looked toward rural life as nirvana. He was someone who had traded dragsters for tractor-trailers, racing for presidency of the Rustic Fence Company. The center Durbin fled, metaphysically, was that urban center which could free him from the dominance of cars. There was no reason to expect him to give up automobiles, they were his livelihood and life's passion. But one fretted over this return to the land.

The most successful counterculture utopians in American history were not those communards of sixties past, but economically self-sufficient groups such as the Amish, Shakers and Mennonites, who not only thumbed their noses at Detroit but shook their heads at a reliance on machinery as sheerest insanity.

Watching Durbin in his easy chair, chain-smoking in this suburban living room, I remembered an elder I had met at an Amish community near Iowa City—a white-bearded patriarch of some vanity who drove the fastest buggy in his clan. Amish were not above a passion for speed. But this buggy's limits were communal, its horsepower singular: an ex-flatracer from New Jersey named Rock 'n' roll.

The last hot rod Durbin had fooled with, in deference to feelings for his mythic '57 Chevrolet, had been a '55 Chevy Nomad, restored, with a 396 big-block engine . . . now five years sold.

"A guy offered me a job driving a dragster the other day," Durbin said. "I turned him down. Nothing I'd rather do than go out here and drive two hundred miles per hour. But she wouldn't let me," he laughed, smacking his fist against his palm. Joan Durbin smiled.

"I'd be driving if it wasn't for family responsibilities," Durbin said. "Way things are, suppose I'll settle for the country, sit on my back porch, get drunk and say fuck it."

While Dennis Durbin was dragging his '57 Chevy out of the Bethesda Hot Shoppes in 1960, Michael Collins was caroming out of Edwards Air Force Base in supersonic jets, scudding across the desert floor at five hundred miles per hour, transgressing co-opted Muroc like a space-age cameleer—fifty feet above the sand in an F-104, say, checking terrain avoidance radar systems, low altitude capabilities, or hot rodding for the hell of it . . . returning from a flight, having done everything required on that mission, and diving to the deck for a twenty-mile joy ride at half a hundred feet, landscape streaking past incredibly, the desert an outstretched palm begging to be slapped. The further one soared away from earth the more speed retreated to a number on a dial, without reference to calamity; one might fly fifteen hundred miles per hour at thirty thousand feet and sense imperceptible motion. But fifty feet above Muroc objects hurtled by with recriminative alacrity. The first moon shot awaited Michael Collins in 1969, acceleration of draconic rockets, a speed of twenty-five thousand miles per hour, top-seeding him as fastest man in the world* ... a mere exercise in Newtonian physics. Down there above Muroc one still felt the dust in one's teeth. Adrenalin pumping and that cold sponge under each armpit which let you know you were alive.

Collins knew nothing in 1960 of what Lake Muroc meant to disenfranchised hot rodders. He had read what Muroc meant to aviators, specifically to the Air Force, in which Collins was a captain. Muroc meant Edwards Air Force Base, home of high-speed flight testing and the USAF Experimental Flight Test Pilot School, where Collins was a plebe. Over Muroc the first American jet had been flown, the sound barrier had been broken, and space-age rockets would be tried. More importantly to Collins, Muroc was that arena where he would compete for admission to the exclusive fraternity of high-speed test pilots. Collins had been flying F-86 Sabrejets out of George Air Force Base, so he was neither stranger to Muroc nor to high-speed flight. Edwards proved another step in that fairly precise career which had chauffeured Collins from prep school, West Point, flight school, day fighter training to Fighter Ops, and ultimately the moon. Muroc stretched rhapsodically toward space. One could take his F-104 from fifty feet above the desert to ninety thousand feet, where "the sky overhead is so dark blue as to be almost the pure black of space."**

Or, one could run.

Intrigued by NASA's expanding astronaut program, Collins applied in 1962 and began training for a five-day physical examination which stood as prerequisite. The killer would be a stress EKG, a treadmill test, ramp tilted ever steeper as the exercise proceeded. Collins started running up a mountain near Edwards in anticipation. Something atavistic strove to mesh. Something ego-swabbing, non-mechanical, anti-technological, suggestive of inner space. Running toward the sky was such a relief after flying at it, pummeling the heavens so catalogued by machinery. Collins dug his sneakers into the alkali of Muroc and soared. A

---

* Twenty-five others since have traveled as fast.
** Michael Collins, *Carrying the Fire* (New York: Ballantine, 1975), p. 33.

program of one hour's running was instigated: two miles at a clip, four times a week.

By July, 1977, Michael Collins was running fifteen miles a day, in preparation for his first marathon. He was forty-seven years old. He had been to the moon. He was director of the Smithsonian's National Air and Space Museum, a post he had accepted in 1971, after an aborted State Department career, a year and some months out of NASA. He was bored, hunting a new job, and in pain. His knees were killing him.

"My knees are my problem," Collins said. "My knees are giving out on me. I just got a new pair of shoes, these Nike LD-1000's. They're supposed to be good for people with ailing knees. I've had them three days now and I think they're helping. So I'm optimistic again. What I really want to do is run the Boston Marathon and write a book about it. But I've never been able to go over fifteen miles. It's not my wind. I have the feeling I can keep going but my knees just drop off."

Collins flaunted the gaunt physiognomy of a distance runner; otherwise he appeared unathletic. Clad in ill-fitting suit, white shirt and narrow tie, black military oxfords smartly polished, he looked the ad man's model astronaut. He dressed with a career officer's disdain for civilian livery, as if suit and tie were bathrobe and sash between uniforms of the day. He carried himself easily, with social grace, but not without discomfort. Collins was a shy man; private. Here in his office, high above Washington's megalithic Air and Space Museum, in its very crow's-nest, Collins as commander moved like an outsider.

A military person, Collins had reason to feel dislocated. Born in Rome, the younger son of a career Army officer—a horse cavalryman—he had endured that peripatetic life of perpetual reassignment, through West Point, graduation, and a military career of his own. Like most career officers he had lived around the world, never establishing a permanent home. Like a few, he had disaffected himself further, breaking earth's hold with rocket fire and braving the moon's gravity. Who could say what restlessness that presumption might have engendered?

On his museum's first floor was a sliver of moon, slate-gray in countenance, bared and mounted upon a pedestal. The public was invited to touch it. Few accepted; relatively few. The piece of moon lay beside other relics of man's striving toward flight— *Spirit of St. Louis,* Goddard rockets, Mercury spacecraft—like a stone washed ashore. If the Air and Space building resembled a launching site along some deserted cape, couched amidst Beaux Arts Washington like a computer in a Victorian drawing room, its turreted facade hinted of World War II gun towers still dotting the Atlantic coast, its aged artifacts so many wrecks drifted ashore. Nubbed spacecraft, gray or scorched black, were rusted anti-ship mines. Collins' own command module, piloted to the dark side of the moon, resembled more a discombobulated fuel dragster than a flying machine. Fired by computers, super-quick, accelerating to twenty-five grand.

Collins was wary of speed, wary to speak of it.

"That was never my goal, in flying, to achieve speed. I always was kind of startled to find it was an interesting and pleasurable byproduct of where I found myself. Speed is not well understood. We're doing, what, a thousand miles an hour right now? Just the rotation of the earth? We should feel a big wind down around our ankles. But in most modern planes, in most situations, speed isn't something you feel viscerally. Mostly speed is a number that says you're going .7 Mach or 1.8 Mach. Now if you're close to another object, like the ground, then whew, that's totally different. Then you get very much a visceral feeling. You know you're about that far away from killing yourself. Pshew, you really see things race by. But in the space program speed isn't that obvious. You fly all the way to the moon and back, practically, and never have a sensation of great speed."

Did Collins nurture experiences as a young man, in terms of vehicular motion, that served as backdrop for his life as a test pilot?

"No, I have to say I really didn't. I used to drive faster than I should. Any kid wants to get the family jalopy and floorboard it once or twice to see what it will do. But I had no extraordinary proclivities in that direction. I'm not very mechanically inclined, for example. I was more interested in English literature than I was in auto mechanics."

A surprising statement from a man who had spent the 1960s in

tech school, memorizing mechanical ins-and-outs of complex
machines he would fly only a few days in the decade. But not
surprising that Collins expressed a fascination for English literature. His book on the moon shot was the best of any astronaut's,
and promised to endure as literature long after less sensitive accounts had sifted into the sands of technocratese.

"I'm writing a novel about flying to Mars in 1990," Collins
confessed. "Writing is all-encompassing enough to sustain me.
But Jesus, from my reading, for every hundred writers there's
one or two that are making a decent living."

Making a living, outside the confines of military or government, beguiled Collins. Providing for his family, for himself, in a
more satisfying way after years of programming in the space
program, of egocentric nonegocentricity (*I* want to fly in space,
but *I* can't do it alone), of guinea pig malaise, harsh compromise,
indignity after indignity; the moon shot dangled at decade's finish, rich dessert after a dull meal. Like most white American
contemporaries, Collins had spent the sixties in school. From
Edwards to Houston; after prep school West Point, basic training, flight school, ad nauseum, ad suppression beyond suppression. Small wonder he would turn away. To have accepted
directorship of a museum—not an atypical seventies move, com-
piling artifacts was taking stock—cataloguing, collating, coordinating programs and personnel which smacked of military if
not academe. Collins was a corporate man, his life had been
subjugated to corporations, but he remained a corporate maverick. He was a loner, that if nothing else separated him from the
corporation. He was a writer.

Further ironies of his position cried for enumeration. He had
sacrificed years in Houston to be excluded from a step across the
moon—nevertheless, as Command Module pilot, he'd experienced some paradigm of driver/pilot aloofness in his orbit alone
round the moon's dark side; he had stayed in the driver's seat
while others walked. He had dreamed of space, of lunar intercourse, some romantic congress expressable only through poetics
of his prose, and suffered seasons of technical drudgery for the
chance; the deal was Faustian. He had relinquished life as a test
pilot for near-life as an engineer, a monkey shot through cloud-

banks in a tin can. He had downplayed instincts toward excess for fear of offending Public Relations, in Houston, the *real* Wild West, more a frontier town during the sixties than ever before— but buttressed, constrained. He had been frontiersman, pioneer, navigator of seas more intimidating than those sailed by Magellan, yet indulged no native lass, not one demijohn in public, no lynching nor mutiny on some anonymous cay ... everything crisp and studiously accounted for, under the lights and open for inspection. Frustration must have run rampant.

"A guy's in this pool competing against his peers for a flight to the moon. Now is he going to go out and have four martinis, drive his car ninety miles an hour, and greet the public with four-letter words? He's too smart for that. He's come too far. He's all mother and apple pie. He's very much with NASA and NASA's never made a mistake in its life. That's where the deception came in. On an individual basis. People not wanting to admit to being anything less than perfect, lest their boss read about it in the newspaper, and they've just shot themselves down in flames as far as getting the first lunar landing flight. Apollo *was* frontier in a way, a pioneering effort, but it was one of such high technology that it was absolutely necessary for it to be this huge team effort. And everybody knew it. So that you always find astronauts saying in their welcome home speeches, hi mom, gosh, I couldn't have done it without the help of thousands. And that was nothing PR told them to say. It was true."

Someone at Houston had described Apollo 11 as a "triumph of the squares." Yet Collins was anything but square. Perhaps he was anomaly as an astronaut; clearly he was different. Of aristocratic bearing, privileged background—his mother had grown up in El Paso, Wild West El Paso, daughter of the town's principal banker; his father, a cavalry officer, had swept her off her feet— Collins no doubt felt the isolation of all privileged minorities, the exultation of adventure percolating in his genes, an intolerance for bores exuding from him as strongly as musk. Popular on the surface, Collins must have known fierce opposition in the space program. If the American aristocrat sensed early that his bearing proved offensive to the majority, he won no solace from his peers, taught from prep school the rigors of competition, not friendly but cutthroat, the simulated weightlessness of laissez-faire capitalism, a space where one dared love no man as friend lest contingencies of the marketplace demand his evisceration. No, Collins was perfect to orbit the moon, had been toughened by a lifetime of seclusion to weather exclusion from that first step across an alien sphere.

He might take frustration out in handball, thrashing his fellow astronauts, or upon family, with his decision to join the Air Force (five of Collins' relatives knew successful careers in the Army, his brother was a colonel, his father a general, an uncle a general, a cousin a major, his father's younger brother Army Chief of Staff). He might complain to Houston of no chance for "play" on his Gemini EVA: "Work, work, work! A guy should be told to go out on the end of his string and simply gaze around—what guru gets to meditate for a whole earth's worth ... I am in the cosmic arena, the place to gain a celestial perspective; it remains only to slow down long enough to capture it . . . ."* He might hone his wit to razor's edge or cloak the sinistrality of his competitive nature (Collins was left-handed) with near-cloying humility. Yes, NASA may have been triumphantly square but Collins was its round peg, smooth in his camouflage as the smoothest hipster on the roughest suburban turf.

What of the atmosphere about Houston's Space Center during the sixties, one wondered? Was there a sense of that decade outside NASA's confines? Of Houston itself as pioneer community, of people who soon would be living on the edge, if not already?

"I think one of the interesting things about people working in the space program in the sixties was that they were in a compartment with fairly solid walls around it. They were focused on this goal of getting to the moon by the end of the sixties, and they had a hell of a lot of work to do; they worked long hours, and their energies were focused on their work. They tended perhaps not to be as introspective as some other disciplines. Because they were primarily engineers, not social scientists. You found them more focused on their own little program and ignoring other things that were going on in the country. We knew there was a Viet-

* Michael Collins, *Carrying the Fire* (New York: Ballantine, 1975), p. 245.

namese war going on and we knew that this was creating great rifts in our society, but that was somebody else's problem. You just heard a murmur. You weren't there on the ramparts. Other things that were going on in the sixties, the things of great change . . . I'm not saying we were impervious to them, but man, don't bother me with that. I've got enough problems . . . we were very insulated, isolated. Had I been a neurosurgeon or a farmer or what have you, I might have found that compartment to be equally information-tight. But I don't think so. I think we were more isolated than most people."

About pioneer activity—was there any sense of the edge? Or was everybody thinking in terms of a technological feat to be performed by decade's end?

"That's hard to answer. Yes and no. Yeah, people thought that breaking away from our planet's gravity for the first time was a pioneering effort. And if you read the standard speeches that NASA officials make, they're always comparing their effort to that of Christopher Columbus or . . . we were going to the moon and there was going to be a Rosetta Stone that would open the secrets of the universe. You had that feeling, of being involved in a pioneering program. But there were so many complexities involved with the going-to and coming-from that, unlike, I would imagine, Columbus, who probably focused all his thoughts and worries on what he was going to find in the new world and how much money he was going to make selling tea . . . I mean, his *destination* was what was important; outfitting the ship and hiring the crew probably were more routine. That had been done before. In the case of the Apollo program, we were doing things that had never been done before, like how do you navigate to the moon? How do you make sure you don't hit the damned thing? How do you design systems that can find themselves three days away from home, so that any malfunction must not require a solution in less than three days' time? We were so involved with technicalities of getting-to and going-from that we almost became experts in the *voyage* itself, rather than what we were going to do when we got there . . . or the implications of what we were doing."

What were those implications, on hindsight?

"I think, ultimately, building toward the capability of deciding whether we want to live on this planet or somewhere else. I think that's the direction of the Manned Space Program. That's the ultimate challenge: to give ourselves that option. And that's a great philosophical question. To stay or to leave. Throughout the history of this earth, we've never had that option."

What would Collins do if he could leave?

"What would I do?"

If he could live on another planet, during the next ten years, would he go?

"No, I probably wouldn't. That gets all bogged down in petty details like how old your kids are and what they're doing, and this kind of stuff. But if I were a young man embarking on a career, and leaving Cape Kennedy was a twelve-billion-pound space ship carrying a crew of 2,500 people, going off in the direction of Alpha Centauri, never to return ... and I knew I had the choice of going, and my descendants might end up somewhere ... or staying here on earth ... I think I'd be strongly tempted to go."

He doesn't lie around fantasizing on it?

"No, I don't lie around fantasizing on that. I really don't."

Collins' novel, about flying to Mars in 1990, had been causing him some trouble. Based on his knowledge of current technology and characters he had known in the space program—astronauts, senators, administrators—the novel strove for accuracy through realistic detail, and, one hoped, offered the peculiar revelations of Collins' sojourns in space which had illuminated *Carrying the Fire*.

"If I could write a novel based on what I know about flying in space, and if I could do that successfully, then I feel I could write a novel about almost anything. Therefore writing would become a fairly substantial part of how I might spend my time for the rest of my life. But I'm finding fiction at least three times as time-consuming or difficult as non-fiction. It does not lend itself to nights and weekends. If I could take a month off I have the feeling I could go like gangbusters—"

Collins appeared reticent to speak of particulars of his novel.

"It concerns a crew of five people flying to Mars in 1990," he reiterated. "I'm not one of them in disguise, and no one of them is really anyone I know. They're amalgams."

Was Collins superstitious about talking of his novel?

"Uneasy, I guess. It's something I really don't want to discuss. I'm kind of embarrassed. Wait until I write it and then read the book, then you'll see if it's any good," he said, laughing.

Was there anything else which filled that creative space, served as balm or catharsis, when Collins' writing was not going well?

"This damn running."

Did he find ideas coming into focus as he ran, themes coalescing, et cetera?

"Occasionally, but I'm a little disappointed. Usually my mind goes to trivia. I'm more sensitive to my surroundings: strange bushes and trees and rocks, and people going by. They divert my attention. Plus the pain. I don't get this euphoria that people talk about, where they're gliding along and they imagine they're omnipotent, and try to run through automobiles, and feel that their feet aren't touching the ground. I never get that. For me it feels good when I quit. I must not do it right. I can lift my head out of my body sometimes and take off somewhere, but it's for pretty short intervals. Then I come back to, God that hurts, or, how far have I gone? I end up looking at rocks in my path, very aware of my surroundings."

Working near city-center, Collins could not have failed to be aware of runners whose numbers had multiplied a thousandfold since 1961, when Collins ran alone up a mountain at Edwards—in the wake of Kennedy's pledge to assault the moon by 1970, and, one assumes, his scolding of Americans to get back in shape. Runners jogged around Washington's mall by the hundreds, past neoclassical monuments, Tidal Basin, Reflecting Pool, Capitol and galleries, as if recalling Kennedy's admonition, acting on it or flying in its face. Where none but tourists had plodded twenty years ago, city-center had blossomed with joggers, Washingtonians employing the city, its magnificent grounds, in a fashion previously held as taboo. Where ten years past police had clashed incessantly with demonstrators, armies of marathoners trooped through calisthenics like driven classicists. Classicists they were. Marathoners were nothing if not mythic beings, bred of Pheidippides' heroic run from Marathon to Athens, pronouncing victory. One could point to few contemporary victories: a raised sexual consciousness, new respect for environment, the capability to launch men into space. Richard Nixon's expulsion from the White House was no small victory; Washington shuffled to the beat of ten thousand Pheidippideses bearing news. Runners clogged America's highways, enraging town fathers, who drew ordinances against them. Nothing would curb the flow. Running was nadir to bureaucrats—by analogue, technocrats—and America, off on some indulgence of the carnal more primitive than Ecology, more sensual than Sixties, came and kept on coming.

The sport of running had boomed during the nineteen-seventies even as technologically based pastimes such as drag racing, Vietnam and Space had peaked during the sixties. Yet running was technology's antithesis. "You don't have to depend on bicycle spokes going around," Collins had noted, of running, "someone pumping up the tires with air or any of those things. There are no mechanical contraptions. It's just you and the world. You got to have shoes, that's about all. You don't even need those. You could run bare-ass if you wanted to." Like counterculture agrarianists, runners were retreating to the land. What had been cross-country running now was LSD: Long Slow Distance. LSD, as acronym, had retreated from chemistry lab to earth and sky; from artificial hallucinogen to aerobic high. Running alone was a most primitive human activity. It harkened to the Paleolithic, when man survived as nomadic hunter . . . pre-agrarian, dependent upon his range as predator, his legs, his lungs. Anthropologists had asserted that distances braved from cave or cliff-dwelling by Paleolithic man, on hunting forays, averaged ten miles.* That would bracket his daily run at approximately twenty miles, the distance contemporary man found psychologically (and physiologically) most difficult to break. A man running alone was in the strongest and most vulnerable of states. Strong because his senses were alert, his big muscles working, his rawest instincts alive. Vulnerable because he tested exhaustion,

* Hal Higdon, "Running and the Mind," *Runner's World,* February, 1978, p. 43.

and motion targeted him as prey. No animal ran in nature which was not attacking or being attacked. Except in playfulness—simulated attack. Or rut. Running was an aggressor's sport in which the line between attack and retreat, fight and flight, was blurred. What pre-seventies runner could forget rages encountered on deserted country roads from hysterical rednecks, the glimpse of a runner inciting some atavistic proclivity to maim? Insults from passing automobiles were so familiar as to barely bristle the runner's consciousness. Assaults from lupine Fidos, frothing at the muzzle, trembling with fear, were expected as rain. The runner alone was on attack; primitive beasts responded.

There was no boredom in running. What masked as boredom was pain; the pain of testing limits. How far, how fast, how long. How hard need one work until the body flushed, sweat ran like blood, and the hole in the center of one's brain opened like a maelstrom, thoughts pouring in, swirling through the trap and lodging somewhere near the base of the spine.

To win that one ran alone.

Yet a disturbing tendency toward group-running had occluded the mid-seventies. If running alone had proved expedient in the late sixties-early seventies—was indeed Paleolithic in sympathy—it stood as reaction to the hearth-bound agrarianisms of a more Neolithic concern. Agrarian communes stepped back from technocracy, to be sure, but in a stultifying way. Possibly they were miniature suburbs, ex-urban, familial, smacking of Mom Dad Buddy & Sis. As first-step-back from asphalt, they moved with proper deportment. But to many, communes were square, a perpetuation of Togetherness where severer possibilities called. Why dig one's hands in Mother Earth when one could lope across her back? Why implant roots when one could hunt nomadically, living blade to mouth, existentially if you will, stalking prey? If communalism was square, it likewise was beat; suggestive of fifties sensibility. The seventies were reminiscent of fifties culture in myriad ways, but previous to running the standard dichotomy between seventies beat and seventies hip had lain obfuscated. The fifties beat had been tribal, bookish, anchored to neighborhood, physically evasive and herbal (marijuana). The hipster traveled alone, often was illiterate, black, despised turf, gloried in physicality and, not uncommonly, abstained from drugs. Back-to-nature, as response to technological overkill, was healthfully regressive but not fully realized until it eclipsed Neo and approached Paleo in its lithicisms. Running alone was the hip side of that recidivism. It recalled dusty natives striding across the Serengeti. Plowshares were being beaten back toward spears. America's primitive psyche applauded.

As did her corporations. It was estimated forty percent of all shoes sold in the United States were running shoes. Jogging polyesters had replaced denim as preferred leisurewear. Magazines such as *Runner's World* knew phenomenal sales, promulgating their lifestyle through editorials and advertising which, amazingly, turned millions on a sport which decried equipment. *Runner's World* was the *Playboy* and *Hot Rod* of seventies chic. As surely as those publications had revolutionized sex and speed during the sixties, *Runner's World* shaped new joggers' attitudes toward running. Psychiatry was not spared; running therapies, in treatment of neurotics and psychotics, were being developed. Marathons had become big business, attracting thousands. A man such as Frank Shorter, 1972 Olympic marathon champion, was a culture hero revered as Arnold Palmer. Like Palmer, Shorter sponsored a line of sports equipment, emphasizing wardrobes.

Something had been gained, yet something threatened loss. As speed, space, sex and war each had come out of the closet during the nineteen-sixties, so had they been transmogrified through huge influxes of corporate cash. Call it a loss of innocence—even Vietnam, that "secret" war, at some point existed as the fancy of a few CIA spooks. Corporations would sully anything. Space—a dream old as man's first glance skyward—told the tale of corporate thrust during the sixties. What may have begun at the '39 World's Fair, behind concepts of streamlining and "Building the World of Tomorrow," bolstered by Kennedy's vision of man-on-the-moon by 1969, had culminated in corporations-on-the-moon: Junked North American Rockwell hulls, freeze-dried wrappers, minicams, and that plastic American flag.

The Smithsonian's Air and Space Museum was as much a monument to those corporations which had manufactured flying machines as to the spirit of men who flew them. The "Spirit of St. Louis" commemorated equally the derring-do of its financial backers as that of Charles Lindbergh. Michael Collins (for whose book Lindbergh had composed a foreword) must have felt this. On his daily runs, often down the Mall, past the Kennedy Center, up Capitol Hill, around Hains Point or along the Potomac toward Alexandria, Collins exorcised lingering traces of techno-virus. An exorcism which had begun, that summer of '69, previous even to breaking quarantine. More Paleolithic than Aquarian, Collins had jogged around corridors in Houston quarantine, post-moonshot, until he "drove everybody crazy." The first step outside, back onto the surface of earth, Collins recalled with primitive relish:

"It was night. There was a lot of excitement, press and PR, crowds, people calling out our names. I couldn't really see where I was going but I was walking on a sidewalk. There wasn't any feeling of the earth mushing up around my feet; what there was was a *smell*. I hadn't smelled the earth for three weeks. That Houston night air smells a little different—I don't know if it's the Gulf of Mexico or the dirt or the grass or what—but it was a very pungent earth smell. I remember thinking, sniff, God, I'm back."

Collins' attitude toward earth had been forever altered.

"Early on, some psychiatrist said that space was going to be like deep-water diving. There would be a breakaway phenomenon. Some divers, the deeper they go, find an exhilaration; they don't want to go back to the surface, they want to ever probe more deeply into the beautiful water ahead—and they drown. I think that's due to nitrogen gas in their systems, a physiological thing, nitrogen narcosis. The shrinks said a similar thing might happen in space. You'd have this breakaway phenomenon and want to keep going. My experience, and the experience of people I've talked to, has been exactly the reverse. The earth acts as a powerful magnet. You like to know where it is. You like to look at it. You think, God, isn't it lovely, aren't we fortunate to live on it . . . I'm looking forward to getting back! When I get back, I'm going to think what a beautiful, little, nice, lovely, fragile place we have. Today I *do* have a different feeling toward earth. A feeling that it's this tiny, little, precious, unique, fragile, above all else, fragile thing that we have to care for, nurture. As we stand here it seems very rugged and flat and infinite. It's all around us. But from space you don't have that feeling. You think, God, we really better protect it, take care of it."

So Collins ran. His feelings toward earth seemed to overlap an aggravated response to himself as human being.

"Running is an introverted thing to do. It's communication with your body. You're listening to it and it's telling you things. Running's a self-centered, inward-turning, ego-nourishing kind of activity. You have the feeling you're doing good things for your body, you're prolonging its life, or you're increasing its ability to cope with stress.... When you're undergoing training which is highly technical and complicated, you *have* to have breaks of one sort and another. Running is good because it's catharsis, where you get rid of these inner tensions through sweating, by building up your body temperature, by exercising your muscles. So that physically you eliminate a lot of worries and fears about the technical nature of your training."

Slowed from 25,000 m.p.h. to seven and one half, Collins trained now for his first marathon. And wrote. Having traded a manipulation of spheres for a manipulation of words, Collins, nevertheless, was skeptical about the future. His heightened sensitivity toward earth was not immune from earthly ennui.

"That's not physiological. It stems from the fact that you have the knowledge—or the suspicion, the very strong suspicion—that you've already had the most interesting job you're ever going to have in your life. You're in your forties and you know you're never going to have a job that's as interesting as the one you used to have. That's kind a bummer. When I've been bored I've always gotten up and moved, I guess. I always was a lousy student and I always hated to be trapped in a classroom. If I couldn't move physically I'd move mentally. You know, I'd get my mind out of that classroom somehow. I don't like to be programmed.

And boy, I sure was programmed in the space program. Kind of a contradiction right there. But I did want to fly in space—"

POSTSCRIPT: In April, 1978, Michael Collins successfully completed the Boston Marathon. Later that year he was appointed Under Secretary of the Smithsonian Institution.

Sport

Rose Bowl, Hula Bowl, Sugar Bowl, Peach Bowl, Gator Bowl, Orange Bowl, Liberty Bowl, Super Bowl, Cotton Bowl ... *nobody* works out in Dallas. Absolute football capital of the universe—by its own standard if not the world's—where are its athletes? Read about football in the papers, see it touted on TV, endure endless predictions on the radio, avoid conversations. *High school, college, pro.* Football is everywhere. And women: cheerleaders all, with long china faces and satin legs, tapered as plastic golf tees. Dallas women are sleek and dutifully exercised ... but where? Where do they do it? *Nobody* works out. To run through the streets of Dallas in cutoff Levis and a faded Lacoste is to invite apocalypse. If the blacks on Live Oak don't get you, the Tex Mex on Pacific will—*runner mon, he need a drink, cat thirsty,* and you are hustled to an alley, doused with Ripple, neutered like a spaniel and stuffed head first in a sanibin—left to bleed to death with your Adidas in the air.

To live is to suffer—humiliation at the hands of lesser beings. Living is exercise, physical perfection. The goal? Bob, weave. Is it isolation? Will ten miles a day separate one from the uninitiated? From the weak ones?

Conditioning. In America, a man makes or fakes his breaks. And Dallas, as the children say, is a heavy town.

* * *

Concrete fades quickly though, east of Dallas; to farm road and black macadam, stoplights; 26 million acres of pine, oak and cypress forest; crossroads towns like Wills Point and Grand Saline, Fruitvale, Big Sandy, Crow—even Greenville, infamous as the scene of Duane Thomas' marijuana bust—so that one may take time to remember 1963. And Joe Don Looney, who, of all the young men from Dallas-Fort Worth with a talent that year for football, was the toughest, strongest, fastest running back, and if rumor hinted truth, absolute meanest sonofabitchin' white boy ever to play the game. Joe Don Looney (the name *rings* with all that was 1962), who, as legend goes, joined coach Bud Wilkinson's Oklahoma team his junior year ('62) after high school stardom in Fort Worth and intense family pressure from his father, himself an ex-NFL pro who had set out to raise Joe Don Looney as "the greatest gridder ever." After three colleges, disciplinary trouble, and a Junior Rose Bowl championship at Cameron Junior College there were scholarship offers from many big schools—but to Oklahoma University because as Joe Don easily confessed: "I can make any college football team in the country, but I can make All-American at Oklahoma." Looney's dreamstuff first appearance at Oklahoma where, late in the Syracuse game, he told quarterback Monte Deere, "Just give me the ball, I'll score," and the subsequent run, an unlikely end-around, where Looney broke seven tackles and outsprinted everyone 60 yards for the winning touchdown—a magical run which sportswriters dubbed "impossible," causing at the moment absolute havoc on the field and two fatal heart attacks in the stands.

Joe Don Looney: already "Oklahoma's Bad Boy" for quirkiness on and off the practice field; who led the Sooners that season in rushing, touchdowns; was an All-American Honorable Mention and led the nation in punting, averaging an amazing 45 yards.* Looney, who at 230 lbs. could sprint the hundred in 9.5;

---

* Of Looney's punting, John Unitas would remark: "In Baltimore one day, during warm up, Looney got off the highest punt I've ever seen. He

who ran 61 yards for a touchdown that season to tie Gale Sayers'
Kansas team, 84 yards for a touchdown against Colorado, scored
three touchdowns and passed for a fourth against Iowa State ...
and who later was thrown off the Sooner team by Bud Wilkinson
after a brawl with an assistant coach (a controversial move by
Wilkinson—but Looney's dreams of All-American, down the
tubes), only to be picked up the following spring by the New
York Giants as their number one draft choice.

Joe Don Looney: who in 28 days of training camp drew more
fines than the rest of the Giants together had drawn in *three years*
... for not taping his ankles ("I know more about my ankles than
these trainers do"), for skipping practice ("I'm in great shape,
aren't I, coach? I know all the plays. Then why do I have to make
practice?"), for violating curfew ("Say I'm 10 minutes late? I got
in an hour early last night. You owe *me* 50 minutes."). . . . Still,
from sportswriters and coaches: "Looney can be the *best*, god-
dammit." Then the trade to Baltimore and a 1964 Colt backfield
dominated by Lenny Moore (who would set an NFL record for
touchdowns that year) and Tom Matte and Unitas, where
Looney was exquisite when given the chance to perform—82
yards on eight carries against the Chicago Bears in his first appearance rushing as a pro—but brooding and frustrated with
coach Don Shula's lack of confidence in him ... enough so to
court trouble off the field: a '64 election-night arrest for kicking
down the door to a nurse's apartment, a fine, lawsuits and one
year's probation; articles in the *Saturday Evening Post, Life* and
later *Sports Illustrated*, with titles like "Bad Boy of the Pros" and
"Football's Marvelous Misfit"—followed thereafter by Looney's
widely publicized trade to the Detroit Lions, for Dennis Gaubatz
... a season or so with the Washington Redskins, 14 months in
Vietnam (rumors of an attempt to sue President Johnson) and a
hopeful comeback trail with the '69 New Orleans Saints, after
two years' lay-off . . . cursed, relegated to the injured waivers list,
more trouble; reports of afternoons alone lifting weights, stereo
booming; more hell-raising off the field, radical politics, Ayn

---

stood there, hands on his hips, watching the ball go up, up, up and yelled
'How ya like that, God?' "

Rand objectivism, sleeping in cemeteries ... but always, "—he's got it *all*, why—" Or as Sam Baugh inveighed: "If Looney ever made up his mind that football was for him, he could be fantastic."

1970, 1971, 1972 and nothing. Looney?

Then:

EX-REDSKIN LOONEY
LOSES COURT RULING

NEW ORLEANS, July 6 (UPI)—A federal appeals court today ruled a confiscated submachine gun could be used as evidence in the firearms trial of Joe Don Looney, a former NFL running back who played with the Washington Redskins.

The gun was found by federal agents in a search of Looney's father's ranch near Diana, Tex., in April 1972. U.S. District Judge William Steger ruled in October that the weapon was found during an illegal search for which agents had no warrant.

Looney was arrested with Ronald Frick, an accused cocaine dealer who allegedly tried to make a deal with undercover agents to sell the smuggled drug.

"More importantly," the 5th U.S. Circuit Court of Appeals said, "he (Frick) had agreed to pay them (the agents) $5,000 to assassinate Federal Chief Judge (Ben C.) Connally to keep him from sentencing Frick's girlfriend for possession of cocaine."

Connally is chief judge for the U.S. District Court for South Texas.

The night of the arrests, five agents of the Bureau of Narcotics and Dangerous Drugs went to the Looney ranch to arrest Frick on a warrant charging him with obstructing justice.

Looney answered the agents' knock on the door and told them Frick was not there. But agents entered the house and found Frick hiding behind a book shelf next to two loaded rifles.

"Looney said that there was some grass (marijuana) in the back bedroom and for the agents to help themselves," the court said.

The agents, who said they feared for their safety because they believed Frick to be dangerous, checked out the house, and in the process found the World War II submachine gun in a bedroom.

Agents said Looney told them the gun was a souvenir from Vietnam, where he served 14 months.

Looney was arraigned for possession of marijuana Oct. 2, 1972, in Henderson, Tex.

Looney played college football at Texas Christian University; Cameron, Okla., Junior College, and the University of Oklahoma. Coach Bud Wilkinson kicked him off the Oklahoma squad after Looney fought with a Sooner assistant coach.

Looney also played professional football with the New York Giants, Baltimore Colts and New Orleans Saints.*

"What's happened to Joe Don Looney?" a friend asked.
"Don't know, but I'm thinking of doing a chapter on him."
"Jesus Christ. You might have to *talk* to him."

Legs are what one remembered: Looney's terrifying weight-lifter's legs which could press 650 lbs. in repetitions of 30, several sets in an afternoon's workout (photo cutouts of Joe Don, adorning a university weight room; strain, pop, and dream of such legs), thighs like oil drums, so overdeveloped the Colts had to special-order pants to fit them. *Legs*. Lifting weights and running. The legend of Looney alone in Texas, working toward Next Season. Behind his daddy's ranch, along sand roads which wound through oil fields, pastureland and East Texas pine forest ... working those mothers. *Legs*.

We had been speaking of God. "It's concepts," Joe Don Looney muttered, "words. That's what gets in the way. Always has. Will, until people take time to ... sit down and see what *is*. Know what I say to a Jesus freak? I mean first off, before he gets lost in his rap? Say, 'Jesus wasn't nothing but a four-foot-tall, wool-headed, pimply-faced African nigger—and if you can't get behind that, brother, you don't know nothing of what the cat was about.' People get hung up on that blond hair, white robe and the pretty beard ... like in picture books, like they want to *fuck* the cat or something, and," Joe Don laughed, "face it, whole lot of them do. They're searching for something *outside* themselves. Jesus knew where that was coming from. They'd only *read* the cat they might get into the far side of that other bullshit, which is ... fucking *prison* man, is what it is."

Joe Don Looney shivered. It was cold in Diana this evening.

* The *Washington Post,* July 6, 1973.

About 40 degrees at the high school stadium, where Diana's Eagles were getting the pus stomped out of them by Troup's Tigers. The legs *were* remarkable. Down from a pro weight of 225–235 lbs. (Jim Brown's size) to an incredible 157, Joe Don Looney carried a phantom of his former musculature, most of it packed into his shoulders and biceps. After five days of fasting and a summer and fall of nothing but fruit, Looney's terrifying weightlifter's legs had shrunk to the stockiness of chicken wings.

"If I could just get 'em warm," Joe Don complained.

He had forgotten his jacket. He was dressed in a cowboy shirt, old Wranglers and a light wool sweater. Not enough. At 6'1" and 157 lbs. Joe Don had zero fat to burn at night football games. I offered him my leather jacket; reluctantly he accepted it.

"Now if I could just have your pants," he said, grinning.

Who could have thought it? Smart money would have bet 270 lbs. by now: exploding gut, an ex-jock surliness to the manner . . . black Mansonesque hair perhaps, a thick beard. Looney's light brown hair was clipped. He wore no beard. He was not ravaged. His 31-year-old face was smooth as an 18-year-old's. We were quietly discussing coaches Looney had known. Joe Don stood under the high school floodlights, splay-footed, his hands stuffed deep in his pockets. He spoke with a soft Texas baritone— ghostly and unsettling, for it was the voice of a larger man.

"Now look!" Joe's daddy interrupted. Troup's fullback had scored on a three-yard plunge, heisting the score up, 20-7. "Shoot," Don Looney said, toeing a chunk of dirt with his cowboy boot. Big Don Looney—number one NFL pass receiver for the Philadelphia Eagles in 1940, and an ex-NFL official—cursed again, ineptitude seeming to oppress him. He leaned forward on the wire fence, shushing Joe Don and me. The point-after was good. Both teams jogged off the field toward dressing rooms. It was halftime.

"You can do it without a coach," Don Looney said, "but *hell* it's tough. Joe Don never had any good coaching in the pros; and he never had much of a blocking line, neither. These here Diana kids had them a fine team last year. Poor little East Texas town, nothing but a steel mill and some dirt farming, but the high school bought 'em all new uniforms and was behind 'em a hundred percent. My father give 'em land for this field. Course that was way back. Joe Don's great grandaddy settled this town, round 1900—at one time owned nearly everything here. Diana lost their first three games this season and everybody's tails fell off. Can't say it's the coach, you can't actually *blame* this coach—but how could he be worth much if he was coaching here in Diana? Huh? You tell me."

"Maybe he likes working with poor kids," Joe Don offered.

"Now it is better since they integrated," Don Looney said. "Town was real tough on that subject. Diana was *segregated.* People still don't like to wash their clothes at the laundromat in the same machines as colored. That sort of thing. Damn if the football team hadn't improved since they put 'em all up in one school. Somebody'd teach some blocking though, wouldn't hurt." Big Don Looney straightened, stretched, and passed a stream of whiskey-brown tobacco juice. A tall man—6'2" with modest paunch, a small boy's face and darting eyes—he spotted someone he knew near the concession stand and ambled over in that direction.

Troup's band had taken the field. They stepped across limed hash marks to a martial beat with precision, grace. Their tone was clear as Sousa's. The evening had taken a surrealistic dip: Hundreds of people crowded in the freezing-cold middle of nowhere, under powerful floodlights, steer breath rising; no actual *town* for miles, but lonesome forest and winter pastureland, 120 miles east of Dallas, practically to Louisiana; no *buildings* to speak of—just cars in a big lot, football stands and this piercing brass band of Troup's surprisingly together but haunting, extinct—like some shiny Packard in a 1930s musical. DALLAS SECRETARY SHOTGUN-BLASTED IN TRUNK OF CAR, I had been shuddering to hours before.

"One-A ball," Joe Don was explaining, "that's the small school rating. Got so much football and so many high school teams in Texas, need four different statewide ratings. Diana's one-A. That don't mean they're not good. Some of these kids are strong enough to play college ball. But they don't get taught much at Diana. Too bad, 'cause some of 'em could get away . . . be more than just steel workers or truck farmers like their fathers. I played AAAA ball in Fort Worth, that's the big school rating and supposedly what's hot."

Joe Don and I had moved toward the cheerleaders. We stood for a moment, staring.

"Tell you a story," Joe Don said. "First realization I had about art or music or drama or however way you want to categorize it—and football—happened in high school at a night game like this. Was going with a little cheerleader—and in those days, man, I didn't have money for nothing. You remember that corsage you were supposed to buy girls for football games? Well, old Don was working a gas station in Fort Worth and we were living out back of it. I didn't have *any* money. I got my cheerleader a cheap corsage, one of those with a cardboard backing, flowers pasted on cardboard. About halftime I glanced over from midfield, and with all the bouncing and cheering she'd been doing, wasn't anything left pinned to her sweater but a piece of bare cardboard."

Joe Don grinned. A play broke near the sideline and Diana's back with the ball hurtled toward us. Instinctively I ducked behind a heavy steel railing. Joe Don reached forward, just as instinctively, and broke the young man's momentum. Joe Don had moved fast.

"You were the star though, right?" I said, panting. "I mean the one she was bouncing up and down for?"

"That's so. Point of my story was not that little cheerleader, but this whole cosmic sideline scene. The *band*, really. I thought that if you were a stud you didn't play in your high school band; you know, the band was for pussies, real men were on the field. I was into weightlifting then, and there was this guy I admired for his neck—a *huge* neck this kid had. He was a starter on the team. First game of the season, we're all lying around the locker room at halftime, pissing and hacking and worrying about each other's muscles—but this cat is hustling out of his pads and into a band uniform. Guy I envied played *clarinet* in the school band—well as being one of the major studs on the starting team. Turned my head around. *I* wanted to play in the band after that. But never could figure how to blow one of those clarinets." Joe Don smiled, lassitude settling across his features.

"Diana could have done something this year," he said, "with the football team they have. Like what these Troup kids did with their band. You got to really want it, though. Can't let things set you back. Diana just gave up."

"Ever think about teaching in Diana, Joe?"

Joe Don looked amazed. "Me?" he said. "What could I teach these kids wouldn't fuck 'em up worse than they are? I mean, having to stay in Diana."

We had wandered near a bake sale. Several women were seated at a folding picnic table, slathered with homemade pies. Joe Don eyed a coconut cream and leaned down to sniff it. Kids milled around: black kids in Afros and apple hats, white kids in farm jackets and high-top basketball shoes, girls in knee socks and pleated skirts, everyone ecstatic. "Lord, Toby," Joe Don sighed, "Which one of these pies you like? Think we're gonna have to liberate this coconut cream. Break my fast tonight with a big slab of that mother." The bake sale women wore smiles; one of them jotted "Looney" on a slip of paper and taped it across the cellophane.

We looked around for Big Don. He was talking with an old black man, standing near the gate. We strolled over that way. Both teams were ready to take the field. The black man eased off as Joe Don and I approached. But he stepped back closer. "Mistah Looney so *rich,*" he laughed. Then he disappeared.

Big Don glanced at the scoreboard, passed some tobacco juice and ruminated.

"Let me tell you somethin' 'bout that colored man," he said. "If the guvment had gold in the bank that feller has in his *mouth,* world monetary crisis wouldn't be nothing to slip a disc about. What say we leave these Eagles to their fate worse'n death, juke on up the house, get ourselves warm."

Joe Don Looney was eating dates. "If there *are* extraterrestrials smart enough to travel here," he was saying, "they're not going to communicate the way we do, with language and all our word games. It's got to be vibrations. Energy flow. Mind talk. I've seen UFOs. Got an uncle, Bill Looney, has been all over the world studying UFO phenomena. Egypt, India. He wrote a book about Light Angels he met in Israel. *Radix,* Bill's book's called. About love, light and power—or father, son and holy ghost as the Christians would call it. You ought to read Bill's book.

"Let me tell you a story," Joe Don said, stoking the fire. I cut the volume on Big Don's color console, Big Don having fallen asleep. He'd made it through talk of the energy crisis, oil derrick fires, the comet Kahoutek, milk fund scandal, several TV serials, most of Johnny Carson and the beginning of a discussion between Joe Don and me concerning LSD therapy for terminal cancer patients. "I don't see how that LSD could do an old fucker like me any good," Big Don had said, before drifting into sleep. He lay the length of his Barcalounger, supine and largely invisible from where Joe Don and I reclined on the floor. Joe Don performed stretching exercises as we talked. Big Don's cowboy boots stuck out toward the color TV, absorbing what was left of the Carson show.

"It's 1970," Joe Don drawled, "the Saints have put me on injured waivers. I been back from Vietnam a short time, my marriage is busting up, I'm into a heavy bit of this and a heavy bit of that. First thing I know it's 1971 and I'm in Hong Kong on a Chinese junk, and there's this amazing cat named Fred living naked except for a loincloth on this junk moored next to us; this black dude Fred who'd been a well-known musician around New York it seems, but now, since we'd turned him on to some special ganja that only *we* had in the entire city of Hong Kong . . . this ganja being the straw that broke Fred's spiritual back, so to speak . . . he'd forsaken his career and everything to sit in the sun, on the deck of this junk doing nothing. Now I'd met a lot of strange people in my time, lot of weird doggies, and there never was anybody more cynical in those days than me. But this cat Fred was another something else. I just couldn't cut a corner on him, he was so real. Old Fred was a *ballbearing* you know, and you can't *get* a corner on a ballbearing. Well, these friends of mine and I were on kind of a last trip ourselves, Hong Kong being a big business venture, $100,000 worth as a matter of fact, a *last* business venture and then we were buying a sailboat, easing off into the sunset, and to hell with everything. Hong Kong was going to be it, no more. We'd have all that money, more than we could spend, plus the boat, then . . . into the sunset. That's all we could think about, particularly the money. There were several of us—friend of mine from Fort Worth; guy named Ray we'd met who was an electronics genius and one of these guys so smart and so charming and so together, you wouldn't think life could ever present him a problem; and this woman Rhonda, from a wealthy family back in the States, a TV model, very successful in New York, and beautiful, had everything a woman could want; and well, there were a couple others. My head was starting to turn around then—those years I played football I'd never so much as smoked a cigarette, let alone a joint. Remember late as Halloween, 1970, I was with some friends in Washington and we were headed to a party. Party was about fifteen miles away, and somebody starts floating a joint around the car. 'You know I don't smoke cigarettes, man' I said, and everybody broke up. But I got a little high that night . . . Halloween. Anyhow, I couldn't get *any* kind of corner on Fred. He was the first wise man I ever met. Taught me meditation, yoga. Fred would do yoga all day—called it sittin' and stretchin'. That's right. Fred and I would sit out on the deck, naked mostly, smoke some weed, do yoga and talk. People were coming from all over to talk to Fred. They'd heard about him, this crazy nigger living like a . . . saint in Hong Kong harbor. Heard that he was a holy man, really. That sort of information travels fast. They'd come and offer Fred all kinds of money to teach them what he knew, to follow them, be their guru. One of my fondest memories is of old Fred sitting on the stern of that junk tossing dollar bills into the wind and watching them drift off into the harbor. Sometimes he'd go with people. Never needed a passport, he'd stroll off the plane in his loincloth and customs wouldn't ask him anything. Fred traveled to the Himalayas that way, never spent a cent. Somebody always paid for Fred, they were honored to have him along. Fred wouldn't do *any*thing on his own. He'd forsaken it all. I'd say, 'Fred, the moorings on your junk are loose, goddammit, you're gonna drift away,' and he'd do nothing. 'Dammit, Fred!' I'd say, but he'd shake his head and insist he'd only fuck up if he touched it. One night we had these heavy typhoon warnings. Everyone evac-

uated the harbor except Fred. Wind was blowing, rain . . . I went
down there and pleaded with him. 'Nope,' he said, 'I'll only fuck
up.' He's sitting out there in the wind and rain, in his loincloth,
saying 'I'll just fuck up, Joe Don.' So a tidal wave comes along,
hits the harbor—and everyone's saying, 'Oh Lord, wonder what
happened to Fred?' Sonofabitch's boat had carried half a mile
inland and settled right-side-up in a boatyard. Unbelievable.
That was about the time I *really* started paying attention to Fred.

"I'm still dreaming about that $100,000 though," Joe contin-
ued. "Goddam, I couldn't wait. But we *had* to wait, was the
problem. Had to wait for everything to come through just right.
So I kept dropping acid, smoking weed with Fred, talking to him
and doing yoga exercises naked with him, watching the lights of
Hong Kong harbor—and fucking women. Man, in those days, if
I wasn't getting laid at least once a day everyday I thought there
was something wrong with me, that I wasn't a *man,* you know.
One night I'd dropped a half a tab and was sitting out on the
junk with Fred, not too high you understand, but tripping off
against the lights and stars, thinking what a beautiful warm night
it was—when old Ray comes screaming onto the boat, 'Let's go!
Let's go!' He's high as a motherfucker on his own crazy nervous-
ness, from having to wait on our deal this long, and he's just
screaming. Shit, I think, it's all coming down, we're going to have
to fight every Chinese in Hong Kong and I'm not even wearing
my pants. But Ray gets us up and explains that we're going on
Charley's boat, Charley being this bad news cat with All the
Money in the World and the hugest most beautiful sailboat you
ever saw, which happened to be docked nearby. That's how we
met Charley. Guess we were neighbors. But we'd never been invited up on Charley's boat. He'd come down and see us, dig
Fred, take us out and spend money on us, but we were never
asked up on his super-yacht. So Ray screams, *'Come on! We're
going out on Charley's yacht!'* And he is crazy, like I tell you,
from his own anxiety and terrible vibrations. But somehow he
gets me and Fred up to the boat and settled.

"I'm sitting with Fred and Ray and Charley and Rhonda, out
on the fantail of Charley's yacht, and that half a tab is still working on me some, though not much—enough to emphasize the

lights, the breeze, the stars—and I'm thinking, wow, this is really
it, this is everything a man dreams of in life: beautiful women,
good friends, lots of dope, Hong Kong harbor, old Charley and
his fucking sailboat—when all of a sudden I start seeing it in another perspective, for what maybe it *really* was. I started seeing
Charley, this miserable cat whom I'd never liked, with All the
Money in the World, as what he was, money-mean and miserable. I looked at the fancy drinks and food Charley was passing
around, expensive dope, and I saw how crazy my friends were to
be suckered into Charley's nightmare. I thought of that $100,000
we were busting our guts to get, and ... I said 'fuck it.' I looked
over at Fred, who was sitting in his loincloth staring at the stars,
and I thought goddamn old Charley and this sailboat and floating off into the sunset. Just then Fred passed his hand over mine,
which was resting palm up across my knee, and blue electricity
zig-zagged between us. Fred held his hand over mine, maybe five
minutes. Blue electricity stayed there. I said 'yes!' and I could feel
all that nasty diseased stuff being sucked out of my body, being
replaced with ... a *clean* glow. Old Fred was healing me! Filling
me with his healthy vibrations, etheric fluid, or what the Hindus
call *prāna,* the vital substance. I climbed down off Charley's boat
and went back to Fred's junk. Couple of weeks I was in
Thailand."

"Your friends?"

"They sailed off with Charley. Don't know what happened to
Fred. He's got someone to follow him though, you can bet your
ass on that."

Joe Don glared into the fire. He stretched and preened, pinch-
ing at his triceps. He settled into a sprinter's crouch and was still.

Flashing stroboscopic lights intruded from the color console.
David Bowie had popped up and was flouncing about in a kind
of feathered Tinkerbell costume, wan titties shored up by two
black ostrich plumes. Joe Don stared.

"What is *that?*" he said.

It was a harsh transition.

"David Bowie."

"A ... man?"

"Yes. He's married, got a wife looks just like him."

Joe Don stared a second longer. Then he reached forward and cut up the volume, shoulders swinging into the beat.

"He'd have to," Joe Don said. "Couldn't fuck no one but himself." Pause. "I can dig his rhythm, though—like *grinding* with a woman."

Joe Don's shoulders twisted and shook from where he lay against the foot of Big Don's Barcalounger.

"I still respond to that."

"Still?"

Joe Don laughed. "Like I told you, Toby. Used to be I couldn't have sat through a conversation like we been having, especially if I was out in public and there were women moving around. Every fine looking piece would step through that door, I'd think 'Lord!' or if she came on to me I'd be coming on to her—and wouldn't be any way I could concentrate on what you and I had been saying. That couldn't happen now, though, I don't *see* women that way anymore. This is ironic . . . I have to want to *make love* to them, have there be some actual *gift* of love flowing between us. Kid stuff, you say. But I was a cat, Toby, right up there with the heaviest in the stud department. I couldn't concentrate on nothing else, except maybe some guy who'd climb up in my face and I'd have to get pissed off and say, 'Okay motherfucker, let's see your *biceps*."

"And it was Fred—"

"It was Fred, yoga, the drugs, me, plus a whole lot of other things. Yoga—with sex—that's ironic too. Now I don't care about sex anymore, I'm a better ball. Got control of my body with yoga. But it has to be the love thing. Lord, Toby, I've rolled off too many."

Joe Don ate the last of the dates and ran a finger round the edge of the bowl. He had wolfed down maybe three pounds of dates since we had started talking.

The coconut cream pie lay in the kitchen, untouched.

Books were everywhere. A library of strange literature: *The Way of Chuang Tzu* by Thomas Merton, *The Chakras* by C. W. Leadbetter, *Rational Fasting* by Arnold Ehret, *The Urantia*

Book, several volumes of Paul Brunton, Baird T. Spaulding's *Life and Teachings of the Masters of the Far East,* some Annie Besant, treatises on yoga, assorted fiction, drama, science fiction, philosophy, King James Bibles, Bible concordances, and notebooks filled with Joe Don's scrawl. Notes on books he'd been reading, what he'd been thinking. An ancient black maid pushed some of this away and served breakfast coffee. Joe Don was in the back bedroom, doing sittin' and stretchin'. It was morning. I hadn't heard from Big Don.

I was seated on an overstuffed couch. A coffee table in front of me was cluttered with Joe Don's books. Several had overflowed to the sofa. It was becoming clear that my preparation for this adventure had been focused in an oblique direction. Talk of yoga, Christianity, astrology, Buddhism, Hinduism, theosophy in general and Joe Don's philosophy in particular had continued late into the night. I carried my coffee to a big picture window. The window framed 250 acres of Looney ranch, brown pastureland, pine forest and pond. The ranch house was just that—a modern ranch house, adapted from Joe's grandfather's place, which had been a ranch house in the antique sense. The end effect was not unpleasant, merely parthenogenetic. One puzzled over sire and dam.

Furnishings in the Looney household were plain. Two Barca-loungers, two lamps, the big color TV, a painting of a much younger Joe Don and his daddy, a plastic statue of a football player, one or two silver trophies. A big fireplace. The floor was carpeted wall-to-wall. It was a masculine atmosphere. Nothing extra. Everything utilitarian. Like trailer camping.

I sat down on the brick hearth to finish my coffee. The maid was banging dishes in the kitchen. She had the washing machine and dryer going, too. Joe Don emerged from the back bedroom, dressed in pajama bottoms. He nodded. I followed him toward the rear of the house. In what once had been the famous Looney weight room, Joe Don swung onto a trapeze-like mechanism suspended from the ceiling and hung upside-down like a bat. His fingertips brushed the floor.

"Gets the spine," Joe Don said. "Stretches it . . . good."

Joe Don sounded groggy. He hung there, not speaking. Upside-down, his mouth fluttered near the center of his forehead like a third eye. Joe Don was far away. I walked outside. It was a lovely day in Texas, about 60 degrees and sunny. Football weather.

I could not get over how thin Joe Don was. When he'd swung down I asked why he'd decided to lose weight. Was it a gradual thing or had he dropped down all at once?

"Gradual. More a result of cutting out all the crap I used to eat than a drastic fast. I been on this mucus-free diet since summer—that means no meat, no starchy vegetables, no nuts. Primarily fruit. I'm not fanatic about it. I've gone off a couple of times. But that's how I lost the big weight. Shit, I used to eat junk all the time. Was always stuffing hamburgers or cupcakes into my mouth. I thought weight was cool. And working out—*always* jacking those barbells around. I've got my weightlifting schedule back in the bedroom someplace. Amazes me when I see it today. Everything was preparation for football. My *life* was a preparation for football. One season would finish and it was getting ready for the next . . . running, lifting, eating and repeat . . . running, lifting . . . it was *crazy*. I really thought that 230 lbs. was cool. I see now that the strong man . . . the really strong man, is not one who can press 250 lbs. or run X-number of miles, but one who can sit still for 90 days without eating a thing. He's the man who'll survive. Not that cat with cheeseburgers on his mind. We don't *need* all that food. It's wasteful to overeat. Just as it's a waste having all these damn electric appliances running. I lost weight to become more healthy is the answer to your question. Healthy in body and spirit. Fruit cleans you out."

Big Don Looney appeared, wearing Stetson, tooled cowboy boots and an extraordinary one-piece jump-suit—top half done like a fancy embroidered cowboy shirt, bottom half like separate Western slacks. His trouser bottoms were tucked into his boots. Big Don extended hearty good mornings.

"Got a man coming over, see about one of them oil wells," Big Don said. "Went by saw GW this morning. He's okay. Got hisself in trouble up there yesterday, though. Knocked one of those old gents on his butt. Said he was interfering with his privacy. This here's Joe Don's grandaddy I'm talking about. Last man of principle. Lives in the Old Folk's Home up Gilmer. Was his house here, before we remodeled it. Anyhow Joe Don, he's got 'em in an uproar. All this gent did was lay a hand on GW's shoulder while he was in the toilet. And GW let him have it."

"Tell that story, Don, about GW and a lie somebody said—"

Big Don Looney grinned and passed a squirt of tobacco juice into a paper cup. "Sheriff come round one evening to GW's place, when GW was young, and accused him of running a still. GW said, Sheriff, you search this place, but I want to know who told you that lie before you leave. Sheriff mentioned one of the men's names. GW got his pistol and went down to the man's house. Said, who else was in on this lie, son? Tell me or I'll kill you. Man told. GW said, come along with me. Man went. GW collected the other and drove 'em both to the County Courthouse at gunpoint. Marched 'em up the Courthouse stairs and made 'em swear out an affidavit that they had told a lie about GW Looney, and regretted it. That piece of paper is still at the County Courthouse. You can see it."

"How old is GW now?"

"He's 93. You ought to see him, he ain't going to last. Here, Joe Don, take this money when you go." Big Don laid a crisp one hundred dollar bill on the table. "Buy some fruit. What's Maybelle got there, pot roast? Lord. Best buy a *mess* of fruit. Whole lot of football games got to be watched this weekend."

Joe Don Looney bought $24 worth of fruit at the supermarket in Gilmer. That's a lot of fruit. Joe Don beamed. "Every time I walk out of a food store I feel guilty," he said. "I got all this good fruit to take home and all they have is that dirty money."

We stumbled out to the car, a Mustang I'd rented in Dallas. Joe Don stashed his fruit in back. He eyed the little Mustang skeptically.

"One thing I'm thankful for," he said, "was a time I had the cash for a fine automobile. Had all the hot rods when I was a kid—'61 Chevy with 348 engine, cam, headers, slicks, the works—but when I went up to Baltimore and got that money, first thing I bought was a 300 SL Mercedes, one of the old ones with gullwing doors. Man, that was an automobile. It was a privilege to drive. Got 150 m.p.h. just like that. You didn't *have* to drive that mother, it drove itself."

"Own a car now?"

"I don't own nothing but my books, a few clothes, down bag, back pack. I sold it all. None of it meant anything."

We pulled out of the parking lot and rode a ways without speaking.

"Your father was a professional baseball player too, wasn't he?"

"That's right. You could play both in those days. Professional sports weren't anywhere near as specialized. Old Don's an interesting character. You ought to talk to him. He's been through a lot: roughnecking the oil fields, running gas stations, refereeing ... but he's done all right by himself. Oil. Investments."

"He only played one or two years in the NFL. How come he didn't pick it up again after the war?"

"I think old Don saw the light. He had a family to support, and he hadn't done nothing in the service but play football for one general's team, then be transferred to play for another's someplace else. He saw football for what it was, I think. A bunch of bullshit."

"Did he lay a lot of pressure on you to play ball?"

Joe Don dug into a bag of grapes and thought for a moment. "I don't know about that." Then silence.

"Can .... What's your first recollection of football? Can you place that? I remember vividly the first time I got into a neighborhood football game. Bunch of kids fooling around, then I've got this ball under my arm and I'm being chased and goddamn! This is football. You recollect anything like that?"

"I used to like to hit," Joe Don said. Then silence.

"Jim Kiick or Larry Csonka or one of those people has said that a running back is a guy who loved to be chased as a kid. Csonka talks about how he used to take off across fields and run fast as he could, for as long as he could. Through briar patches, fences, everything. He'd even throw rocks at cops to get them to chase him. He says he believed he couldn't ever be caught."

"I can dig that. I used to like to run."

"What was your opinion of yourself as a running back, Joe—when you were playing pro?"

Joe Don looked at me. "I thought I was the best. There wasn't anyone else who could touch me." This said in absolute humility. Then silence.

"And looking back?"

"I was the best."

"Why do you suppose you had so much trouble in the pros?"

Joe Don Looney laughed. "Trouble? Make a right here, Toby. Let's quit all this talk about *football*, and go see GW."

GW Looney sat propped up against the sunless wall of a dayroom—alone but in company of twenty other residents of the Old Folk's Home in Gilmer. He spotted Joe Don and smiled, raising a thin hand. The other residents stared. Joe Don crouched beside the old man's chair and took his hand.

"Brought you some fruit," Joe Don said. The old man grinned eagerly, exposing one or two ochre teeth. He was very thin.

"How you feel?" Joe Don asked. The old man held Joe Don's hand and said, "All right, but ah'm going away from here in a few days."

"That's okay," Joe Don said.

"Ah'm going away," GW said, "and ah want you should take care of your father. Watch after him."

"I will," Joe Don said. "Don't you worry."

"Do believe ah'm going away," GW said.

"That's okay," Joe Don repeated. He stood up. "I'm putting this bunch of bananas in your room." He walked away.

GW looked at me. I smiled, hunkering down beside him, like Joe Don. The old man took my hand.

"Had me a *good* life," GW said. "Ah lived with a good woman. Never done no man harm. Ah got sons who do well. Ah got one down here who made $600,000," and GW laughed as if it were inconceivable to him, "*$600,000*," and squeezed my hand. "Had a good life," GW repeated.

I could feel old people around the rim of the dayroom watching us.

"Those bananas are in your room," Joe Don said, crouching back down. "We're going along, now," he said. "Be back in a couple of days."

"Ah might be leaving 'fore I see you," the old man said.

"That's okay," Joe Don said. "That's natural." And we left. Old folks' stares trailing us down the hall.

"He always talk about dying?" I asked, once Joe Don and I were outside.

"I never heard it before. Spirit must be leaving his body." Joe Don arched his backside out of the Mustang's bucket seat, avoiding his seatbelt, and I started the engine.

"I'm much closer in consciousness to that old man in there than I am to my father," Joe Don said.

We rode along in silence.

"Maybe GW *is* the last man of principle," Joe Don said. I turned left on Rt. 154 and headed back toward Diana. A quiet country blacktop, through hilly East Texas pastureland.

"I had a grandfather on my mother's side was a cowboy on the old Chisholm Trail," Joe Don said.

Then we were home.

Racked out full-length like regulation space cadets on Big Don's two Barcaloungers, Joe Don and I stared at the big color screen. Tennessee and Mississippi were kicking the shit out of each other someplace several hundred miles away. Big Don was down at the near tank, snagging crappie with a cane pole. If we stood up and looked out the window, we could see him. But we settled for Tennessee-Mississippi, flat on our asses full-length on the Barcaloungers. Eating grapes. Joe Don had a whole shopping-bagful set out between us. We spit pits and stems into an empty sack. Occasionally Joe Don would contribute a bit of mucus.

I'd asked Joe Don about Bud Wilkinson. No comment. I'd asked if the Oklahoma team had voted concurrence in Wilkinson's decision to dismiss Joe Don. "No," Joe Don had said. Nothing more. I described for Joe Don a scene in Don DeLillo's *End Zone* where the hero goes into a football game stoned, stands and stares through one down, then leaves the field to get something to eat. Joe Don laughed. "If anyone did play football stoned, sure wouldn't take more than one down to quit."

"Why?" I asked.

Joe Don glanced at me like I was crazy.

"Twenty-two grown men on a patch of grass, running full speed into one another, to control possession of . . . a worthless value-object? The football? A value-object of *no value?*"

I shrugged. "The British actor Robert Morley has a rap about footballs. He maintains that balls and sports involving balls are the root of all wars, psychoneuroses, envy and interpersonal strife. He says balls should be confiscated and destroyed. Further production of balls should be outlawed by international decree."

Joe Don spit a grape pit toward the fireplace and missed. "You see the fallacy in that though, don't you, Toby? Robert Morley's *playing* football when he talks like that. He's putting it all on the head of the ball. Same old transference. He's still *playing games with a ball,* when he talks that way.

"It's like a Jesus freak with Jesus. Exactly the same. If I get hold of Jesus, he's going to save my ass. If I get this football they're going to love me in the stands, and I'll be a winner. Or in the case of Morley, if I get *rid* of this football they're going to love me and we'll all be winners. Bullshit. It's all inside. Balls, Jesus—you can't put that value *outside* yourself. God ain't in Jesus or that football. He's in you. Jesus would be the first to've admitted that. He knew he was God. But he knew everybody else was God, too. Tried to show people. But they were dumb then as they are today. I was an atheist for twenty-nine years, Toby. None of this agnostic shit, man I *knew* there was no God. I wanted—wanted to see there was God so bad—for that twenty-nine years, but I couldn't. Somebody start rapping about God, I'd say, okay, come on over here, let's *talk* about it, brother. And I'd always have a counter to the cat's argument. I was so tight. Was like my legs. Took six months to get loose enough to make a full lotus. I was the tightest cat in the world. I took 100, maybe 150 acid trips before I had an hallucination."

"How—"

"Willpower, Toby. That old Looney will. *I will not hallucinate.*

Used to think I could conquer the world with will. When I did let go—remember the night, was in Hawaii and this chick I was tripping with, she could see it, she told me later, she could see it rolling across my face. Tranquility. God. Knowing it was all inside.

"Let me tell you a story about willpower. When I was a kid in high school, back in Fort Worth, I'd been working out with weights—had just started again, 'cause I remember I felt sore— well, I went down to the track that afternoon and had myself timed in the hundred yard dash. For fun. No blocks or nothing . . . and I was under ten seconds. I said, Joe Don you can be the best at this. So I started training. Was only one other kid in Texas who could beat me, whole time I was in high school. We ran about even, actually. First year I got hurt before the statewide competition, and he took it. I was furious with myself, I knew I was better than this kid. I knew that my willpower would have broken me loose and I'd have beaten him. But this kid had a beautiful zen-like attitude toward running. He *knew* he could get from this point to that point faster than anyone else. Was nothing willful about it. Once I realized his secret, I knew he was right. But I also knew that *with* his secret I could beat him worse. I did, too. Won the statewide championship next year. Was nobody who could catch me."

"Is it true you once ran a 9.5 hundred?"

"I ran a 6.2 sixty, which is comparable."

"That's amazing, at 230 lbs."

"Well," Joe Don said, hacking a gob of mucus into the stem bag, "I used to amaze myself fairly regular."

We watched the Tennessee-Mississippi game, bare feet stuck out over the toes of our Barcaloungers to the big color TV and an ever-reddening Texas sky.

"Got to run before it gets dark," I said.

"Now look at that!" Joe Don said, pointing at the screen. "See! There!" He laughed. "That business of helping each other up after the play. That's *exactly* what I'm talking about. Used to bust my ass going downfield, and then lie there with my hand in the air, waiting for somebody to help me up. One day I said to myself, you stupid sonofabitch, all you're doing with your hand

in the air is wasting *time and energy.* You can get up by yourself
and be back where you're supposed to be, spending half the time
and energy it takes to wait on someone else. You don't need that
help. Nobody does, Toby. I'll show you the road where I used to
run."

"Maybelle can cook that pot roast," Big Don was saying, "but
she's awful slack with a dust mop. Gonna catch the gawldern
beriberi around here, she don't mend her ways and clean up that
kitchen."

Joe Don hid in the rear bedroom, doing evening yoga. I hid in
the Coors. Big Don and I had polished off a major portion of
Maybelle's pot roast, plus carrots, turnips, okra, potatoes and
blackeyed peas. I felt as if I'd eaten a whole calf—hide, hooves
and hair. Big Don and I were spavined out on Barcaloungers,
watching *Hee-Haw.* Big Don had been entertaining me, between
Hee-Haw skits, with tales of John Connally, Lamar Hunt, H. L.
Hunt and Lyndon Johnson, all of whom he seemed to have met.
He had switched to war stories, however. I sat up and reached for
another Coors. Big Don was not drinking. He chewed a plug of
tobacco, every so often spewing into a paper cup.

"How come you didn't pick up football again after the war?" I
inquired.

"For one thing, Pittsburgh—team I'd been playing for—didn't
have a quarterback worth ten cents. I went back there after I got
out of the Air Force, told my coach I wanted to go down to
Washington, play with Sam Baugh. I mean, I was a *receiver*—
right?—and what good's a receiver without a quarterback who
can throw? Coach up at Pittsburgh said, 'Don, you play here or
you don't play nowhere.' Coaches had power like that in those
days. So I hung it up."

"But you played football through the war?"

"Right! I was better and faster than I'd ever been. That wartime ball . . . let me tell you something. One day I was playing a
football game for Pittsburgh against New York, *in* New York.
Next day I was in Texas in the Air Force, headed for Randolph
Field. In that one day, with no sleep, my ass busted up and sore

from that New York game, I'd flown all night to Texas, seen my wife give birth to Joe Don, ridden all next morning on a bus to an Air Force induction center, spent all day drawing shots and gear, then rode all that night down to Randolph Field, where some general was waiting to speak to me about what kind of football team they was going to have on base that year. In the space of forty-eight hours, my life had completely changed. I was no longer a professional football player, I was a father and an *airman* to boot!"

"Then they jockeyed you around—"

"They jockeyed me over the *globe*. Made me a phys-ed instructor, see, which was excuse for not calling me ... full-time athlete. We had a football team down there at Randolph was the best in the service, Toby. Which meant the world then, 'cause all your football players had been drafted. These generals would do *anything* to keep us from being sent overseas. Soon as one season was over and the weather got cold, we'd be transferred someplace like Puerto Rico, where another general would have a softball team he'd be winning a pot full of money off of, and our MOS would be switched to 'guard at a fuel depot' or something. All we'd do would be lie around in rope hammocks, drink papaya juice, play a little softball and deal cards. Then come fall and the chance of a new invasion, chance one of us might get *hurt* or *killed*, they'd ship us back up north for football season. I never been so frustrated in my life. Day I got my discharge, I walked into the office there at Randolph, and this sergeant is giving me the pep talk. You know, 'You stay in, Looney, you keep your stripes,' that talk. Well, I stripped out of that uniform, down to my shorts, and left it there in front of his desk. Not before I told him what he could do with his stripes, though."

The television fluttered. Newsfolk broke into a skit between Junior and *Hee-Haw*'s mule, mouthing inanities about— The picture rolled and caught. Big Don lurched forward.

"What?" Big Don said, slapping his Barcalounger to the floor. He reached out and adjusted the picture. It was the tail-end of a Presidential news conference. Junior and the *Hee-Haw* mule were gone; Dan Rather flashed onto the screen to begin a discussion of what evidently had transpired.

"Would you think they'd interrupt *Hee-Haw,* show what the President has to say?" Big Don said, settling back. "Now would you?"

Joe Don strolled out of the rear bedroom. He was shirtless and shoeless. He had his tongue in a terrycloth towel, and he was stretching it.

Big Don looked at his son in amazement. Then to me, shaking his head.

"He's always fooling with himself," Big Don said. "Joe Don, what in *hell* you doing now?" Joe Don did not answer, but grinned as best he could, with his tongue in a terrycloth towel.

"I think he's stretching his tongue," I said. "It's, uh, preparation for a yoga breathing exercise."

"Stretch?" Big Don said, coming out of his Barcalounger. "Stretch his tongue? What's wrong with the length the good Lord give him? Joe Don, what you think someone'd say, walk in here and see you *stretchin' your tongue?* Boy, they'd toss the net over you so fast your head would swim."

Joe Don released his tongue and moved it back and forth around his mouth. "What's this on TV?" he asked.

"President just give a speech," Big Don said, reclining with a squeak, "and they never even stopped *Hee-Haw* to show it. Man's talking about it now."

Joe Don looked unimpressed.

"Well," he said tiredly, "I hope you two get the *particulars* straight."

I reached behind my Barcalounger and shot Joe Don the finger. He laughed. "I'm going out and do my hangin' now," he said, ambling slowly across the wall-to-wall.

I took a pull on my Coors. I tried to concentrate. Had I really just given Joe Don Looney the finger?

"Feel ... weird doing this," Joe Don said, from the *Matsyendrasana* pose. "Never done yoga before with someone watching. With a woman, yes. It's real nice. But a woman ... who's doing yoga."

Much later now. Big Don had retired for the evening, to

shower, shave and cap off his night with a John Wayne movie. "Can't top the Duke," he'd winked. Joe Don had urged him to stick around: "Sit down," he'd said, "come on over. We're having a conversation. Nothing particular. But come on, join us." Big Don had looked tempted for an instant, then suspicious. He'd begged off. So Joe Don, at my request, was demonstrating basic yoga postures.

We'd run through *Bhujungsāna,* the cobra posture, *Pashchimottanāsana,* the drawing-back posture, *Halāsana,* the plough pose, *Padmāsana,* the lotus seat, and were finishing with *Shīrshanana,* the head pose.

"My legs are awful tight."

"Don't force anything," Joe Don coached. "Everybody's tight at first. Remember how tight I was. Takes time. Let it happen gradually."

Joe Don was in extraordinary condition. Despite the weight loss, his muscular definition was precise. His every move catlike, facile. Reaction time equaling that of a bantamweight fighter or professional dancer. Joe Don spoke softly, easing me through each posture with a voice that was deep, powerful, and half a continent away.

"This exercise . . . gets . . . internal organs," Joe Don said, moving rhythmically into an abdominal lift. His stomach rippled and sucked. I could see his backbone snaking through his belly.

"Goes . . . high as the heart," Joe Don said, relaxing. "Shouldn't do that one right after you eat." He lay back against the wall-to-wall in *Shavāsana,* the corpse posture.

I was cold, slightly damp from yoga exertion. I slipped on a down jacket of Joe Don's near at hand and fought to get back into a modified lotus.

"You exercise any more . . . in a traditional manner?" I asked. Joe Don lay motionless, hands at his side.

"Somebody's got a chinning-bar, I might take a few pulls."

"Drugs?"

"Would be wrong for me now. Drugs were useful. But wrong now." Joe Don was speaking haltingly. I pulled myself back into *Matsyendrāsana* and asked about the submachine gun bust.

"You see that UPI clipping?" I said.

"No, you got a copy?" He sat forward, touching his forehead to his knees.

I fished a Xerox from my briefcase and passed it over. Joe Don ran through it once and smiled.

"Was reading Sartre's *The Wall* the day we were busted," he said. "That story, begins: *They pushed us into a big white room and I began to blink because the light hurt my eyes.* I'd dropped a tab of acid that afternoon, Windowpane, I recall, and everything was very, very strange."

"You realize Ronald Frick had arranged to have this judge iced?"

Joe Don straightened from a neck twist and glared. "Toby, I had no idea Ron'd do anything that stupid."

"Was he hiding behind a bookcase, like the story says, with two loaded rifles?"

"Old Ron was back there where you're sleeping, *completely* wasted, arms and legs tangled up in two stereo speakers. They carried him out."

"And the Thompson?"

"Something I brought back from Vietnam. Lot of guys did that. But it wasn't a Thompson, just a little grease gun, like the paratroopers carry."

"Ever get the chance to fire it?"

Joe Don smiled.

"You ever kill anybody, Joe Don? In Vietnam?"

"No. I wouldn't have. I couldn't have killed anybody."

"You like the Army?"

Joe Don raised up from *Shavāsana*. "You talk about *crazy* people. You think there's crazy people in insane asylums, you join up with the Army! People in those asylums are fine, there's nothing wrong with them. You go ahead and do your thing in the goddamn *Army* once and see what I mean. I got along in the Army. Duty I had was absurd. Guarding a supply depot. It was soft ... like *M.A.S.H.* or something. But goddamn, I couldn't wait to get out of there."

"Worry about getting killed?"

"Toby, I come so close to getting killed so many times *outside* the Army ... that's one thing turned me around, those close calls

I kept having. Like I held something inside me wanted to survive all this bad shit. Something spiritual, had an extra ounce of lift in it, would pull me out of impossible situations. Like I was in Peru à couple of years back ... and I'm being chased, see, I mean there's all kinds of fuckers after my ass. I'd rolled this car I'd been driving, totalled, it's the middle of the night and *cold as a mother*. I've got to swim for it. Toby, my ass is exhausted. It's pitch black and cold, I'm tossing around in the surf, and I say to myself, 'Joe Don, you may have bought the ranch this time.' I'm moaning Lord if I get out of this one I'll hang it up for sure. There didn't seem any way I was going to come out of that surf alive. But I did. Something in me just came to life and I swam out of there and got away. Don't ask me how. But close calls have dogged me, Toby. As for death ... well, like I said to GW: it's gonna be okay."

"And jail? You're still facing this firearms thing—"

"That's right. And we're fighting it. I don't *want* to go to jail ... but let me tell you a story. Was this kid I grew up with in Fort Worth. My absolute best friend on this planet. We did everything together. First piece of ass we got, we got it together. First fast cars we had, we had 'em together. First football, first acid ... I mean, whatever there was in this world we figured worth seeing or trying, we did it together. Couple of years ago this buddy got busted. Sent up to prison, long term. He cut his throat alone there in his cell one night and bled to death. I've thought about that a whole lot, Toby. No, I don't want to go to jail. But I had a dream about this buddy, straightened me out some. In the dream he came back here to the ranch. I answered my front door one day, and he was standing there, grinning. 'Man, you're dead!' I said to him. 'You *can't* be standing there!' He said, 'No I'm not, Joe Don, I fooled 'em. All I did was open this hole in my throat, let out some blood, and they *thought* I was dead. Easy.'

"There were always three things I was most afraid of Toby, about going to jail. One, that a bunch of guys would beat my face until there wasn't nothing left but pulp. Two, that these same guys would hold me down and fuck me in the ass—hold me so I couldn't do *nothing* to protect myself. And three, that ... somehow I'd die in there with those people, that I wouldn't ever get back outside. Now—I don't know. It doesn't matter so much about jail. I see they can't really lock me up. And the other stuff—it don't matter, either."

Joe Don and I sat quietly on the wall-to-wall. There was the noise of Big Don's portable squawking from his bedroom.

"Something I didn't tell you, Joe Don. Something weird. When I started research for this trip, I wanted to read the big articles on you published while you were playing ball. I located bound editions of *The Saturday Evening Post, Life* and *Sports Illustrated*—that wasn't a problem. But I had to visit *three* different libraries before I could find articles in those bound editions which hadn't been ripped out and stolen. *Just* the stories about you."

Joe Don looked shocked. "Man, I don't want no disciples. Disciples equal *prison.* That ego business. Like dealing cocaine and being *addicted* to it at the same time. There's no one in this world more selfish and egotistical than a cocaine addict. Except an evangelist. And when you start to *sell* your religion like you would your cocaine . . . no sir. Let me tell you about the Maharaj Ji. I went up to Memphis to hear this little cat speak, this Maharaj Ji . . . . I didn't know much of what he was about, but I'd *heard* a lot about him, for what that's worth, and I wanted to see for myself. So I got up there to this rally, and as usual when I go to these meditation sessions, it's me there, plus a whole lot of women. Don't seem like anyone else goes to these things but me and a bunch of women. I listen to what the little cat has to say, and it's okay, I'm grooving on it. Afterwards I go up and I'm talking to a couple of his lieutenants, and they see I understand what's being put down, that we're thinking along the same lines, so . . . they hit me for $75 or whatever it was to take this course. I said, 'No! You can't be serious! You're *selling* it?' And the cat starts hitting on me about expenses, that bullshit. So I left. No, Toby, last thing in this *world* I want is disciples. Somebody wants to hear what I got to say, okay, I'll sit down, talk, give 'em everything I know. You owe people that. But no more. Not *bondage.*"

"That is a moral for you—telling people the truth as you see it? You believe that to be an obligation?"

"A man should pass on the truth as he sees it," Joe Don said. "That *is* an obligation."

"The only obligation?"

"The *only* obligation, as I see it."

Then Joe Don did a peculiar thing. Without stretching a muscle, he extended an etheric arm about my shoulder and said: "It's gonna be okay, Toby. Believe me. Everything's gonna be okay."

Morning again. Early. Hanging by my heels from Joe Don's trapeze, fingers brushing the floor, spine tweezed out straight and stringy. A bubble gum spine. No one else up. Hanging alone in the Bat Room. Feels . . . good. Head heavy, neck and shoulders full. Serpent-fire stirring, rising to *Shiva* and the thousand-petal lotus. I checked my notes.

1. Football as day-to-day, extended life-of-violence in the *corporate structure* of America. Hitting and being hit "for the team," training and childish self-denial. Drag racer, test pilot, hipster work in ejaculatio-praecox. Theirs the one-shot, narcissistic plunge. Often ending in calamity. Which more violent?

2. Rise of professional football in the nineteen-sixties concomitant to rise of corporations and corporate violence. What had been largely a schoolboy activity prior to World War II grew during the sixties to America's number-one viewing pastime, eclipsing baseball. Because of football's violence; corporate violence. Owing its greatest popularity to color television and TV's corporate support. Looney's climb through the ranks—corporate ranks—of Texas high school ball. Big Ten college ball, to pros and his eventual disaffection.

3. Joe Don Looney as *corporate maverick* (bad nigger) whom owners tried to founder. Look on Joe Don's face during the sixties of a powerful, exhausted field hand. How could the sixties have been "fun" for Joe Don Looney?

4. Kids idolizing football players during the seventies—they identify with team or individuals? How we idolized baseball players, i.e., Mickey Mantle during the sixties (connection between Big Don's raising of Joe Don to be "greatest gridder ever" and Mantle's dad forcing him to switch-hit as a boy, though it made Mickey cry).

5. Baseball still the sport of individual heroism in America. That and running. But does anyone care?

6. Success of a book like Dan Jenkins' *Semi-Tough* (partly suggestive of Looney's career) lies in its depiction of a "scene" which is sexually exciting, witty, violent, and which the reader can envy. Reader
envies a *group* of people whose lives are fuller and more exciting than
his. Can't picture a *Semi-Tough* of baseball, the lone cat sport. Di-
Maggio? Williams? The greatest, but never part of a scene. DiMaggio
lived it with Monroe, but a private, religious affair.

7. The "scene" as corporate security.

Behind me, what was left of Joe Don's weightlifting equipment lay stashed in a far corner of the Bat Room. From my perspective it stuck to the ceiling like mud daubers' nests. A heavy
canvas punching bag rose from the floor, an obese pussy willow.
Back door was open. During the night a near pasture had filled
with cattle. They grazed along a fence not twenty feet from
where I hung. I closed my notebook and skimmed it across the
ceiling. Still early here in Texas. Sunday. More sleep was required. Many big games to view today. I disengaged myself from
Joe Don's trapeze and tiptoed back inside the house, trying hard
not to disturb individuals. Two old footballers who had hung it
up, so to speak, before their prime.

"You stick around one more night," Big Don said from deep
inside his Barcalounger. "We'll grill a mess of burgers there in
the fireplace. Got a couple more games worth watching, too."

I thanked Big Don and told him no. We said goodbye. Joe
Don walked me to the car. I had a folder of Xeroxes under my
arm. There was an old story about Joe Don on top, and I pulled
it out.

"Remember this?" I asked. It was the "Bad Boy of the Pros"
article, from a 1965 *Life*. Joe Don read the first line and a half:

*"He hardly knew what to make of it as he sat on the Detroit
bench, bruised and worn from battering against the Baltimore
Colts' line, despondent because he had hardly been able to dent it.
The huge, brooding unpredictable rambunctious halfback . . . ."*

"That's amazing," Joe Don said, handing back the article.

"The prose?"

"No, that guy was *right*. I remember that game vividly." And

Joe Don laughed. "I was sitting on the bench there in Baltimore, not knowing what to make of *any* of it. I remember sitting there that afternoon, looking up at the crowd and thinking: 'They cheering for *us?* All those people come to this stadium, pay money, to yell for us? *Me?* What am I doing down here on this field, when all those people are up *there,* yelling and screaming?' I had a distinct sensation that something was wrong that afternoon. And this writer picked it up. Incredible."

I tossed my junk into the Mustang and dug for my keys. "Sometimes a writer will pick things up," I said.

"Books are my friends," Joe Don allowed.

Then we said so long.

POSTSCRIPT: As of 1977, Joe Don Looney was living in an ashram in India. His firearms conviction had been overturned. A note in May, 1979, said: "Toby, the best consideration you could show me is to state at the end of the article that I now live with my Guru Baba Muktananda."

War

At college we stood locked into the war before it became the war. Our deferments were ligaments roping us to a conflict most did not know existed. Freshmen in 1962, at a land grant university like Delaware, we stumbled through ROTC four sessions a week, learning the intricacies of the M-1 rifle, how to field-strip it, fire it, pirouette it through a manual of arms and, as our master sergeant leered during the Cuban Missile Crisis, entertained the possibility of using it "quicker'n anybody thought." ROTC was involuntary then, to remain at Delaware one must endure— a sort of muffled induction. ROTC was painful, a bore, but they had you. It interfered with the real business of college—sex, speed and sport—to a degree that one felt mutiny approaching murder, distraction plummeting toward disaster.

No one spoke of Vietnam in ROTC. Outside that military enclave we encountered few veterans. Mostly tight-lipped. Estranged. One such was an early Special Forces adviser who wove tales wired as his demeanor, an old man at twenty-five, raked as a pug boxer in this freshman world of mock-Ivy League. He had a story about Vietnam which bit into its heart of darkness. He played it out for us one day, a tale of Communist monks so wedded to terror they could take an orphan boy at birth, wean him, rear him, teach him a life of obeisance to one master, his monk, one idea, the possession of his soul. His soul was a black ball presented to the boy at infancy. To be separated from the ball was to be separated from his soul, the boy was taught; he would die. His monk had authority to possess the ball. No one else. As the boy grew he was trained to retrieve his soul at any cost. The monk took the ball, placed it on the ground, the boy snatched it back. The action became reflex. Consistency of impedimenta was thickened. The ball was dropped in water. The boy's hand snaked out. Sand and water. The boy's hand thrust. Dry sand. Dig and clutch. Behind bamboo, thick lumber . . . until the boy was man, knowing nothing but the ball, that to lose it was to die; the boy a man with power in his arm to thrust through solid matter, shatter barricades, to retrieve his soul. On market day his monk might lead him to a village. This Communist monk of terrorist intent. A village chief suspected of collaboration with anti-Communist forces would be targeted. The monk would take the young man's ball. He would secure it. Standing before the village chief he might point "There!" to his charge, at the village chief's chest. The chief's heart would be torn out, message plain as blood, the monk sifting back into the crowd, black ball hidden beneath his robes.

That was the horror. The horror of romance.

Then there was technology. An ex-SEAL lived in a hovel off campus with a claque of beatnik types. Brooding, aloof, he hardly fitted in, except that he loved his grass, lived to vipe, and was intimidated by the out-of-doors. One never saw him outside. He'd been to Vietnam, wouldn't say exactly when. What he spoke of were the tools, complicated weapons for killing men in interesting ways. Mostly commando devices. Esoteric knives, guns, garrotes. The enemy existed to prove these weapons, he believed. Stories wafting through green haze on Choate Street, 1963, and the terror on this veteran's face mellowed from goofing, receding into reveries of snaps and clicks, righteous machinery fulfilling its design.

We raced motorcycles, some of us flew planes, we drove Cobras, Jaguars, 'Vettes and Mini Coopers. We were no strangers to machinery. Delaware was a state founded on the romance of technology, or was it the technology of romance. The du Pont fortune, extracted from gunpowder during the nineteenth century, ran full tilt during the sixties, fueling corporate purgatives for Vietnam. Everyone in Delaware, it seemed, was a du Pont or worked for the corporation ... an arrangement so feudal in its psychopathology that touring chateau country outside Wilmington one anticipated thatched roofs of a different kind lining perimeters, thatched roofs of medieval varlets. For that's how subordinates were treated. One afternoon I argued in class with a black friend about Stokeley Carmichael, both of us grooving; that night, dressed in knee britches, he served me drinks from a silver tray at a debutante party. Corporations ruled the state ... Delaware's tax laws were written for the corporation; corporations by the thousands claimed Wilmington addresses. At the apex rested du Ponts, Gallic in their affection for society, princely in their pursuit of leisure, medieval in their disregard for vassals. Once you were in, you could really have some fun.

Those of us who infiltrated did so with no small guilt, for the wars we'd been fighting were Motorpsycho Nitemares of early Dylan; Dylan as heavy domestic artillery who rearranged our perceptions drastically as had r&b during the fifties. Dylan himself the infiltrator, a Jew, the kid from Hibbing with barbed wire for nerves who jackknifed chords into your head like spider crabs, horned anemones previewing a harsher flower decade, one that saw the holocaust in every head exploded by drugs, every brain deluded by the promise of love which had not learned from history. Dylan pricked the Jew in each of us even as he piqued the closet Nazi. Zapping us into the Janus energy still amok from World War II, static to run a war another decade.

As sex, speed and sport dissipated in the totality of their attraction, war infiltrated emotionally ... a stranger war than that of evening news, one of the senses, of personal romance. We read *Green Hills of Africa* and ached for the primitive, to *smell* game before sighting it, become as one with jungle creatures before gunning them down. We read of Tommy Barban in *Tender* and envisioned home life of the professional soldier as "war, any war," his business "to kill people." Le Carré, Saint Exupéry, Stendhal, Ian Fleming ... the selection was arbitrary but hideously precise. Books that became movies: a double dose. The world of James Bond—beyond elaboration. Nowhere else did sex, technology and romance meld so seductively.

A game we played our senior year was the Tenth Victim. From a Marcello Mastroianni-Ursula Andress film of the James Bond milieu, an idea generated by Fleming (an ex-intelligence officer), author of books transmogrified by Hollywood into the cold-war consciousness of a generation. The premise being this: Ten people, one of whom could win, played a deadly game. Secret lots were drawn. Five naming killers, five naming victims. Killers knew their victims, but victims ran scared. If you were victim, you sought your killer's identity so that you might eliminate him first. If you were killer, you schemed creative deaths. Your victim must expire in style. We channeled much energy into the game. It was our first war game, really. Both men and women were eligible. That added a sexiness. One girl studying deep in the stacks fell to a tarantula draped across her neck. Another, in a women's dorm, opened her door to an elderly maintenance man (hair dyed gray, fake mustache, carrying mop and pail) and was shot, fainting in a tangle of Bondian underclothes. A motorcycle was detonated with a smoke bomb wired to its ignition, a most creative kill. One girl was doused with acid. Another strangled while making love, the most lascivious ... that belonged to Di Giacinto.

Di Giacinto was one of two close friends who would become Special Forces officers in Vietnam; two friends more removed from consciousness of that debacle during the early sixties than any I knew. One was a poet, a songwriter, philosopher, a dreamer who spent seventeen hours a day in bed; he would join the F.B.I. after Vietnam, a transition that remains a mindfuck.*
And there was Henry Di Giacinto. Both were outsiders, Henry even more so: of Pennsylvania coal mining stock, a tall, dark-haired Italian kid from anthracite country who came down to Delaware on a basketball scholarship and who infiltrated feudal ranks with the charm of a Rubirosa.

You couldn't tell about Henry. He had the air of a man who

---

* For elaboration, see: "Lt. Troll," *US#3* (Bantam, 1970).

wanted stability from life, when what he wanted was to fuck off and get drunk. He'd been financially independent since his nineteenth year, he'd had a long affair in high school with a coach's wife, lifting sex from sport, and both these factors lent him a maturity which aced his charm. He lasted three semesters on that basketball scholarship, quitting to work through school. Odd jobs were the work he did: janitor, clerk. Henry never studied. He had an ease with women that was the envy of everyone who met him. That ease translated nicely to his relationships with men, for he never flaunted his victories. At 6'2", 200 lbs. he was easy-going but possessed of a capacity for violence, once provoked, which shocked even him.

The original pacifist, one remembers Henry as slovenly, unkempt, loafing in student union or fraternity house, usually with a woman, open for anything. When in fact he worked hard to support himself and to pay for school, with no goals, no ambition except the vague directive of being near the action, running with a wild crowd. At Delaware that crowd ran from Theta Chi, roughest jock fraternity, where Henry was brother, to the du Pont sector, dream palaces of the protected, where Henry was outsider. A life as perpetual student would have suited Henry. He took his law boards, did well. No real drive persisted to study law, however. Henry was cutting finals, flunking courses, gave no shit but for women and punctilious dalliances of the rich.

A break was needed. A break with goals cemented to a time slot. A break for maturation. Then return to college. In December, 1965, Henry joined the Peace Corps. Went to UCLA for training, where he undertook a life of courses and fucking off not dissimilar to what he'd known at Delaware.

The Peace Corps, love child of the Kennedy administration, was an organization geared toward disenchanted young Americans—listless, skeptical, regressively idealistic—which trained them to live abroad where they might help underdeveloped peoples realize potentialities. Peace Corps volunteers built roads, hospitals, sewer systems, taught a variety of post-industrial skills. Henry's Peace Corps class was preparing for Nigeria, where they'd work to set up a school system. Instructing elementary school teachers. Henry studied education, language, descriptive linguistics, Ibo; Henry's group was slated for the Ibo region. About this time riots in Los Angeles were popping off like fire-crackers. Peace Corps directors thought good training for Nigeria, and not bad domestic politics, would be to insert the class into black families across Watts, to teach in neighborhood schools. Henry's class arrived on Monday, the second Watts riots erupted on Tuesday.

"That's the first time I was personally shot at," Henry would recall. "The original pacifist had been dropped into a combat zone."

Muslims and Panthers had warned Peace Corps directors that if white volunteers were shuttled to Watts they'd be iced. A fat allowance was offered as boarding fee; most black families relented. Henry and five dissidents complained. To deaf ears. Girls were raped by families they'd been staying with, fires raged, gunshots sounded. Volunteers were maimed. Henry was riding the bus one night when the driver shut down his interior lights. "Don't want my bus shot up with your white face on it." Henry was eating spaghetti in a neighborhood bar, spaghetti as only a black can prepare it, when a patron pulled his gun. "I'm gonna shoot your hat." Fired two rounds and missed. Then came right down. Henry offered a profile. "What was I going to do, dive under the table?" Third shot went in the ceiling, plaster flying. Fired a couple more, spattering dust. Out of ammunition. Folks stood about drinking. They took up a collection to buy more bullets. When Henry threw a buck onto the plate he was safe, he was cool, a brother . . . but the experience gave him pause.

About Watts and the Peace Corps. Henry returned after three weeks to UCLA—to a decimated class. People missing. Some in the hospital, some in rest homes, some fled. Henry and the dissident five were called out; their class would embark for Nigeria within a week. Henry and the dissidents were sacked. Quickly Henry was drafted. A draft notice he never received. He was back at Delaware and the F.B.I. was looking for him. The pacifist was pissed.

During pre-induction rigamorole for his Peace Corps experience, Henry had taken a psychological evaluation test which listed his most suitable occupation as that of career military officer. Flooring him. The original pacifist was no ingenue in military affairs. He had been fascinated by war games as a child. But at age twenty-three, soldiering was far from his mind.

Henry's grandfather had fled to the United States before World War I, evading the Italian draft. Hunger, poverty, lack of a future, he also evaded. Coal mining was a step up. Henry was descended from peasants of the Abruzzi region outside Rome, "Landed aristocrats," Henry would joke, "they came with the land and worked it." Many of Henry's relatives were coal miners. His father had been a postal clerk during World War II, but various uncles had served in army, navy, marines, and they'd brought home souvenirs. "It all comes down to supply channels," Henry would laugh. "If you got the supplies you can have your army." Henry owned uniforms, equipment, gunstocks. He could outfit a platoon of neighborhood kids. He was their general, obsessing on combat games. He owned toy soldiers, designed uniforms for them, painted their colors intricately. Enormous numbers which partook of elaborate battles, hundreds of soldiers with air support, model planes which Henry constructed, sixty-odd planes, three aircraft carriers—the whole machine. "I was a dedicated militarist at thirteen." In high school he owned an M-1, loaded ammunition, competed nationally for sharpshooter badges. He joined the Air Scouts, an air ROTC program for high school kids, but lost interest gradually to sex and sport. He read. Science fiction, adventure, titles like *Galactic Soldier*—offshoots of military hype. Still, in 1965 that psychological evaluation alarmed him. There had been James Bond during college: "Fascinating books, depicting a life every young man envisions, of killing enemies with impunity, having an endless expense account and budget, a whole government providing you with goodies and toys, a constant stream of voluptuous women...." There'd been two years of involuntary ROTC. No inspiration there. Yet Henry as history and political science major had become intrigued by the Vietnam war.

Henry told me about it one afternoon in August, 1977. Henry back from war games, reserve operations intricate as any combat extravaganzas he'd orchestrated as a child. Henry was fat; a sizeable gut bulged from his jungle fatigues. He worked as a commodities specialist in Allentown, Pennsylvania now, a thirty-four-year-old family man with responsibility, but he retained his commission in the Special Forces reserves.

"I started to inform myself on Vietnam about 1965," Henry said. "Bernard Kalb came to Delaware and gave a little talk. He was recently back from Vietnam, and two hundred-fifty people showed up. He was shocked. It was the first interest he'd seen expressed. I knew about Vietnam because of our friend Scott, who'd been over in '62-'63 with that first Special Forces group. I'd begun to read heavily into guerrilla wars, wars of national liberation—started to fascinate me. I was *studying* now, now that I saw these governmental conspiracies taking control of my life. I was mad. The army drafted me with two weeks left of my final semester. I got no marks, lost all that money, and was inducted. I was offered asylum abroad by some Persian friends . . . but I felt it my duty to serve. During Officers Candidate School I intensified my reading on Vietnam and the type of war going on there. I read all of Bernard Fall, saw Viet-Minh newsreels, studied Che Guevara, Mao Tse-tung, men who had involvement with creating a military force out of a peasant or urban, non-military group."

Peasant seemed to hang Henry up.

"I knew it was a matter of time. Once you finished OCS you had maybe eight months, and then, whoosh, to Vietnam. Those were the great cannon fodder years, '67, '68. Rough on platoon leaders. I had no intention of going to Vietnam with a bunch of amateurs. I was familiar with Special Forces through my reading and figured they were the best the army had. If I was going into combat I wanted to go with people who knew what they were doing, thereby increasing my chances of survival. So I *volunteered* to go to Vietnam. A big deal. I mean if they can get you to stand up and say take me, they'll help you out. They'll *take* you. I said, by the way, can I go over with the Special Forces? Sure, they get killed too, we need plenty of them.

"The mission of Special Forces already intrigued me. Its guerrilla nature. Infiltrating, running in to organize a resistance movement. To free those who were occupied or oppressed. I dug on that. That was philosophically my cup of tea. I'm sort of a man of action. I'm a dilettante as a scholar. Intelligent yes, but that doesn't mean anything unless you act on it. So Special Forces suited me more than, say, the Peace Corps. Which I found to be another fucking Washington bureaucracy."

And nowhere as romantic. Henry might discount romance as his motive, but few could discount the romance of the green beret. Jaunty as Jack Kennedy, upon whose grave a green beret rested. Cocky as that Irish American, an outsider, war hero, jungle fighter, commander-in-chief with a grace acute as his British forebears, but minus their stuffiness. Descended from British commando units of World War II, the American Special Forces had been tempered through incarnations as Darby's Rangers, Airborne Rangers, and Green Berets. They were American as PT-109, yet alien. Nothing of the Marines' sailor insouciance rumpled their demeanor. They were Boston Irishmen in English broadcloth. Hostile, yet chic. Hostile-chic.

That ethos had been promulgated by Kennedy, and he stood as its apotheosis for the nineteen-sixties. Kennedy's personal commitment to Vietnam had been decisive, but no less so than the unspoken will-to-conflict adrift in America since World War II. It came again to a rage against technology. There had been hand-to-hand combat in the Pacific Theater ... providing catharis after great, impersonal invasions flooded by megatons of air death ... but Americans could not find it in their hearts to forgive bureaucracy for having dropped the atom bomb ... not for the destruction it wrought but for the opportunity it cheated, of taking Japan by hand, on the ground, with garrote and blade. Korea offered another swirl toward that most primitive dance, thwarted by armistice. And multinational considerations. It seemed technology had robbed the infantryman of knowing his enemy in the ancient manner. Land wars were hopelessly outmoded. A band of loyalists need be formed. A specialized elite to forge a spearhead.

The Special Forces was spearhead of that American infantry, which, during World War II, synthesized much of what would be realized post-war as hip culture. Infantrymen sloughed through mud, they were land-bound; their soldier's language reflected that commitment. The forties image of the hip infantryman, promoted by Mailer in *The Naked and the Dead* and Jones in *From Here to Eternity,* was blooded ancestor to peacetime hipsters of the fifties and early sixties. Montgomery Clift in the film version of *Eternity* was paradigm for the displaced infantryman, displaced from his role as foot soldier by bureaucracies he could not comprehend, prototype for a generation of battle-torn malcontents. Through G.I. language, ever a conduit for hip talk, the hip manner of Clift and characters like his Private Prewitt—their phrasing, military garb, jazzmanship, four-wheel-drive mania—infiltrated the culture. Protestors raged against the Vietnam war during the nineteen-sixties, but did so clad in World War II fatigues, Jeep Wagoneers at the curb. Hollywood exploited the sentiment ruthlessly. Who could forget Audie Murphy in *To Hell and Back,* starring in the film version of his autobiography, reliving Congressional Medal of Honor valors for the silver screen, for the world to envy? World War II proved a media windfall: movies, books, photo essays, cartoons, comics, clothing, cars, toys—the icons of war were omnipresent; we fondled them like rosaries. And learned. Dividing ourselves socially as children of fathers who had served and those who had not. Hostile went beyond chic, it permeated the fabric of our existence.

If hip language was province of infantry, Special Forces probed a kilometer further. Nothing G.I. Joe about Berets, they appeared clonish, androidal, beyond sloppiness of ordinary language. They went beyond language; they worked some perimeter between technology and ritual most Americans had not faced.

It was their primitiveness which attracted. America knew firepower, planes, aircraft carriers, helicopters . . . but Green Berets knew the jungle, blade in hand, knew reliance on a minimum of technology. They sought blood knowledge, intimacies of warm flesh. Green Berets were hipsters of the right; conservative, reactionary, non-communal, primitive and attracted to primitives. If Vietnam was the apotheosis of America's journey to the East—a hegira begun with Columbus, intensified by frontier expansionism (where West was East, native Americans were Indians), fueled by drugs during the nineteen-fifties, transformed into a middle-class lifestyle during the nineteen-sixties—then Green Berets were hip explorers charting bleak territory. If what Che

Guevara said proved valid, that guerrilla bands were the armed vanguard of the great popular force that supported them, Green Berets were the Janus face to Haight Ashbury, LSD, consciousness expansions of meeker varieties.

There aren't any politics where I'm going, another friend had said, before shipping out to Vietnam as an S.F. lieutenant. *No emperors, no Nixons, no Lairds.* Had I slipped backstage before a performance to watch actors applying makeup? Watch them paint last touches of characters they'd portray? *A beautiful thing,* he said. Having rehearsed parts, memorized lines, they awaited the curtain. Guerrilla teams painting up before a night raid were like that. They knew the script but for its finish and that's where creativity emerged. Opportunities such as Malraux spoke of in *La Condition Humaine* for terrorism as a religious act . . . possession of oneself, absolute knowledge for the instant. No vague ideals, but an antithesis of romanticism, an exquisite realism. One could participate in that most primitive rite and hope for a bristling of creative sensibilities . . . toward an understanding of violence. A dissolution of fears.

The fear came differently for Henry. It came not with that first shot, not with a first barrage of incoming mortar rounds—but with the realization he was under the charge of maniacs: a bureaucracy of field-grade officers, deranged or incompetent, who manipulated toy Waterloos from the safety of bunkers, Waterloos they'd never seen.

"It started my first day in-country," Henry remembered. "October, 1968, some months after Tet. I'd been assigned to the Fifth Special Forces Group, Nha Trang, but it was obvious at Long Vinh replacement center they'd send me where they wanted. I didn't wait for that. I hopped a plane for Nha Trang, met the S-1, told him I'd like to join the MIKE Force—a mobile strike force of Montagnard and Nung mercenaries, commanded by Americans, who went where the action was . . . all sorts of good operations. S-1 said, Gee, lieutenant, like to oblige but we only assign experienced officers to the MIKE Force. We'll forward you to Pleiku. So I flew up there. Spent one night in Pleiku, next morning I saw the S-1. Told him I wanted to join the MIKE Force. Gee we'd like to have you but feel we can't assign inexperienced people . . . we'll send you to B-24 in Kontum. Every one of these goddamned stops was getting me progressively further inland, progressively further north. I was nearing the front, if you could find one. They were flying me all over the country. I didn't know where I was. I got on a helicopter that afternoon for Kontum and if it'd come down I wouldn't have known which direction to walk.

"Each post was a little smaller, a little less secure. At Kontum bullet holes were everywhere. People were on guard, carrying weapons within the compound. I still didn't have one. I was in my khaki uniform carrying my duffel bag from California. Kontum province is this huge province in northern II Corps, adjacent to Laos. Beautiful country: triple canopy jungle, rolling foothills. Reported to the S-1. Glad to have you aboard, lieutenant, but . . . don't know how to say this . . . we can't assign you to an A-site, we've got to send you to the MIKE Force. You're shitting me! I thought they only sent experienced people to the MIKE Force? Yeah, well, as a matter of fact you'll be leaving on a thirty-five day operation tomorrow morning, better get over and meet your company. What? I don't even have a *gun*.

"Three days in-country, I was battalion Ex-O and a company commander in the MIKE Force. I didn't know shit. I had six hundred Montagnards under my command. Plus two Americans, one lieutenant and a sergeant who'd been there four years. Fucking company carried M-2 carbines from World War II, two BARs, two radios, one machine gun, and one sixty m.m. mortar. Awfully light. That morning we flew down to LZ English and headquarters of the 173rd Airborne Brigade. Back along the coast, thirty miles from where I'd started. Back with troops to go to combat.

"A gang-fuck from the word go. Our Montagnards *hated* going down there—this wasn't their country. They were highlanders. They *hated* the Vietnamese, hated humping along the coast fighting Vietnamese's battles. But they went. Because they had faith in their leader. Me. And I didn't even have a weapon.

"Three plane-loads of us flew down. Five-thirty, six at night, we checked in. Where'd you guys come from? We weren't expecting anyone. Well, okay, you're here, we'll put you in this area of operations to move as directed—try and locate the enemy. Puzzlement. I walked back to my people and there's a big fucking flap. The Vietnamese didn't want our Montagnards in their camp overnight. Almost dark and they were putting us out of the wire. You've got to be kidding me! Well, we have to keep the Vietnamese happy. But be careful, we've got ambushes out. You assholes better coordinate, I said, 'cause we're walking through there!

"Marching to combat. Out the gate to the edge of town, past rough terrain, garbage dumps, empty fields, a river, rolling hills and into the mountains. Was just about dark when our point man spotted Americans. Dead ahead. With claymore mines out. A LURP* team on ambush, with no word we were coming, and we're standing in their killing zone. I could have got waxed right there. They did not fire. Were going to but couldn't understand why we were walking *away* from camp. Incredible. We avoided several other LURPS and got deeper into the country. That night, my first in combat, I set up in the pitch dark in a pouring rain, not afraid but a bit confused.

"Everything could have gone so wrong. I was anxious ... to get away from these fucking Americans. They weren't coordinating things. Still, they were experienced field-grade officers and I was a second lieutenant who recognized he didn't know a hell of a lot. My troops were experienced, had seen a lot of combat.

"We were at the teat of the An Lo River, an area so hot with NVA they wouldn't order American units there. We were one hundred thirty Montagnards but for two Americans. One had walked home. It was quiet for five or six days, we fucked around, finally headed inland. No real problems with battalion head-quarters except that they were so defensively oriented they were doomed for failure. Our liaison detachment was two fuck-off sergeants who were constantly drunk and who spent all their time figuring how to get out of there. Still, I knew no fear. Suddenly we were before a white frame house, battalion headquar-ters for NVA; they were in there and the fucking shooting

* Long Range Reconnaissance Patrol.

started. We seemed to be winning. I got on the radio and requested gunship support. Sorry, no gunship support, we're saving that in case an American unit's in contact. Hmmm. We assaulted the house and captured a cache of American grenades, ammunition, M-16s—the latest American weapons of which we had two in our company. We were *outgunned* by our own weapons. We made contact again, and again I cranked up the radio. I called for artillery fire and helicopters, holding the microphone so rounds could be heard. Denied. Then this colonel comes on and says someone has spotted *six* VC on the far bank of the river; we should drop everything and head them off. What, I said? They're right *here,* we're shooting at them. No, cross the river as ordered. Fucking *madness.* But—we crossed over. Just one of our men was wounded. I called to request a Medevac. Sorry, we can't commit a helicopter in case there's an American unit in contact, have to give them first priority. Is there an American unit in contact? No. Why can't you come out and pick up my man? Carry your wounded, hustle down and cut off that road.

"I was getting really fucking bitter. More than anxious, I was afraid for the first time. That I was in the hands of madmen. Maniacs who were running a war from bunkers thirty miles away. Insanity. That's when I decided I'd do it *my* way. The next fourteen days we were in contact. A firefight morning, afternoon and evening, with breaks for meals. That's too hot. A division-size operation had had their clocks cleaned there two years earlier and I was hiking around with one hundred thirty guys. Our mission, in MIKE Force, was not to defeat the enemy but to fix him. Every day some one of my men would be wounded. I walked in with one hundred thirty people, walked out with seventy-three. Heavy attrition. It got so shitty, with no fire support, the Montagnards *quit.* They fucking stacked arms. A bitter experience for me. But I learned quick. November 22, I still remember, was our heaviest action. Got the shit kicked out of us. We had bodies, some of theirs, some of ours. A cache of weapons. Again I called for a Medevac. First helicopter landed had a camera crew. From CBS. Second the Battalion Commander who hot-dogged it around for folks back home, *after* the battle, while my people were lying around wounded or dead, *needing* helicopters. From that day I considered myself independent of Americans. I shut down my radio, avoided conflict. I was commander-in-chief of my own fucking unit."

Henry sensed the war was in trouble because American brass possessed no knowledge of the enemy, had never been out of their bunkers to take a look. But that was behind him. Most of it, anyway. On Christmas Day, 1968, Henry flew up to Dak Seang, eight kilometers from the Laotian border, to take command of that Special Forces camp. Further north and further west. Dak Seang had suffered a major attack; the camp was in ruins. An elaborate matrix of concrete tunnels and bunkers underlay the compound. Dak Seang's senior officer, a captain, had not been above ground for thirty days. "A bit whifty," Henry recalled. The man was terrified. The morning after Henry arrived he was hatting up, gone on the first helicopter. Henry, now a first lieutenant, was Executive Officer to a decimated A-team of five Green Berets, four to six hundred Montagnard mercenaries, one hundred Vietnamese, and sixteen hundred Montagnard dependents.

Dak Seang was at the lip of the universe. No roads, no villages; dense jungle. Nothing but enemy for miles. NVA were so close one could hear the thump of mortar rounds as they dropped into tubes. Helicopters shuttled in once a week, hovered, took off quickly; supplies were parachute-dropped from cargo transports. Radio contact with the outside world was minimal. No tactical air support could be counted upon in event of a major attack. Henry had three companies, two recon platoons, two artillery pieces. His camp was at the center of the Dak Poko River valley, on a major NVA infiltration route—old French Route 14, from Pleiku to Da Nang.

"It was a place you couldn't get away from very easily," Henry remembered.

It was a place with problems: the camp had to be rebuilt, troops retrained, discipline established. An Executive Officer underground for thirty days did little for camp moral. Racial differences had flared. When Henry arrived, South Vietnamese and Americans held machine guns trained on each other's compounds. Shots had been fired. Montagnards were restless at this discontent. On New Year's Eve, one week after Henry's arrival, his A-team drank itself into hysteria and discharged four hundred fifty rounds of ammunition inside the team house. Berets were shooting bottles out of each other's hands with .45 caliber pistols. Henry retreated to quarters and hid beneath a concrete wall.

Henry stayed at Dak Seang seven months. He established order, rebuilt the camp, conducted operations. And tasted the fear. He dropped from two hundred to one hundred sixty-five pounds. Tension was steady. Still Henry thought himself to be immortal.

"I believed I was immune to bullets. I'd been shot at—a lot. Had automatic weapons-fire trained on me at close range, had rounds pass through my rucksack, my clothing. A Chinese priest had given me an amulet to wear and told me I could not be killed by bullets. I thought, why not agree with it? Makes things easier.

"First four months at Dak Seang weren't bad. Then we began running into contacts around camp, tension built from Vietnamese versus Americans versus Montagnards, and time started working on you. Intelligence reports sifted in about attacks building up, frustration mounted from discussions with our S-3 at supporting headquarters, where he'd say you're on your own, we can't help—if you get attacked do what you can, we have no reinforcements even *planned*. We were so far away it would have taken an hour for tactical air support if air support had been available. It was us and the indigenants."

Which, theoretically, fitted Special Forces to a T. Its mission, as designated by the *Special Forces Handbook*, being thus:

1.) To plan and conduct unconventional warfare operations in areas not under friendly control.

2.) To organize, equip, train, and direct indigenous forces in the conduct of guerrilla warfare.

3.) To train, advise, and assist indigenous forces in the conduct of counterinsurgency and counterguerrilla operations in support of U.S. cold war objectives.

4.) To perform such other Special Forces missions as may be directed or as may be inherent in or essential to the primary mission of guerrilla warfare.

If that primary mission, on the deepest psychological level, was blood knowledge, its fiercest imperative was blood knowledge of the primitive. Montagnards—indigenants of the Central Highlands—were Vietnam's most savage inhabitants: silent, brooding, blasé about battle, painted of body, dour in countenance, tribal, nomadic, and wedded to magic. Closer in temperament to North Vietnamese than South, they fought not for territory but for spoils. Were mercenaries in the simplest sense. That they fought North Vietnamese, a people more closely related than lowlanders of the south, and fought for Americans, placed them in similitude to the American Indian—whose dissidents likewise had hired to fight against their kind. The guerrilla experience for Americans was in some sense a rekindling of Indian wars. There we first had suffered guerrilla raids, there our European-style conventional warfare first had proved wanting. Blood knowledge of the Indian, through massacres, hand-to-hand combat and learned rituals, had stood as a powerful totem during the nineteenth century. Who could say that America's venture into the jungles of Vietnam was not a continuance of that obsession with the primitive which had colored Westward expansionism? That Green Berets, knife in hand, bodies swathed in tiger stripes, faces painted black (after Cochise or Al Jolson?), were not the spearhead of cultural volition, armed vanguard of a great popular force which supported them?

There was no border at Dak Seang. There were no boundaries. "Just empty space," Henry remembered. Eight kilometers from Laos and a perimeter which did not exist. "A border suggests sovereignty, and there was no sovereignty there. It was whoever took it. No people, no government. Just empty space." Beyond bureaucracy, beyond technology, beyond chemical megadeath of mother corporation—Henry descended into the primitive. A descent which would mark him for life.

"I absorbed a lot of pecularities. I was *strange*. The whole way through. I was like a tiger on the prowl. That tension, quickness, alertness became a part of my nature. Totally out of place in a civilian situation. A state of affairs which made it supremely difficult to adapt once I returned to civilization."

Henry remained in Vietnam's Central Highlands ten months,

having extended six months, indefinitely in the Special Forces. But bureaucracy finally ensnared him, assignment fuck-ups through behind-the-lines ass-kissing enraged him, so he pulled out early.

"I flew home via Germany. Had a girlfriend there, my fiancé. In late '69 the war did not exist for Europe. Except in the left-wing circles my girlfriend frequented, where I was considered the archetypal imperialist aggressor. I did not speak German well enough to counter that argument, and, like I said, I was strange. This was the time of My Lai. I grew tired of the arguments. I stayed in Germany two months and told my girl I was heading home to the States. She could come if she wanted. She didn't."

What a different America Henry encountered in early 1970. Where in 1968 the war had been a modest feature of the evening news, it now riddled every aspect of American culture, media most thoroughly, to embrace longhairs, rednecks, middle Americans, bureaucrats, artists, rock stars, politicians in a dance of death macabre as any one might have imagined in Vietnam's Central Highlands. Where the antiwar movement in '68 had seemed a few thousand disreputables at the steps of the Pentagon, by 1970 it included middle-class citizens of "respectable" demeanor, most college faculties, and the collective student body of America. If Henry had felt the archetypal imperialist-aggressor in Germany, imagine his discomfort upon returning to the University of Delaware. A campus, like most, under psychological siege. The lines had been drawn and everyone played a role. You were for or against, shadings did not exist. Hair was long or it was short; you were hip or you were straight. The veteran guerrilla stood aghast at mock-guerrilla domestics, would-be Guevaras in Weatherman fatigues, street people from the suburbs polemicizing Marxist tracts with gruff voices of the proletariat. I recall asking Henry quite soberly in 1970 if he'd collaborate on a book about guerrilla warfare, which could serve as handbook for domestic subversives to shut down every major city in the United States. Henry stared at me but a second, then laughed, shaking his head. I was finishing a book about Bob Dylan that winter, had been living on a six-thousand-acre estate outside Wilmington, guest of a friend whose parents were abroad, and the irony of my leftism was not lost. Henry and other veterans visited that estate. Where Vietnam vets had been unheard of eight years earlier, everyone had a war tale to tell. The war's obsession with technology ran ragged through domestic culture, two men on the moon that summer had not helped; friends home from 'Nam brought war toys with them, pistols, rifles, even automatic weapons. One alumnus commandeered Army Reserve helicopters for weekend parties, tethering them to his parents' lawn, touching down at wedding receptions, private galas, orgies of the Wilmington rich from Rehoboth Beach to Philadelphia, tanking up to fly revelers *beneath* the Delaware Memorial Bridge on nightly raids. Rock 'n' roll cranked out the megawatts and pulsed chopper thuds into the metabolism of everyone. Most folks packed a gun. Permanent casualties flecked the peace movement, moratoriums and millionfold marches took on the cast of great, nineteenth century battles, Gettysburgs in their formality, honor at stake, position the platform, not individual expansionism of guerrilla ethics. The nation charged itself up in a manner unsurpassed since World War II. Economy boomed. Cash was there for the rifling, and Henry, howsoever bemused, shook himself alert and set up shop.

He started a company importing coats from Iran and hookas from Turkey, capitalizing on the hippie trade. That paid bills for about a year, while Henry finished college and weighed career options. His attitude toward school had changed. "I was a different person." He was serious, a dean's lister, composing papers on topics such as "cultural politics and intercultural communications—problems of politics between cultures," and "limitations imposed on the Red Chinese economy and military by their lack of railroad transportation."

He was also in the Army Reserves.

"The army was still in my blood. I was going to Reserve meetings Friday afternoons and coming home Monday mornings. The only place I wanted to be was in the army, in Special Forces. That lifestyle—of being outdoors, in volatile situations with responsibility, challenged constantly by fluid situations, not humdrum—I found totally seductive."

Henry returned to active duty before the year was out, assigned to the Tenth Special Forces Group at Fort Devens, Massachusetts. There he underwent training in winter warfare, warfare oriented toward Europe. He stayed seven months at Devens, an entire month of which he spent living in the snow, deep in the mountains of New Hampshire. He attended German language school; his group traveled to Germany, where they undertook various exercises. Then, in September, 1971, Henry was reassigned to Lop Buri, Thailand, where he became the S-3 plans officer to the 46th Company, commanding an augmented A-detachment with a training mission to advise the Second Royal Thai Army Special Forces Group.

"That gave me an opportunity to see how plans within the army came into being and were executed. An overview as to what one should be doing to achieve goals of the United States. Problem was determining what goals of the United States *were.* If you talked to someone in the embassy, they'd tell you one thing, someone in intelligence another, someone in the army . . . promoting his career. Goals of the United States hithertofore had been fairly clear to me, when in fact they were not clear at all, even to the people who were making them. This is what I saw. I took a wider view of setting up operations and executing them, rather than being at the end of a chain, as I was in Vietnam—out there not knowing what the fuck was going on, wondering what they were thinking. I was not reassured at what I found: More disorganization at the top than at the bottom."

Henry made enemies. He had been a maverick, a renegade in a world of efficiency reports and attitude grading for which he never had given a fuck. He had enjoyed close association with a general officer instrumental in condemnation of the army for its handling of My Lai. These deficits, combined with the army's winding down, its reduction of size post-Vietnam, did not bode well for Henry's career.

"If you were not a West Pointer with maximum efficiency reports, your chances of remaining on active duty were nil. I had never cared about making points, winning medals, promoting my career—those things weren't important to me. When in fact the people to whom those things were important stayed in the army. Particularly West Pointers. West Pointers were attuned to how corrupt the army was, because they learned it at West Point. That's succinctly put. They were the worst officers I encountered, the most self-serving, unreliable, dishonest; everything you would not desire in an officer. They adapted well to a political environment. And rightly so. The army could not tolerate the fact that West Point was producing officers inferior to a six month OCS course. I got caught up, again, in something beyond my abilities to combat."

Henry left the army in February, 1973. Unsettled. He came down to Washington to visit me. He was restless, awake all night reading, sleeping when he slept with a pistol beneath his pillow—same pistol he'd carried strapped to his back in Vietnam, a Walther, James Bond's gun. The pistol traveled in Henry's glove compartment, in his pocket, in a briefcase. Again the society had shifted gears. The sixties were winding down, love children but a memory; casualties lurched out violently at every crossroads. The seventies locked in. You could not run for public office without drawing fire; you could not drink at a neighborhood bar without risking fights, at the least a leaden sense of dread. Henry caught hepatitis, was sick for months. As if infected by the new world, by this strange decade unfolding, he took his time recovering.

Government still beckoned. Contacted by the CIA, Henry was interviewed at Langley, then not activated. The mission, he said, was never funded. Henry retreated to the world of business. Like many sixties renegades, he thought to create, in the nineteen-seventies, a firm economic base for future operations. The dedicated militarist went to work for his uncle in Pennsylvania, at Mr. Red, a chicken wholesaler.

"That was an interesting job. It taught me business. It opened doors for me to make a substantial living. I worked there two years. Problems developed within the company, so I quit, moving to a securities company. What I wanted was a job with no limits on what I could earn. I'd had it with a salary. The big money was in commodities. That's where I went. Today I'm way ahead of schedule. I'm measuring everything on the bottom line, now. I put numbers on my goals. That's a more realistic approach. You don't deceive yourself then. You're either producing or not. If you're *not* producing, change something: work harder, work smarter. Without quantifying your goals there's no accurate way of measuring yourself. You tend to think you're achieving goals when you're not.

"Business gave me a perspective on civilian life I'd been lacking. I really didn't take it too hard about the army. I'd seen the army's faults. I still had this burning patriotism but realized I was approaching it from the narrow end. The army was so confining, unexpressive, conservative and rigid in its attitude toward everything that I decided to indulge my patriotic feelings from the outside. To become successful financially via endeavors which would improve my position materially in life, at the same time obtain for me influence over those who control the army. Run for public office. Get an elected post. This is how you can assert yourself in society. In the army you really can't."

Despite what that personality inventory had stated in 1965, that Henry was a natural as a career military officer, business wooed him away. Not as vassal to the corporation, however, but as investor, independent—though he wore a corporate hat. Henry married a Canadian in 1974. They settled in Pennsylvania, where Henry joined a securities firm. Henry moved there knowing one person, his employer, and within two years felt secure enough to run for public office.

"I ran for county commissioner and lost, but with a respectable number of votes. I doubt that I would run next time for anything less than U.S. Congress. It wouldn't be worth the cut in pay. I'm still a patriot. I can be a *better* patriot by producing a better income for myself. The more I make, the better patriot I can be. If it's good for me, it's good for the country—I'm more productive, I'm paying more taxes, supporting more welfare bums, more bureaucrats in Washington who do nothing but pass papers to each other. And I'm a very liberal person," Henry laughed. "Far be it from me to be a right-wing militant.

"We've got to get our congressmen squared away to start helping American business. Instead of fucking with it. 'Cause that's the golden goose, and Congress is trying to dismember it. I don't have that much confidence in government to serve up a better replacement. Everywhere American business has gone in the world it's improved the lives of most people it's touched. The same cannot be said for American government."

I watched Henry sip Coca-Cola before a revolving fan this hot Sunday afternoon in 1977, and tried to recall the fuck-off kid I'd known fourteen years earlier. The kid with no goals, who now quantified his every activity. The lithe athlete, now an overweight executive in exploding jungle fatigues, approaching middle years. The guerrilla patriot, self-assured in his patriotism, of his part in an absurd war.

"I never expected tangible rewards for being a patriot. Never expected a victory parade in New York after going over and liberating Vietnam. A lot of fellows did. I didn't have those jingoistic tendencies then, I don't have them now. I don't think my basic philosophy has changed one bit. Gross mistakes have been made in American policy; being in Vietnam was not a mistake but how we were there and how we behaved. We have business putting our nose anywhere in the world we can affect the outcome of a situation. We should and we have to.

"The experience of Vietnam was valuable to me. I enjoyed most of my time there. War is fun. It's just those days of combat which aren't. People get killed. The camaraderie of men at arms is seldom duplicated in civilian life; one exception being a rather small group of friends in college—who shared a common ground to touch upon for many years.

"Vietnam does not exist in the U.S. army today. It's ignored as if it did not happen. Today, all we're concerned with is an aggressive, expansionist Soviet government. In the mid-sixties, even late-sixties, I felt we could still achieve something meaningful. By the end of my second tour it was cut your losses and run. That sixties strength of character has been eroded at every level of American society.

"But I feel no guilt. Perhaps for not having *acted* in certain situations. Specific guilt, nothing general. Nothing about Vietnam. I did as much as one person could."

What happened to that hypersensitivity and catlike awareness Henry'd described? Had that dissipated in this peacetime situation?

"It's still there but on hold. The circuit's active but the breaker switch is open. Wouldn't take much to get it back. That combat training's made me very perceptive about what's happening in business. But I have no desire to fight again. The opportunity's there. Anyone who wants to join the South African or Rhodesian armies can do so. I'm not interested. So far as being in the reserves, I do that to keep in touch.

"I've quantified a few of the goals I've had since college. And eliminated others. Such as wanting to be an international grand master in chess. And a world-class tennis player. They're unrealistic. I'm still hoping to publish a book, hold public office, earn a net worth of one million dollars. I want to paint well. I work at that. I've achieved one goal, and that's to reach a higher rank in the military than any member of my family."

Those goals seemed so romantic, even Gatsbyesque, born of college and collegiate sensibility. Had Henry nurtured similar feelings for the Green Beret? Some romantic notion of the Special Forces which that overseas cap symbolized?

"Not really. I personally found the hat uncomfortable. I rarely wore it. Whenever it rained, water got on my glasses and I can't stand that. It was colder than shit in winter, didn't shade your eyes in summer. It's a fucking worthless hat. A piece of paraphernalia. In Vietnam, around camp, I wore a baseball cap. Made it a part of the uniform for my troops. We wore the Beret when the colonels came around, 'cause they thought it was cool. But I never did."

Dissent

At Christmas, 1974, one month after my marriage to an ex-lieutenant of the Army Nurse Corps, Joe Don Looney came for supper—a Vietnamese dinner. He came bearing gifts (*Sri Aurobindo and the Mother on Love*) and driving a new pickup—"You can't hardly own nothing else in Texas"—eagle feather dangling from the rear-view mirror, down bag fluffed out under a camper lid. Looney appeared tired; he wore six days' growth of beard and his hair, longer now, was touched with gray. It had been a year since I'd seen him. We embraced in the drive then ducked into my small log house where a cackling fire cut the chill of this December night.

Corinne had the fixings out. Already the musk of *nuoc mam* fogged the room. A friend, a Vietnamese woman she'd known in Saigon, helped spread various delicacies about the kitchen. I introduced Joe Don and the three said hi with the deference of those who have dwelt near the oriental sensibility. Joe Don presented a companion, a tall grinning fellow in his late thirties, Kevin Walsh*, who was looking forward to this Vietnamese meal. Walsh had lived in Vietnam during the early sixties, as a civilian, a merchant seaman, and had developed a taste for the cuisine. Corinne had spent three years in Vietnam; Thiên-Kim*,

* Both Kevin Walsh and Thiên-Kim are pseudonyms. Identifying characteristics have been altered to protect their privacy.

over twenty. Looney, his tour. Neither veteran nor refugee, my taste for the cooking was domestically acquired.

This Christmas was an anxious time for the South Vietnamese. Armistice had been in effect since January, 1973, but fighting never had stopped. It would be five months before the fall ("Sigh-gone. Hi-noi!" a friend would quip*) and the tension of interim circumstances weighed upon America even as it weighed upon our dinner party. Corinne held a penumbra of memories in Saigon; Thiên-Kim her family; Walsh a Vietnamese "wife," Looney the recollection, perhaps, of having first encountered a culture much like that he presently embraced: War-torn emblemata of an Eastern path, bombed-out reps on the lotus trail. I saw it from another side.

The same side, really. As college deferments had locked us into the war, so the peace movement at home had provided us with phantoms terrifying as many stalking the Central Highlands. Whether through guilt, righteous indignation or dedicated protest, we had plunged into dissent hysterically as others had plunged toward the draft. Vietnam was our common demon— not the country but the concept—the monkey on our backs each fought to extirpate. Years had wasted every vestige of romance from that conflict. We shared something real now, no matter who we were.

Looney had never tasted Vietnamese food. Had spent a year there and never tried it. He picked gingerly at hors d'oeuvres, the anchovies in *nuoc mam* and sugar, the clear beef soup with dumplings and noodles, then began to devour each course as it was presented. We sat in a semi-circle on the floor, before the fire, reaching communally toward steaming platters of the richly scented food, reaching behind chopsticks toward each other with morsels too wonderful not to share, palming rice bowls like fielders' mitts to shag the overflow. A fat casserole of white rice rested at the circle's center. Surrounded by grilled chicken on skewers, *Ga Nuong Xien,* in a bed of lettuce leaves, pork fried in *nuoc mam* and sugar, sautéed beef, fragile meat rolls of crab, shrimp, pork and chopped vegetables, *Cha Gio,* wrapped in translucent sheets

---

* Scott Wright, to David Halberstam, in conversation.

of rice paper, colored shrimp chips fried in oil, cabbage sautéed in *nuoc mam,* tossed with chicken bits and fried egg ... everything in technicolor, *nuoc mam* pungent as finger paint, *nuoc mam* the sturdy easel upon which this meal had been constructed.

Looney—a vegetarian these eighteen months—tasted meat as if for the first time. He could not help himself. Even adversaries were brought together over the artifice of cuisine.

Post-romance, we sat comfortably about the feast, happily seduced by gustatory evidence of a culture more rich than anything suggested by the evening news. Looney unsnapped the button on his jeans and dug in. Walsh smiled ecstatically. Kim and Corinne, architects of this pleasure, picked lightly, chattering. *Nuoc mam* flowed thick as plasma in the collective vein. Who could think that rotted fish sauce, rank as death, could mortise such feelings of contentment, of righteous sensuality?

The cooking itself was ethereal: half real, half imagined, half molecular, half metaphysical. The scent of *nuoc mam* (despised by G.I.s in Vietnam, they would machine-gun stray vats of it) was the stench of decay—yet sexy, alive, the aroma of love. Juice of dead fish rotted by the sun, it was metamorphosis incarnate; as protein-base of the Vietnamese diet, a veritable phoenix. Insufferable when cold, under heat it rose to the senses with a salient fluttering of wings. One meal was sufficient to alter a decade's thinking on Vietnam.

Corinne and I had come together over a Vietnamese dinner. A single course and I knew some elemental knowledge had been withheld. Corinne had been to war and I had not. We had grown up in comparable circumstances. Each had suffered through private education, had endured attendant rites of puberty: dancing class, debutante parties, selective isolation. Corinne's background was thoroughly military, however. Born in occupied Germany to a career army officer and wife, she had moved across the globe haphazardly—relegated to boarding school by the second grade. Her great uncle had been first U.S. ambassador to Vietnam under Eisenhower, her father had served there, as had other relatives, so it made a certain sense that, out of nursing school, she should hightail it to the front. That was what she wanted. Attributing her curiosity to the desire for professional experience, she responded to some genetic program several generations old. Her first day in-country she had been shelled. At a dormitory near Tonsonnhut she spent her first night under a rusted cot listening to rockets whistling in and exploding about the airport. It was Tet, 1968.

She was assigned to the 36th Evacuation Hospital, Vung Tau, a French resort along the coast. There she spent five months treating Vietnamese civilians—women, children, older men— primarily burn patients, people who'd gotten in the way. Then she rotated to a medical I.C.U., where she dealt with American G.I.s—drug addicts, heart attack victims, pleurisy patients. Then to a surgical I.C.U. She had wanted a M.A.S.H. unit but Vung Tau was what she'd drawn. Hours were long on the ward but mornings were spent at the beach, sunning, sleeping, lolling in the backwaters of war as if on extended summer vacation. Vung Tau was an in-country R&R center, G.I.s were everywhere, constantly partying. But G.I.s weren't Corinne's cup of tea.

Any Vietnamese who could wrangle a job on an American base would take it, and many worked at Vung Tau. Corinne met Thiên-Kim there. Kim worked as a translator. She spoke good English. She was bright and precocious. She had spent the midsixties as a Saigon bar girl, having left home at thirteen. She'd pulled herself away from that. She and Corinne became fast friends. Kim took Corinne home to meet her family, introducing her to Vietnamese cuisine and hospitality. She helped her meet a Vietnamese boy as well. A tall, good-looking Vietnamese who likewise worked at Vung Tau.

He was married with children but that did not matter. He was separated, he said. Corinne met him the last two months of her tour and for those two months they were inseparable. When her tour was up, she returned to the States but waited only until her discharge to fly back to Saigon. He had an apartment for her there, he still worked at Vung Tau, but they lived together on weekends. It was the fall of 1969. Corrinne had returned without a job and it would be eight months before she landed another as a nurse. It was during this time she began to absorb Vietnamese culture: Saigon with its frantic streets, Asian cul de sacs, Parisian architecture, driven natives, exotic cuisine and studied nonchalance in the face of war. Saigon was an armed camp, death lurked at its perimeter, infiltrated via sapper raids, rocket attacks, entropies of unnamed phyla. A bunker mentality existed at the base of Saigon frippery which rendered it all the more seductive.

Corinne took a job with American Express at Tonsonnhut. She did volunteer work as a nurse for the Salvation Army, where eventually she was hired. That job ended in June of 1971. She returned to the U.S. Romance and the war had not worked themselves through. She obtained a position with the International Rescue Committee and went back to Vietnam in December, 1971. She worked in a plastic surgery hospital for children. Within five months she'd left, but returned again in November, 1972 with no job, to stay another five months. The war, the romance, the excitement all were winding down. By April, 1973, she was living in Washington, working at George Washington University Hospital as a nurse. By January, 1974, we had met.

Met for the second time actually. In an earlier excitement we had swayed to a different orchestration of sixties energy, the Washington debutante bash. Had embraced in the pink light of artificial dawns as Meyer Davis spun out the tunes, "Nice Work If You Can Get It," "But Not for Me," "This Could Be the Start of Something Big," fizzle of champagne and the perfume of bacon at post-midnight suppers, fuel required to maintain this frantic pace. *Most extravagant parties since the twenties,* columnists wrote. *Displays of wealth more Fitzgeraldian than Fitzgerald.* It had to be true. No telling how much those "introductions to society" cost. More than a college education, in many instances.

We partied in circus tents, by swimming pools, along vast, freshly cut lawns; we populated hotels, private clubs, river liners sailing to Mount Vernon; private estates we overran for weekends, barracks were constructed to house us; we overtook resorts; charged anything from club chits to taxi fares, hotel rooms to hamburgers. Everything went, our mandate was the exhaustion of pleasure; it was a grueling pace, one that culminated in violence often as romance. Energy being that intense.

Accompanying a notion that much was being done for us was the suspicion that something was being done to us. Deb parties were—required, an extension of private education, like prep school or college. Specifically, they were extensions of dancing school, the graduate program to that social curriculum in which our parents had enrolled us years past. The energy was ecstatic and very much a corollary of sixties *joie de vivre.* But it was our parents' energy; we were nothing but the fire, the puppets dancing to this, their ultimate realization of postwar wealth.

Deb parties were as much a by-product of that hot sixties economy, beyond responsibility, beyond morality, as was America's fascination with hot cars, hot sex, violent sport, war and unbridled technology. They harkened to a prewar sensibility, to a thirties sophistication of style, and in that regard they were archaic. But the cash flow they engendered was thoroughly sixties. They were our parents' fantasies of postwar prosperity, and for that reason we knew their days to be numbered. All the more impetus to kick out the jams. We introduced a few of our personal obsessions, notably rock music (one party featured Count Basie for dance, the Four Tops for rock 'n' roll—at a time when the Four Tops had two Top Ten singles on the charts), but in the face of such baroque spectacles we were surprisingly blasé. This was how it *always* had been, we felt. For purer spectacle we felt more akin to what was going down in the streets.

Next to experiencing rock concerts live, the most powerful intimations that our years of isolation were at an end were those great civil rights marches of the early sixties. Notably, Martin Luther King's march on Washington in August, 1963. Here a more appropriate manifestation of energy was apparent. *Don't go near there,* parents had warned, rioting would result in a bloodbath. Of course they were mistaken. The day was a giant picnic graced with music, visual spectaculars, oratory and an overwhelming sense of community. Once again a notion insinuated itself that we were no longer alone. And it walked hand in hand with black culture.

There was a schizophrenia at the heart of the debutante experience which confused us who sensed we were dwelling on some societal Lip. In one regard, deb parties were the apotheosis of our parents' values, the quiddity of middle-class hauteur; in another they were expressions of an elitism refined as . . . Special Forces or championship sports. If there was a Valhalla to the middle-class ordeal, it was reflected in the sixties deb party; if there was an aristocracy of spirit in that specialized dose of energy, we felt compelled to subscribe. Deb parties were an elitist's pocket of sixties hysteria, elite as the damnedest empiricisms of sex, speed, sport or war. We felt driven to oblige. An imperative demanding as the pull toward experimental rock. Deb balls were the purple-hazed, Hendrix-riffed artillery barrages of polite society. Doomed to extinction by decade's end (blame economy, blame lobotomy), temporarily they provided an alternative acre of re-stricted playground for those who were privileged to attend.

Corinne was blonde, small, five-foot-two, had a chipped tooth in front which detracted not one smidgeon from her smile. She was total energy. She was hot to be with, to hold, hot to drink with and help laugh away more ridiculous aspects of our condi-tion. We shared the ironies of hopscotching that energy.

Black music raised some height of black energy, we wanted that; deb parties were a cap to white pretension, something there was worth excising. Corinne and I shared motorcycles, smoked dope, shared friends, tried some loving. Last time I saw her pre-war was the summer of '66. We were lying on a private beach at Rehoboth listening to Lyndon Johnson announce intensified bombing of the north. Then we were back in Washington for a James Brown concert at a black theater downtown.

She was off to war, I . . . to some irascible flip side. At my pre-induction physical a gnarled orthopedist yanked me from the line, tapped my coccyx, counted my ribs, and pronounced my arches too high for combat. Three years of college soccer, a life-time of athletics and I could not trot those metatarsals through boot camp. Relief, but not without guilt and a prickling aimless-ness. My father, like Corinne's, was a decorated veteran of World War II. I felt a genetic tug toward combat, had assumed post-grad work would include platoon leader's school at Quan-tico or Fort Bragg. My father had served with Darby's Rangers in at least one major invasion, had sloughed through several others plus a firestorm of less specific action. So there were con-flicts. I spent late '66 trudging through Europe, then returned home for graduate school and another fling at "art."

Art (writing for me) was still the final edge, that dividing line between hip and non-hip which fashion seemed least likely to blur. Nothing sociological, I felt, approached the sophistication of literature or the magic of rock 'n' roll. A fellow approached me one day with a leaflet previewing a colossal march on the Pentagon, celebrities promised. That Norman Mailer would speak injected a certain interest, but otherwise the thing sounded flat. Promised crowds of dowdy political-science students mouthing inane polemics, dull, craven, unhip. I let the date pass. Imagine my chagrin upon reading Mailer's report in *Harper's*. Something akin to art was happening in the streets, something white, collegiate and raucously middle-class.

The Third Reich built our Volkswagens, sired our interstate highway system and suggested the mandate of a transcontinental invasion force; likewise, it lent us a predilection for mass hijinks. "The father of street theater was Hitler," Gary Wills wrote.* That observation carried weight. Albert Speer, architect to the Third Reich, designed stage sets for Hitler's Nuremburg rallies—lights, sculpture, electronic audio-visuals—with a hand adept as that of David Dellinger. Banners, troopers, mass marches, oratory—Speer foresaw it all during the thirties, helped whip National Socialism from a zany clique of violent extremists to a worldwide political force. What had been hinted in '67 on the steps of the Pentagon was reaffirmed at Chicago, '68: Art could influence politics directly; not art removed from the fracas but mated to it, theatrically. Street theater *was* politics, the politics of hip. Or so we thought. It was also war.

Anyone who doubted that did not engage the particulars. Forget Kent State, Jackson State, forget Chicago, forget the Days of Rage, forget May Day, '72. Cite demonstrations peaceful as the '69 moratoriums, take any day on campus post-Cambodia. The lines were drawn. It was hip against straight, longhair against redneck, college student against cop—to venture beyond that was to experience a nation divided as if by civil war. You took your life in your hands stating a position. Many protesters felt

* Garry Wills, "The Sixties," *Esquire's* Fortieth Anniversary Issue, October, 1973.

themselves cascading toward extremes violent as those their fathers had known overseas. The fighting was often desperate as that our brothers were enduring in Vietnam. One has only to recall wide lines of police sweeping across Washington's Mall ... on Bob Hope Remember America Day, July 4, 1970. Police dispersing demonstrators during filming of the National Anthem, police lobbing tear gas into a crowd of one million, grandmothers and babies choking, dragging beach chairs behind them, demonstrators heaving bottles, screaming ... so chaotic Bob Hope shot it four times before he got a take. That was theater, televised theater, but it was likewise war, for real heads were broken, real guns were fired, and the sides were marked. Actors soaked in blood fondling sheep guts wandered through the crowd. Non-actors fell into the Reflecting Pool emitting scarlet flumes, or spat teeth at curbstones. Police were carried off with broken limbs, smashed faces. Horses were stoned, beaten, lanced at one demonstration with a rain of hypodermic needles. Equipment was destroyed: trucks, half-tracks, jeeps set afire, anti-aircraft lamps crushed or dumped into the water. Machine guns were emplaced on the steps of the Capitol, on the White House roof, troops occupied government buildings, 82nd Airborne ready. Running at or from police—waves of blue descending, clubs raised, holsters unsnapped—one had no doubt he was at war: In the heart of spectacle. Real rather than fantasized, more real than any deb ball or Newport weekend. For you could die spectacularly. After dark, campfires lighted the Mall from Capitol to Lincoln Memorial, harmonicas sounded, voices lifted as at Gettysburg or Bull Run. Amid Beaux Arts autonomy of official Washington—Smithsonian's dark castle one's chummiest foe—it was an eerie communion.

That war continued for years. There was no romance to it, romance died, as in combat, with first bloodshed. But there was energy. We had "God on our side." And some semblance of hip. We'd made a choice, we didn't *have* to be there. Self-righteousness was not absent from our cadre, nor disdain for our brothers of the draft. Why subjugate yourself to the vicissitudes of bureaucracy, cut your hair, wear Uncle Sam's uniform, when you could get the same rush in the streets, costumed, bedecked in warpaint, longhaired, stoned, in the company of women, and carry the banner of moral rectitude at your flank? Here was a guerrilla war to sink your teeth into. Dangerous as that going down abroad. You could get yourself killed. Or destroy your head trying.

I sort of let mine slide. After May Day, '72, fun drained out of the Movement like pus from a weeping sore. No morale-boosting extras like frantic music, dervish dancing, candlelight marches, even skull-busting duty-time possessed equivalent energy. The Movement was slipping into "seventies" (read: depression) surely as were maligned segments of the middle class. Protest equaled—Vietnam Veterans Against the War, a courageous but depressed group of patriots tossing brightly ribboned medals onto the Capitol steps. It was everyone who'd been implacable admitting someone else had been right. It was "sixties" (read: style) saturating middle America, blurring ecstasy, clouding position. Who the hell knew where he stood in the early seventies? Everybody *looked* the same. But it was heroin instead of methadrine, hollow visions instead of high. Time to hit the road.

Many of us did, extending Kerouac trips into less-mythic perusals of alternative space. I spent four years on the road searching for the Great American Bar. Thirty bars a day six months at a stretch—work a couple months, then head back out. Away from television, away from newspapers, in some antipodal heartland where people *talked* to one another. I thought I might discover something. We talked and drank and I wrote a lot of it down. During R&R from one of these missions, I encountered Corinne.

She came to my house, took one look and said: "Why can't I live here?" She broke out her wok, got the kitchen steaming, and served me a meal like first sex. She didn't say anything about Vietnam. Just laid out the food. I couldn't tell her what I'd seen. I merely tasted. It was January, 1974. Survivors.

Within a year we were hosting this dinner party—married, Corinne working in an intensive care unit and attending George Washington University on the G.I. Bill, I writing *Saloon* and working part-time selling furniture. It was a life. Like many seventies couples we had entrenched. The restlessness was still there, but temporarily it lay in check while we rustled up an emotional grubstake.

Restlessness played across Looney's face; he rippled with anxiety. Uptight about his firearms appeal, his spiritual affirmations re-expounded rang false. He picked at his muscles, black circles beneath his eyes, dark beard nearly Mansonesque. A football injury pinched his back, he would have it Rolfed this week. It was transition time for Joe Don; he was clutching at spiritual phantoms. The insecurity of that noplace painted him in grays and browns.

Contrastively, Kevin Walsh crouched at Looney's side with a satiated grin. Walsh tickled me. At some point I'd mentioned the merchant marine and Walsh passed round his seaman's card, dated 1963, picturing him in full beard and black Viet Cong pajamas. Later we'd spoken of protest and Joe Don had said, "Kevin here's sort of an expert. Slept on it, you might say. In front of the White House."

"How long?" I asked.

"Two years," Walsh said. Then grinned as if it were nothing.

Walsh, it seemed, was some penultimate seventies street person. A Diogenes of the sidewalk, having lived on the street since 1971, sleeping in doorways, parks, cozy backyards, in Dempster Dumpsters, under cardboard, on the road, in woods, in deserted buildings, and for two years before the White House, protesting the Indochina War. Yet he was *clean.* Even his clothes.

"Guess I know every spicket, unattended hose and swimming pool in this city," he said comically. "Summertime I bathe in the river. Last June I was swimming buck naked at the foot of 31st Street and a tour boat went by, tried to run me over. I just showed 'em the old backside."

Walsh lived primarily in Georgetown—tough to street-sleep in that populated quarter, I had an expert here—but hailed originally from Kenwood, an upper-middle-class suburb of Washington. He'd wandered around the world. Aside from tours with the merchant marine, he'd foot-slogged through Vietnam, Laos,

Cambodia, Thailand, Burma, India, Pakistan, Bali, passing through Indochina at the height of the war unharmed, unhassled, across the Ho Chi Minh Trail in shoulder-length hair, beard, black V.C. pajamas, his possessions in a sack, through Pathet Lao villages where children had never seen a Caucasian and where adults revered him as *bhikku,* blessed wanderer and saint. As mendicant he'd hitchhiked where he could not walk, worked odd jobs when he could not—live. Currently he toiled three or four days a month at Yes!, a health food store, restaurant and spiritual enclave in Georgetown. Looney had played football with Walsh's brother, and therein lay the embroidery of a tale.

Walsh's father had been a star athlete at the University of Maryland during the thirties, had played tackle on that football team, had boxed heavyweight at a championship level. Kevin Walsh was one of four brothers, legendary athletes around Washington. Legendary also for their irascibility; two had died violent deaths, one had taken his talents as far as Oklahoma University, where he'd roomed with Joe Don Looney and played exceptional ball. Several pro try-outs for Jim Walsh, a couple of summer camps, but nothing permanent. He'd introduced Joe Don to Kevin, by the mid-sixties already a character and headed down that spiritual path Looney would hit in the seventies.

Kevin Walsh was an athlete himself, had attended prep school on a football scholarship, playing fullback and linebacker. He was heavy-set, tall, about 6'2", and handsomest of the Walsh brothers. But by prep school he already nurtured a proclivity for the inane. He tried college, returned to prep school, dropped out, took a clerk's job at the F.B.I., then one afternoon in 1956 walked to a recruiting office and joined the Marine Corps. Why? "Who the fuck knows." It was a six-year commitment, two years active duty, two active reserve, two inactive . . . a big chunk out of a young man's life. Walsh was just a kid but already he'd taken a step toward renouncing it: the brothers, the jockishness, the competition, the drive toward success, forced religion, the suburban hopelessness of the prepackaged kit.

Walsh studied electronics in the Marine Corps, inaugurating a fixation on energy which would dog him through the seventies—

great radar baths which haunted him, waves of positive and negative ions nudging him in contrary directions. Out of the Marine
Corps that energy manifested itself in black—black music, black
rhythm, black sex. In 1960 Walsh inexplicably purchased an all-
black bar in an all-black neighborhood in downtown Washington. The 4200 Lounge, on Fourteenth Street. It was more than a
bar, it was a night club with entertainment: rhythm and blues,
jazz, dancing, hustling, razor fights, hip talk, desperate screams
and a thunderous jungle beat which Walsh found intoxicating.
Walsh not only owned the 4200, but managed it, tended bar and
hung out there incessantly. This was unusual in 1960. White men
as absentee owners of black businesses were not unheard of, but
for a kid from the suburbs to show up all smiles, take over a
neighborhood joint, then *run* it, embracing regulars as oldest
buddies on the block, set blades back. They couldn't help but dig
him.

Walsh's suburban friends infiltrated by the carload. They likewise stood in disbelief. Washington was a *segregated* city then,
1960 was early for this brand of backslapping, brother-up-a-
spade jive. The kids from Kenwood tiptoed in warily, but tiptoe
they did. Soon they had black girlfriends and were regularly
hanging out. Walsh, throughout his Marine Corps experience,
had abstained from sex, was in fact a virgin. He got laid quickly
at the 4200. The morning after his first intercourse he attended
mass and felt no guilt. "Something that good couldn't be bad,"
Walsh rationalized.

Blacks were more open generally than Walsh's Catholic
friends. They "communicated" better, were easier in their expressiveness, looser, more sensual. They seemed never to have
experienced guilt. Walsh enmeshed himself in the world of
black. Became some odd brand of benign hipster, unself-con-
sciously, blissfully. And not a touch naively. He married a black
woman "part Cherokee" who came up with an extra husband in
the army some time later; Walsh's marriage was annulled. But
not before it wounded him. A streak of violence began to assert
itself, violence which appeared at predictable moments. Usually
surrounding women. That was the sole trouble he knew in his
bar. One night a black man came on to Walsh's wife, "probably

not realizing," and Walsh slammed him against the wall, slammed him repeatedly until Walsh's wife reached across his shoulder and smashed a bottle over the fellow's head. Walsh experimented with many black girlfriends at the 4200 until 1961 when pressure and responsibility became too great. He sold out to a partner. Kevin recalled his bar life fondly, said he still wandered through black sections of D.C. with impunity, with a bloodied veteran's awe.

He was seeing another black woman in 1963 when she became pregnant. Though not certain the child was his, Kevin wished to keep and accept it. He was overseas when he got the news. He had been working for Coca-Cola as a driver-salesman earning $175 a week, "busting ass," but the pace had been too grueling, he'd eased off and joined the merchant marine. Kevin stayed at sea from 1963 to 1970, with time off to experience Vietnam, acquire a "Vietnamese wife" and trek overland. It was on board ship that Walsh first developed a social conscience about Vietnam, transporting troops, rapping with them, sympathizing as an ex-Marine with men who were "putting their asses on the line."

At some point Walsh returned to D.C. and found his black girlfriend involved with another man. A heartrending scene ensued where Kevin asked her to choose and she walked to the other man's side. Kevin maintained child support but stayed pretty much at sea after that. He maintained his child-support irregularly. Refusing to go through courts with his payments, he sent money directly to his kids, and served time in jail for nonsupport. The sixties he spent primarily on board ship.

He wrangled a steady run to Vietnam on a fruit company freighter. He liked Vietnam, liked the women; as with blacks felt the freedom and openness of their attitudes toward sex, toward energy. Kevin had met a monk in Bangkok who'd taught him to meditate into the sun; Kevin was receiving showers of inspiration from these optic sunburns. Was hearing voices, collating tantric advice. After his hegira through Indochina on foot, carrying a wooden bowl and two pair of black pajamas sewn by his Vietnamese wife, he'd seen the war, passed through its fronts, and the experience traumatized him. He came to live on Con Phoung Island, Phoenix Island, home of the Coconut Monk, once Hugyn

Nam Than, a Cao Dai preaching a meditated peace plan for ending the war.

The Coconut's plan was simple. He wanted various factions at the Paris Peace talk to reconvene at Phoenix Island, *part* of Vietnam, for meditation toward a reasonable solution to the conflict. According to Walsh, the Coconut believed salubrious vibrations of Phoenix Island coupled with proximity to Vietnamese soil would induce a willingness for compromise, a mystical armistice. Walsh's own proclivities toward things mysterious had intensified, but he discovered an anchor in Coconut's concrete proposal and dragged it home to the States. The Coconut explained much in terms of astral forms and etheric construct; but he held degrees in physics and chemistry, taken in France, which lent him Western credence.

Walsh found Washington of the early seventies alive with indignant protest and torn asunder with great antiwar demonstrations, captivating *zeitgeists* of moral rectitude. Walsh locked onto a purpose. He had the Coconut's peace plan, which he presented to every member of Congress with no success; and he had this sensitivity toward energy, communicating directly now, through the sun, the sky, through a hundred thousand riled-up celebrants in the war dance of antiwar. He stayed in trouble with police for nonsupport. He lived permanently on the street. He held no job. His black wife went with another man. None of that mattered. Walsh fell in with communards, a group of Quakers holding a vigil for peace on the sidewalk fronting the White House. Walsh remained two years.

"Was much communication down there," Kevin remembered. "Always someone rapping, always something going down. We ate, slept, made love on the sidewalk. We bathed in Lafayette Park, using toilets there. Never felt lonely. We rapped with tourists, protesters, police, about religion, politics, current events— anything. I'd hip them to the Coconut Monk. It was a high-energy experience."

Walsh had little luck promoting the Coconut's peace plan. Apparently it was vague. At May Day demonstrations, 1972, where New Left forces vowed to shut down Washington in protest of the federal war machine—actually barricading major thoroughfares with telephone poles and refuse cans—Kevin found himself caught up. He'd been standing before the Capitol listening to dissident speakers, a few singing, some naked and dancing, when police moved in and started arrests. Something clicked in Kevin's head, some residue from grade school about the Bill of Rights. Kevin grabbed a microphone. He spoke his mind, making little sense, but rallied two hundred people about him: arrested. They were bused to D.C. Coliseum (in company of seven thousand others, largest mass arrest in American history, later to be ruled illegal), where the scene was primo energy, people dancing, fucking, singing, holding each other in tense webs of intercommunication. Kevin balled a woman in the crowd, her husband nearby, as cops chastized Kevin wiping jism off his jeans. Kevin reacted strangely to his incarceration. He would not give his name nor would he allow himself to be fingerprinted. He refused A.C.L.U. lawyers. Eventually he relented, but not before causing considerable anxiety. "I suffered a tremendous loss of energy," Kevin recalled.

He was on a thirteen-day fast some time later when arrested for protesting without a permit. Kevin's girlfriend had been pregnant; he'd planned to deliver the baby himself; it had died. He was part of a Community for Creative Non-Violence demonstration *inside* the White House when detained; in solitary confinement at D.C. jail he felt the baby's spirit enter his body and became quite manic. An ugly season for war protesters: One of Kevin's colleagues, a Quaker man, was buggered thirty times by black inmates before guards interceded. Kevin sensed the radar fumes. He refused to cooperate with police. He believed some perfidious electronic device was being directed from an adjoining cell to work on his spirit, to destroy it, to get him off the street. At one point he felt he had died. He was transferred to St. Elizabeth's Hospital. Kevin pulled back. The electronics had proved effective. He was not too active after that. Yet the manic phases increased.

Demonstrations wound down after May Day. One or two would follow; sixties energy was dissipating. Everyone felt it, but the demise was most trying for stalwarts like Kevin who had cooked on the spiritual front burner so long.

One of the final rallies Kevin attended celebrated the "divine presence" of Maharaj Ji. Kevin's parents had driven in from Kenwood to pluck him off the sidewalk, remove him from what they sensed would be a trying scene. Kevin rode out to Kenwood; his mother encouraged him to stay, but vibrations weren't right, his mother bugged him; he got his father to drive him back, lugging sandwiches and fruit. Then commenced "the all-time best demonstration ever," music, flowers, peace, tantalizing sexuality. Kevin attained awesome levels of energy that night, what only can be described as manic ... dancing in total frenzy, hopping around, chanting. The demonstration climaxed in a peace march to the White House, a candlelight procession which affected Kevin profoundly. He felt *strange,* like being there and not being there. He felt present in spirit yet not in body. "A dual creativity."

Kevin had tried a few drugs during his sidewalk vigil before the White House, some acid, some mescaline, some grass, but never had liked them. His visions of light increased unfueled by chemicals. His confusion seemed to mirror that of seventies society, energy filtering from the collective psyche like nerve gas, the etheric body wasted, pyrolitic. After the Ji rally he hitchhiked to Charlotte, North Carolina, saw his sister, attacked his brother-in-law when he tried to stop Walsh from performing mantra dances in his backyard, Walsh manic over some exterior conflict he felt being waged inside his body. He was incarcerated in a state mental facility. Sedated with Equamil, Thorazine, Melaril, Kevin hovered on a low plane. He was transferred back to Maryland, spent two weeks in the county installation near Rockville, then hit jail, where he was wanted for nonsupport. Kevin effected a deal to stay as long as the drugs were discontinued. The sun was talking to Kevin, he'd been meditating into it again, and the message was split. Kevin tried going over the fence, unsuccessfully. He spent fifty days at Springfield Mental Hospital, in Sykesville. By any reasonable diagnosis he was insane.

Kevin had been wandering through Kenwood one afternoon, near his parents' house ... bummed out at his mother, who'd been lecturing him about his lifestyle ... Kevin drinking from gutters, creeks, watching the kids play—when he strolled through a High's store, bought a soft drink and encountered trouble. With a black man there, an employee. Kevin was beaten, his shoulder dislocated, his face smashed. Some question as to who was at fault. Kevin felt himself connected to another consciousness, thought himself being tortured in the emergency room as his shoulder was reduced. His pain was transcendental. That was the spring of '74. He'd been planing out since.

Sleeping on sidewalks, sleeping around town, hitchhiking out West, working odd jobs at Yes! restaurant, at seventies-concerned hostels like the Finders in Glover Park, helping with a derelict's soup kitchen run by the Community for Creative Non-Violence in Washington. Walsh renounced the Movement as the Movement died in his arms. Like Diogenes, who'd slept in a water jug, Walsh wanted few essentials. Extra T-shirts, sandals in a ditty bag. You'd spot him around Georgetown, staring into the sun or toweling off at the foot of Thirty-first Street. In summertime he'd disappear. "Living like a muskrat," someone remarked, "Kevin's that attuned." He visited his children, they'd slept with him before the White House. He'd visit his parents, but calls there never reached him. Perhaps that was protectiveness, as Kevin was wanted for nonsupport. Kevin had relinquished activism except for that related to specific people in specific situations, where results could be tallied. Thus work at the Finders, at Community for Creative Non-Violence, which ran a free clinic for street people, a free hostel, free pre-trial service, lectures and spiritual solace. Kevin was both patient and doctor. How it should be. There'd been too much activity during the sixties, the action had driven many crazy. Sport, sex, war— Kevin had worked through a lot. Physical activity seemed anathema to him, though he stayed in shape. Taking meals where they fell, tonight he dined with us.

Thien-Kim was the quiet one of this group. Delicate, she smiled that nervous smile of the Vietnamese, composed in perfect posture, effusing a self-confidence none of us could match. She looked fragile. But she was tough like none of us was tough.

Formed by the war, she carried a survivor's grace to this country, having put herself through high school, college, a marriage and successful restaurant venture. Yet her family remained in Vietnam. Their fate was uncertain, Kim supported them from her earnings—a family of sixteen—as she had since her immigration in 1969.

The sixties for Kim was war, that's all, that's what she remembered. As Corinne and I had been two-stepping to Meyer Davis in 1964, as Kevin Walsh was first encountering Vietnam and pleasures of Vietnamese women, Kim was shuddering to the whine of incoming rockets in a small village seventy miles from Saigon, near the Cambodian border. Her first recollection of war, of anything really, was that constant boom of artillery, no more disturbing than "hearing a car go by outside," until the practiced ear detected incoming rounds. Then children's games would be dropped, fear would hit, and everyone "ran to hide." The war ventured closer than artillery. Communists were familiar as ARVN. Quite early, Kim was exposed to the atrocities of war. A village chief had been beheaded in public. At an intelligence compound, Kim had sneaked in to watch an interrogation: two women being horsewhipped with heavy braided leather, then tortured with electrical charges to their breasts. Kim had watched through a window; the experience lingered. There was much fighting around her village while she was growing up. No wonder she cultivated an early disposition toward violence.

Kim had been a tomboy, she'd led a gang of boys in mock wars with other village children—she was "the queen leading her troops into battle." She beat up fellow students at school with kung fu, and was in turn, beaten by nuns. She suffered beatings from her mother—for her rebelliousness, for her "misbehavior," for no reason at all. Very young, Kim had decided she would not accept the plight of Vietnamese women in village society. Which equaled subjugation, primitive and sexist. She felt superior to other children because of her intelligence, felt "old" in her mind. She felt close to her father, was indeed her father's favorite of seventeen children. Kim's father had been something of a roué. A rebel himself, he was model for Kim, not content with strictures of Vietnamese society. Kim and her mother suffered a final rift over her father. Kim's mother asked one day if she had seen her father sitting next to such-and-such woman at work. Kim answered yes, thinking "that's what she wanted to hear, and to avoid further beatings." Her mother became furious, sniffing an affair. She berated Kim. Kim's father likewise turned against her, once accused. Kim felt alone. At thirteen she hit the bricks for Saigon, her mother's parting words an ironic benediction: "You'll wind up a whore." No, I'll never do that, Kim had thought. She didn't.

Her history was complex. Too complex to detail other than in relief, but too poignant not to sketch. Kim left home with no money, no relatives in Saigon, no hope but to find work. Her determination was impressive. When her bus stopped halfway to Saigon at a Communist roadblock, Kim walked through, braving a mine field to catch a bus on the other side. She walked to Saigon Circle, where she'd heard people found jobs. There she was picked up by a madame and taken to a brothel. Offered maid's work and babysitting (for prostitutes), Kim lived there some months, cultivating great sympathy for the women. "They were human, they laughed, they cried. They were victims of the war like everyone else." Offered the chance to sell her virginity, she refused. "In Vietnamese culture, virginity was priceless." She took a job as a bar girl, hustling drinks but not herself, and "made a fortune" at it. She sent money home. The club where she worked was front for a diamond smuggling racket, it was clean, professionally run and generally aboveboard. It was there, hustling G.I.s, that Kim learned English. Well enough so that within time she landed a translator's job at Vung Tau.

There the upheaval of traditional mores by incursion of G.I.s upon Vietnamese society was pinpointed in microcosm. Kim never recovered from it. Working with G.I.s, living near them, falling in love with them, finally leaving Vietnam to follow one, Kim suffered a dose of sixties energy on the black side. When she came to America in 1969, it was because America represented the sole economic prosperity she'd known. She planned to "get an education," a doctorate in economics so that she might return to Vietnam and "help Vietnamese help themselves." She put herself through undergraduate school—studying in English, her second language—working full-time to support herself and her family in Vietnam. She married and had a baby. Her ambitions modified. Where she'd dreamed of becoming Vietnam's first woman president, now she wanted to write, "to become famous, to help Vietnam that way." She had composed the first draft of a novel. In English. It was a remarkable work. The tale of a Vietnamese girl and the American occupation of her country during the nineteen-sixties.

As I watched Kim help clear our table, I was struck again by the element of survival expressed in her every movement. She epitomized the foreignness, aloofness and shell-shock of a Vietnam I'd not known. An inscrutable suffering. She made me feel alone, guilty and slightly dangerous. I hadn't seen it. Walsh had, Looney had, Corinne, my wife, knew more of sanctioned blood-sport than I, had stood closer to war. One could not say I envied these veterans; I felt excluded. They, but for Looney—nervous, twitching, as quintessentially American as I—had relinquished portions of soul to Vietnam. Their stories were special. Yet I knew others grazed by the war who had made their deals at home. Their stories bore hearing as well.

I had not heard the old man approach.

"You Doc Rock's brother?" he said.

I'd been resting on Sandy Rock's porch, staring off at a blue haze cloaking Walden Ridge, deep in southwest Virginia's Cumberland Mountains, when the old man stepped from the woods. He'd startled me. He was dressed in a blue serge suit, white shirt, tie, stained fedora and work boots. He was filthy.

"Been lookin' for Doc Rock," he said. "You kin?"

"Not actually. Visiting." The old man stepped closer.

"Got this cut won't heal." He hiked up his trouser leg and peeled down a sock. "I give her three days but she just won't scab."

The cut was inches long and oozing fluid.

"I'm no doctor," I said. "Doctor Rock's in town."

"Oh," he said. "Well look at this. I soaked her with peroxide, tried a heavy bandage then no bandage at all. Thought Doc Rock ought to see."

"You call him at his office," I said. The old man rolled up his sock.

"Sure you ain't his brother?"

"I've been accused."

"I seen his van's why I come. Name's Johnson."

We shook hands.

"Where Doc's boys? With the mother? Ain't seen Doc Rock in two weeks; heard he run off with a twenty-year-old woman, was on his honeymoon. You heard?"

"I haven't. Think I would."

"Some people don't like Doc, says he drinks. I like him. Like his boys, too. I drink. Some say I 'tend church drunk but least I 'tend. Doc Rock's a divorced man. Like me. I married the same woman twice. Doc ain't that dumb. Smart . . . 'bout the smartest man round here. He can talk French, them other tongues. I come up one day he had two girls in bikini suits, was talking all that French. Retired steel worker myself."

The old man eyed me suspiciously. "You sure you ain't a doc?"

"I'm sure."

He hunkered down beside the porch, pulling a bush-sized weed from a support. "Doc don't want that."

I glanced out again toward Walden Ridge, over the several acres of blackberry and sumac, broom sage, paw paw, dwarf cedar and sourwood that constituted Sandy Rock's backyard. Across that ridge was Tennessee. Six miles north was Kentucky. The heart of Appalachia.

"Most people hereabouts is poor," Johnson said. "They's coal miners, farmers, lawyers—lawyers 'cause Jonesville's the county seat, seems like even they's poor. Doc Rock does everybody right. 'Bout the onliest doc round here'll make house calls. 'Bout the onliest *doc.* Had two die last year. Other, old Nat Ewing, is stove up and don't treat much. Doc Rock's fair with his bills. Couldn't make much. Built this house though. Bought the land, a pile of lumber, some nails, put at least half up hisself. Pretty spot.

Had some hippies help. Couldn't work full-time and doctor too. Doc Rock favors a beard and his hair's long, but don't mean nothing. To some it does. Not when they's hurtin' though.

"Shame 'bout his boys ... they can't live with the mother. Hear she's up in Pennsylvania, remarried. Doc raises 'em good, but folks talk 'bout that too. Ain't nobody's business.

"They's other hippies in them hills, but none professional like Doc. Seems like they's siftin' in gradual. Lee County's old fashioned. Got us a congressman made it illegal to burn the flag—in them hippie demonstrations. 'Bout all he done. Folks is folks once'd you come down to it. Guess they learned that 'bout Doc Rock."

The old man straightened awkwardly, favoring his injured leg. He tossed off a wave.

"You tell Doc I was here," he said. Then limped into the woods.

"Pete Johnson's typical," Sandy remarked. "People elsewhere will ask why I'm down in southwest Virginia, and I'll say I want to practice in a place where I'm needed, not demanded. Pete Johnson walked half a mile with that cut and asked for treatment then only after three days of his own remedies failed. I don't want to be where people are calling me for a lot of Mickey Mouse horseshit, which is what they do in the city. And where you've got so many goddamned doctors that people are calling doctors that don't need to. Down here there's a need. I want to feel like I'm doing something other than pampering little old ladies who want their hands held. It sure isn't for the money."

Sandy reclined at his desk, flipping the plunger on a ballpoint pen. His office was furnished haphazardly in a hodgepodge of antique styles which fit the incongruities of his situation: a thirty-two-year-old physician with top-notch professional credentials in a region as backwoods-primitive as any in the U.S. The antique furnishings he'd purchased from a retired country doctor. They held modern accoutrements such as Japanese typewriters, tape machines, television, telephone answering services

and medical gizmos tentatively. Sandy himself—red beard fla-
grant against an open-collared sport shirt—looked incongruous
in this small-town, country-doctor setting.

"Jonesville's our county seat and aside from that is really just a
crossroads center for indispensable services. Such as schools,
stores, post office. I treat about two thousand people, most of
whom are dependent on me for all medical care. I cleared eleven
thousand dollars last year, after expenses. I charge ten dollars a
visit, set my fees in accordance with what other doctors charge in
southwest Virginia. I could be making twenty dollars an hour in
the emergency room at Big Stone Gap. But that wouldn't satisfy
me morally or ethically. Could moonlight an extra ten thou a
year that way. But I don't enjoy being paid twenty dollars an
hour for sleeping."

Sandy paused to take a call, then reflected.

"Part of that reluctance comes from my navy experience. I was
in a senior medical student program, offshoot of the Ensign 1915
program, where they were paying me full pay—Lt. JG pay—my
senior year in medical school. Which amounted to good money.
Eight or nine hundred dollars a month after taxes, I think. This
went on all the while I was marching against the war. Once I
realized the depth of that conflict I tried to transfer to Public
Health. Navy wouldn't hear of that. So it was then I went ahead
and filed for CO status. In my essays I remember saying that I
would be willing to serve my country in an alternative way, like
being a doctor in a rural area or in Public Health. But I said I
would not participate in the military. Being in the senior medical
student program, where they paid you through that year, obligated you to three years in the navy after internship. I was all set.
I got my orders for Vietnam the same week I got my discharge as
a CO. In the back of my head I kept thinking, in some way I'm
going to get this off my conscience and repay it. Not that I was a
CO, but that I had accepted money from the navy my senior
year, then got out through CO. That's where the guilt came from.
So I think I've actually paid in a way. Because there are a lot of
things I miss living here."

Like civilization. Civilization and the company of educated
peers. Raised in an urban environment, having attended classy

schools—St. Albans, University of Virginia, University of Virginia Medical School—Sandy had to feel isolated. Though he and I had shared an interest in rural music, rural manners, rural culture since adolesence, I could see how too much of a good thing might grate.

"It would be nice to have a decent *restaurant* in town," Sandy said. "Food really spoiled me in New Orleans."

Sandy had taken his master's in public health at Tulane after leaving the navy, had lived intermittently in New Orleans for several years. "When my marriage dissolved that final time I was working at Model Cities Neighborhood Health Center in the Desire section of New Orleans, finishing up. She'd come down from Charlottesville and spent four or five weeks ... last time we were together, spring of '73. I'd had it with New Orleans, wanted to get back—to Virginia, or this area. Didn't want to be too close to her, not too far either, because the kids had to travel. I was looking for a job. Women were always important in my life. I was dating this girl from Louisville; she wrote me to come up for a bluegrass festival. I happened to see a medical brochure containing an advertisement for Lonesome Pine Hospital in Big Stone Gap, Virginia. Caught my eye because of its crazy name. In bold print they said we'll fly you here to see our clinic and so forth. I looked at the map. Was just a hop, skip and jump across to Renfro Valley and this bluegrass festival, so I took advantage of the free trip. Decided I really liked this area. Liked the music and liked the people and liked the surroundings. Lonesome Pine was a nice hospital, so I came back. I did emergency work there for two years.

"Which wasn't all that satisfying. Emergency work's pretty impersonal. And it's gruesome. It can be rewarding in a technical way. Somebody comes in with an acute problem, and you deal with it, but it's computerized almost. You could put it in a computer and if you had all the equipment right there, just about anybody could treat it. But I had some thinking to do, to get my shit together as it were, so the technical aspect was a comfort. I bought some land down here almost immediately. Didn't build for a while. I camped out, lived in a tent off and on, then bought a camper-trailer and lived in that. Had friends I stayed with in

Appalachia, the town, when weather got bad. The isolation was good. Many thoughts."

I'd first met Sandy in the fall of 1960, when we were freshmen at St. Albans School in Washington. Sandy had transferred from public school and was wearing argyle socks. "We don't wear argyle socks here," I'd said, then offered my hand. The kid intrigued me. I thought of him as "kid" because I'd already endured seven years of private education (ten if one counts preschool) and was feeling like the world's oldest con. Sandy wore a gray striped jacket to class, which reminded me, wistfully, of some long-lost youth. When I ached to be a hoodlum, clattering through halls in fat black loafers and horseshoe taps. Sandy wore a crewcut. He wasn't fooling me. Despite Ivy League camouflage I remained a hoodlum at heart. Immediately we were in trouble: lifting parents' automobiles, drinking underage, crashing black night clubs, racing cars, fornicating, fighting, avoiding fights, playing music, digging music, manufacturing situations where our music could be heard. For that was the positive link. I was obsessed with bluegrass by age twelve; I saw it as country music's rock 'n' roll. Sandy hitched on to that obsession—he played guitar, piano, drums, a little trumpet. Both of us lived for rock 'n' roll. And that predisposition for performance of a medium which proved barely acceptable across suburban airwaves gave us a brotherly bond.

Despite Sandy's rebelliousness, he was the first person I encountered in high school who *knew* what he wanted to study: medicine. My father was a doctor, my grandfather, my grandfather's father. I'd never considered it. Sandy's father had worked around newspapers most of his life, had been a speechwriter for Nixon, was then personnel director for the *Washington Post.* If a push toward medicine existed, it was indirect.

"Socially I felt a certain *grima* for my father," Sandy admitted. "You know the Portuguese term? Well it's embarrassment for another person. My father was well-liked. He had friends. Women really liked him too, which was surprising to me. I felt *grima* for him in that he wasn't a banker, like our neighbor across the street, he wasn't a lawyer, like our next door neighbor, and he always lived in areas that were a little above his means. He was down on the third floor of the *Post* and not on the seventh floor, with the executives. So I directed myself toward a profession where I figured I'd have some social standing. Which is ironic, because at the time I espoused that social standing I also rejected it.

"It's hard to say what my motivations were in high school. A considerable amount was social standing. In the early sixties and late fifties, doctors were enjoying a heyday, because after the war, with the development of penicillin, they had abilities they hadn't had before—with the new antibiotics they could cure things. A lot of vaccines were coming out; before World War II much of medicine was hand-holding and sitting at the bedside. Up through the sixties, medicine was one of the most economically rewarding professions. Epitome of the Establishment. That was before people started questioning things. Throughout the nineteen-sixties there was questioning about everything, and medicine didn't escape that scrutiny. Doctors had begun to realize that people were saying, hey, why are you doing this to me? Why are you putting me on this medicine? I want to know what you're writing down about me, too. And maybe I need a second opinion. The first malpractice suits started during the sixties. At least they hit their stride. Lawyers got into the picture and said, well look, if this doctor's violated you in some way, we should sue him. What's happening now in the seventies is that doctors are countersuing, and I think that in the next five years we'll see a dramatic decrease in malpractice suits."

All that questioning was far from Sandy's mind when he entered medical school in 1966. Married his sophomore year in college, he had two small sons to support. By 1966 the proposition of medical school was formidable indeed. Criticism of that establishment seemed counterproductive if not insane.

"I deified older doctors. I remember looking at fourth-year medical students, or interns, and could not conceive that one day I would be that, that I could attain that status, much less the status of professor of medicine with a position at a university. Still, my attitudes gradually changed. Medical school is one of the most metamorphosing experiences anyone can go through. It changes your way of thinking and your attitude toward all people, doctors included. I realized that doctors were fallible and human; I still respected them. But they lost that pontifical quality."

Throughout undergraduate school Sandy's consciousness, to my recollection, stayed more antisocial than social. Harmless, it centered about a ceaseless striving after women, a dogged interest in rednecks and redneck music, and the brand of "acceptable" private orgies which were the ken of U. Va.—a young gentleman's curriculum geared toward sowing of wild oats.

"The societal issues I became involved with in the sixties were the war or population, and I came to both fairly late. Population growth I was fanatical about earlier than the war. Because I attributed the world's ills to too many people. I still feel that way. I became very cynical in medical school. Felt that most people's ills were related to their own foolish behavior, which probably is true, especially in our country. And that the most obvious foolishness was in having too many children uncared for, too many people crowded, starving. Abusing all the drives that they were socio-biologically endowed with ... which, when you're crowded, increase. Crime rate and the birth rate go up, surprisingly.

"I became very interested in that my fourth year in medical school. I was considering joining Zero Population Growth, Inc. I'd been doing a rotation on preventive medicine when I went up to Washington to an AMA meeting, this World Population Conference. The entire meeting concerned the physician and population problems. A guy named Joseph Beasely spoke there. He was erudite about this whole population question. Seems to me Paul Erlich spoke. Folks like that. It was so easy to say that the ills of mankind were due to overpopulation. Too many people, not enough resources. Our world had become more finite at that point. You could look at it from the moon and see that's all there was, there wasn't any more. The possibility of being able to expand onto other planets was becoming less likely as we became more realistic about the difficulties involved.

"That's why, later, I went into public health to get my master's degree. In population dynamics and family health. My attitude at that point was: Men will always have ailments but they will have many more ailments because of what they do to themselves.

Most of those things they do because there are too many of us. If there were fewer people and more resources, people would be able to enjoy finer lives. And wouldn't be driven to drink and murder and violence, the internal combustion engine, the automobile, all those things that come from too many people.

"I was kind of a Johnny-come-lately on the war. I was getting into a more radical stage in my last year of medical school. Don't know how much medicine played a part in that change, but I joined the navy program my freshman year. I think I had at that point considered going in the navy right after medical school, spending twenty years, then retiring when I was forty and setting up practice somewhere. I'd get navy pay. I kept that in my head a year or two. Then as the war became more prominent in the news, I became interested in it. Once again I was obsessed with man's inhumanity to himself. What he could do to himself. The underlying theme was always there. War was probably the most obvious. You stand there and kill another person. I started thinking how ludicrous the whole concept was. I'm not politically oriented and I couldn't see the need for war. Could see its inevitability, but observing it from a pragmatic view I couldn't believe people were foolish enough to shoot each other with guns and think that was going to solve problems. So the last two years of medical school I became really anti-war."

Sandy's appearance began to change. He became much looser in dress, nearly defiant of his medical peers. His defiance showed in every resolve.

"I started talking about the war. To my classmates. I tried to get them interested in at least signing petitions. There was petition after petition going around U. Va. then. I remember sitting in class and having them go by, signing them, petitions to the President. After Cambodia there was a large popular outcry and a deluge of petitions. I noticed that my classmates were more interested in doing the medical thing and sort of ignoring their social responsibilities. They had no social conscience. Their interests were in learning the nitty-gritty of practicing medicine, one-on-one. I ignored a lot of that. Which in the long run made it tough; I had to catch up on stuff. But I had this enormously archaic social conscience where I felt that you couldn't do anything if you ignored the ills of mankind that were more social ills than medical or biological. So the war, population, related things, became important to me."

As they became important to many young doctors. You'd spot them at demonstrations, bearded or braided, with red armbands over white jackets, corpsmen to combat troops who were getting their guts kicked out protesting a war nobody could fathom. They wrought havoc within medical schools, wearing peace buttons, insignias, letting their hair grow frizzy, flaunting beards, defying that establishment where they need be approved to prosper in the traditional manner. Sandy's predicament was complicated further by his involvement with the military.

"November, '69, was the first giant moratorium; they held that huge rally in Washington around the Washington Monument—five hundred thousand people or something. I was actually on active duty then, my senior year. A Lt. JG. I went up there knowing that I shouldn't, and participated in the march, wore my white jacket and red armband, and helped out with the Medical Committee for Human Rights. After the Cambodian invasion, April, 1970, I did the same thing, but more than just marching and standing around. I got involved. Back at U. Va. there was activity of which I was part. So they called me to ROTC and the commanding officer kind of Article Fifteened me, which is the lowest form of court-martial. Told me not to be involved with anti-war activity. At one point he said, why don't you just get out of the navy? I said, well, I've considered it. I'll get Washington on the phone, he said, and he called Washington. He literally had the phone in his hand when he said, listen: I can get you out of this program right now, and you can forget the military. But you can also forget practicing medicine anywhere in this country. His exact words. I sat there and said, holy shit. What am I doing? Here I've just gone through four years of medical school and they can fuck me out of being licensed to practice medicine anywhere in this country. I believed the sonofabitch. And—I was due to go into a naval internship. I'd figured I'd go out to San Diego and be a naval intern. Good God, I said to myself, you'd better shape up. I decided to stick with it. I realized I could probably keep my thoughts to myself and maybe be anti-war, but I wouldn't do all this outward stuff. I told him that. He told them on the phone that I was staying with the program. I did. I cooled it for the rest of that year. I convinced myself that I could work within the system and change it, so I thought: Okay, I'll be a naval intern. I'll go out there and be a good boy, but I'll still work to stop this war.

"I got out to San Diego and started dealing with guys that were coming back from Vietnam. That was July, 1970. Being in the military, having to wear that uniform with all the hatred there was for that uniform . . . was rough. All my friends were people at UCSD, totally anti-war and actively so. I was constantly reminded that I was part of that military which was perpetuating this horror in Vietnam. Then dealing with veterans who were coming back . . . the guys who were maimed, or killed, or who were dying, paralyzed, whatever. Plus guys who were coming back with other problems not so severe, but who talked about what was going on. And they . . . just talked about killing these gooks. One guy I remember, a sergeant, huge guy, a Baby Huey, told me how he'd blown this gook's head off to get a transistor radio. Actually didn't know if he was South or North Vietnamese. He wanted this radio. So he blew him away. It was right about that time I figured I couldn't handle any more. I wouldn't be a part of it.

"I went and saw this shrink: another guy doing two years in the navy. I forget his name. After hearing me out he said, well, you're really a conscientious objector. I didn't even know what that was. He gave me a booklet. Which started the ball rolling."

No easy ball for Sandy to bounce. Already ostracized by certain quarters of his family for having married at eighteen, he faced the wrath of his parents—conservative, middle-class folk—plus that of his grandfather, a marine brigadier, not only the family's patriarch but holder of its heftiest purse strings. He had paid Sandy's way through medical school. He controlled an inheritance not to be scoffed at. After Sandy's defection from the military, he did not speak to his grandson for three years.

"My father wrote me a letter supporting my conscientious objector stand. Had he not, I probably wouldn't have gone through with it. Don't know if I could have admitted to myself that's why, but I would have found some reason not to. I'd have gotten discouraged, because it was a lot of work. My father played an important role at that point. I was always trying to please him. He died in November, 1971, and if he were alive now I'm sure my life would be much different. I always felt his watchful eyes from a distance."

Sandy left the navy as a CO on April 28, 1971. He finished his internship at Mercy Hospital, San Diego, then worked in Palm Springs for a month after trekking around the West with a friend. That fall he started his master's in public health at Tulane. Spent a year in population dynamics, studying with mentor Joseph Beasely. Afterwards, he returned to Charlottesville and the University of Virginia for a pediatrics residency. That lasted a scant six months. His attitudes toward the traditional medical environment had shifted considerably.

"Biggest change was my attitude toward the social hierarchy, as a professional. You were supposed to wear a coat and tie, for instance. I went back and didn't. It drove some of the older doctors crazy. They spoke to me and had doctors who were close to me speak. But I refused to oblige. I stayed open-collared the entire six months. That's when I grew my beard. I was showing my disdain for things I felt to be unimportant. Dressing up. Being a way you're expected to be if you're a doctor, if you're any professional. So I wouldn't wear a tie—I didn't want to act like a doctor. I didn't want to *be* a doctor. Because a doctor has seven kids, drives a Cadillac, is wasteful ecologically. My interest in pediatrics was really ... if you could get to kids and have them healthy, you'd end up with healthier adults. Keep them from smoking and drinking and talk to them about not overpopulating the world. So my motivation in pediatrics was oriented toward population."

Sandy returned to New Orleans, however, discouraged with academe and Charlottesville, scene of his dissolving marriage and memory-bank of too many raucous affairs. He spent that year working with blacks in an underprivileged section of New Orleans. He'd started to refocus his attitudes toward large programs such as population control, which dreamed of aiding masses of people in impersonal ways, to the more humanistic role of a one-on-one personal physician. He already had his vasectomy. What more could be expected as personal sacrifice to the population crisis? Vasectomies hurt.

"What I haven't mentioned is that I got very disenchanted with these various movements that started in the sixties and persisted through the seventies. Many people did, realizing other methods existed besides marching and becoming involved in big programs. This damned organization I was with in New Orleans, the Family Health Foundation, had so many people on the payroll they were sitting around intellectually masturbating, getting grants to do studies that were practically meaningless. I was beating my head against the wall being involved with that crap, because it wasn't helping anything. It was, but at enormous expense.

"During that two-year period after I'd retreated to Virginia, working in the emergency room at Lonesome Pine Hospital, I went through my most serious thought transformations: how I felt about what I could do to satisfy myself in medicine, and what were the important things. That's when I realized I could provide a service for an area, just do my thing in a small part of the world. So I thought, I'll go to Jonesville, Virginia. I'll practice medicine there and I'll practice good medicine, '76 standards. Even though people might expect a different kind of medical care, I'll get them used to medical care they should expect to see. When you come to a doctor with a sore throat, he shouldn't just blast you with penicillin at your risk. He should culture your throat and see if it's strep, tell you next day. I went through this painstaking dealing with people that said, I'm going to treat you the way you *ought* to be treated, perhaps not the fastest or easiest way. And they've gotten used to that. To where some of them are demanding better medical care. Which is good. They should demand it. Here in Jonesville I'm trying to combine modern medicine with the personal touch of a family doctor—family medicine, being my specialty. I *am* a specialist, not some dropout resident who's bandaging the walking-wounded.

"If every specialist, every *person,* pitched in and worked to the best of his ability, we wouldn't need these major social movements. Things would happen on their own. That's much different from how I felt in medical school, when I clung to this idea of a social elite, a sort of benevolent aristocracy to rule people incapable or incompetent to rule themselves. I still think we need to spread out the wealth. We need people that are capable to infiltrate all areas of our society to pull them together and do right, rather than depending on Washington, if you will. All that hierarchy and bureaucracy . . . but I digress." Sandy scratched at his beard. "Digressions make me hungry. For God's sake let's eat."

Gilbert's Cafe had operated in Woodway, Virginia, for forty-odd years. It was a white house at a country crossroads, obscure sign out front, garden out back, so that if you didn't know it was a restaurant you'd hardly guess. We walked through a porch to a tiny lunchroom. Deserted but for three farmers in sweat-stained coveralls; wrapped around their meals, silent. Gilbert's was furnished with forty-year-old fixtures: Formica-top tables, country chairs, a wooden counter with spindle stools, some antique jars and bottles. The lunchroom was cooled by two electric fans. Over the cash register hung a thirties-vintage Coca-Cola poster picturing a young girl effortlessly quaffing the product. A door to Gilbert's kitchen creaked and out limped an extremely old woman.

Miss Gilbert had run Gilbert's Cafe alone the twenty years since her husband's death. She was seventy-eight. She served one meal a day, lunch, but that she served with style. "You want lunch, Doc?" she asked, smiling curiously toward me. Sandy introduced us. Small banter ensued concerning Sandy's boys, were they away for the summer, how was Miss Gilbert's leg?

"Lunch for two," Sandy said. "I'll have milk."

Milk came frothing and cold, fresh from cow to refrigerator to table. Lunch was *lunch* at Miss Gilbert's, no selection. It came on a multi-sectioned tray and consisted of vegetables from her garden, canned or freshly picked, and meat from her barnyard, home slaughtered. The old lady did the work herself.

"She keeps trying to hire help," Sandy said, "but nobody's up to Miss Gilbert's standards."

Eight or nine sections divided Miss Gilbert's tray, stocked with country ham, chicken and dumplings, meat loaf, potatoes and gravy, macaroni and cheese, greens drenched in hog fat, corn, beets, cole slaw, side dish of fresh lettuce and tomatoes, a jello salad, turnips and kraut. Sloshed down with whole milk, it was a meal anchored to the soil. Nothing empyrean about Miss Gilbert's cooking, it was earthier than a wash-tub riff on a standup bass. Perfect synthesis of redneck culture.

"Now you finished that ruffage," Miss Gilbert said, "you get pie or cake."

"Pie," Sandy belched, stomach resting against the table. "For two."

Apple cobbler came with ice cream on top, milk about its base thick as paste.

"What's this going to cost?" I asked.

"In dollars or triglycerides?"

Miss Gilbert cleared our trays.

"Two dollars," Sandy said. "She rarely lets me pay."

We eased carefully from our chairs and approached the register.

"Two dollars for your friend," Miss Gilbert said. "I owe you that house call."

Sandy protested.

"Next time," the old woman said, slamming the drawer. She hobbled toward her kitchen.

Riding west to Kentucky, four of us now: Sandy, myself, Sandy's girl, a twenty-year-old blonde in a SO MANY MEN T-shirt, and Stan, a deaf fellow from Jonesville and Gallaudet—we traversed the rocky countryside in a Volkswagen van, long-haired, unpretentiously pretentious, locally outsiders. Ten years post-*Easy Rider* we meandered through hollows housing primitives clannish as any pilot-lighting Vietnam's Central Highlands. *"It's a long way to Hazard, it's a long way to Harlan, jus' to get a little brew, jus' to get a little brew,"* we sang, not forgetting one second the nature of that anthem and its ramifications here in coal country. *Any* outsider had best watch himself; ten years past, long hair and a beard would have been invitation to murder rather than colloquy. Today we rode with children of yesterday's adversary, communing. Somebody passed a joint. Sandy flashed fingers at Stan, incurring cynical chuckles. "What's that?" the girl asked. Sandy tried to explain. Not easy. Communication was labored but a possibility. Sandy the trailblazer, medicine man, armed with sign language and amulets of love.

Freaks peopled these hollows, refugees from the sixties dropped in as if on night raids. Like homesteaders in Indian territory or Green Berets nudging the DMZ, they'd fought to protect base camps and their rights to uncivilized incursion. Fighting "rednecks" on the home front had proved analogous to fighting VC in Vietnam. Attraction for the primitive had cost dearly. Lives had been sacrificed to ameliorate that civil front to the Vietnam war. Freaky school buses dotting these hollows were targets easy as bunkers capstaning the Ho Chi Minh trail.

We stopped at one. Friends of Dr. Rock's. The woman was eight months pregnant and Sandy would deliver. The man offered grass, a tour of his bus, muffled conversation. Communication here likewise was partial. Each of us stared in contrary directions. The bus was cleanly outfitted. Efficiently. Like most homesteaders, Hollywood or otherwise, the couple spoke grudgingly. We smoked. A Jeremiah Johnson, peace pipe mystique. Herbs and folk palliatives hung in the air.

Departing, I questioned Sandy about "natural" approaches to medicine and how he pictured himself fitting. "Well . . . I tend to underrate my knowledge and abilities. I sort of forget the years of tedious preparation I had to go through to become a physician. When I force myself to remember that treating people takes a great deal of understanding of human anatomy and physiology, body chemistry, not to mention the human mind, how it works and so forth, when I make myself remember that and not take for granted what I know, and think everybody knows, then I'd say I can't buy the natural path. Now on the other hand, if you mean 'natural' in the sense that if people treated themselves right would they stay healthy—I'd recant. Much of our disease is caused by ourselves. We don't stay in shape. We drink too much or smoke too much or eat too much and fuck too much. All those things are—"

"Bad for you," I snickered.

"Yeah. I mean, in the sense of sexual promiscuity, where you're fucking a lot of new people. You get herpes. You know—"

"Herpes," the girl replied.

"You tend to drink and smoke while you're acquiring that herpes," I said.

"Right. All those bad things. Your body. Yeah."

We rode a ways in silence. Stan flashed fingers. Sandy flashed back. Stan nodded his head, smiling. Coal country crept past.

"Medicine's a specialty," Sandy said. "It's always been a specialty. Even in our age of computerization it's going to require compassion, patience, understanding and a certain amount of guts. All these qualities not everybody has. Not saying I do, but I've got a modest amount of some and lots of others. Medicine's an ego trip. People automatically react to you in such a way that puts you on a pedestal. And I still react indignantly to statements that attack my credibility or that demean me as a physician. If somebody calls me 'Mr. Rock' I bristle. It's *Dr.* Rock, not *Mr.* There are expectations to being a professional—lawyers, politicians, others in higher echelons share these expectations. Not necessarily to the good. So I certainly haven't swallowed my ego. I don't demand, but expect the respect I get from being a physician. Yet when I see people who've lost touch with their humanness, that rubs me pretty raw too."

What was the reaction, I inquired, from people around here to what they must have seen as a hippie doctor?"

"Distrust. Hostility. That was a typical reaction. But I realized I could do anything I wanted and people were going to come to the emergency room. They wouldn't avoid that because of a hippie doctor if they were sick. So I sort of taunted people in that way. I felt like, well, you're going to accept me for myself. And you'll have to change your attitude about people with beards or hair that's a bit longer. Doesn't mean they're bad. Lot of them are good. Lot of real assholes, *bad* people, have short hair and are clean shaven. They were going to have to accept me. And they did."

* * *

Evening now, and we were seated on the front porch of Sandy's house—a remarkable house, modernistic, balconied, lathed in plywood, unfinished ... tools lay about. Sandy had built fifty percent of it himself. Rough cut oak, one half inch thick had been meant to clapboard its exterior, stockade-style. But the house would remain unfinished during Sandy's tenure. He had already spoken of selling it. An unfinished vision, we sat on its porch picking guitars and drinking.

"I got this wild hair up my ass to build a fucking house. I really liked camping on my land. And ... typical of how I do things ... I figured I'd build this house, then somehow discover what I wanted after that. I could envision staying. Figured if my practice didn't work out I'd sell the house and sell the land. At that point I didn't know what I wanted, but I knew I'd always have a job. Knew I could make thirty grand a year working at the emergency room if I had to.

"The house was designed by a friend named Bob Cupps—lives up here in a log house, or did. He'd constructed a cardboard model, I always liked the idea of living in a house with balconies and lots of glass. We thought we'd build the whole thing for twenty thousand dollars. Crazy. It's cost me thirty already and it's still not done."

Sandy strummed a Country Gentleman tune as we stared out toward the mountains.

"I've got sort of a five year plan," he said. "Once I get the kids through high school, this house finished or sold, and my practice stabilized so that I'm not just another doctor practicing medicine, I'll probably take off. Be a ship's doctor, go to East Africa, something like that. I'm restless. I've always felt this terrible restlessness. Because I don't come from an area like this, I don't feel part of these people yet. I'm starting to—and I really do like being a small-town family practitioner. I love hiking down the road and having Pete Johnson say, Hey Doc, what's happening? I like making house calls. And I like dealing with people one-on-one."

Sandy double-bent an empty Budweiser and tossed it through

the door. "Still many changes to endure," he said. I stopped picking and let him catch my eye. He smiled.

"Next time you see me I won't be wearing this beard."

We nodded together and watched the night close in.

Art

Corinne and I split up the night I bought *Saloon* its final ticket on a Greyhound to New York. Galleys polished, drudgery completed, we had meant to share a vacation. Instead there'd been ugly confessions and threats of desertion. My reaction had been to finish the review I'd been writing for Sunday's *Post*. I walked from bedroom to study and coldly, professionally, immersed myself in prose. No way to shift gears. I'd spent the greater expanse of our two years together locked in that room, hitting the keys. Though I'd married Corinne it was *Saloon* I'd consorted with. Both contracts had come through simultaneously. Without one I couldn't have tolerated the other. Nor could she have. *Saloon* neatly wrapped, review properly typed, I invited Corinne along to dump the mothers off. Outside the *Post* and again in a midnight Greyhound depot, each of us wept for something nearly inexpressible.

Saigon's fall had been rough. I'd watched Corinne waver toward evacuation; her nerves shot, her resolve diminished as those American troops garrisoned in-country. She'd volunteered for Red Cross duty; had been refused. A vet, she was angry to help, hungry for an excuse to return. After the fall she'd toppled into a kind of reverse shellshock: working full-time, attending classes, studying—a schedule mated to mine, which left us two hours' daily companionship. As Vietnamese flooded the country and refugee camps popped up like A-sites or firebases, she grew more unsettled. I finished a first draft of *Saloon*. She begged to leave, hop a next plane anywhere. I wasn't able. I kept accepting assignments, decompressing, coming off the hard stuff with profiles and reviews. Refugees poured into the cities, old friends called, friends of friends; the war intruded as maliciously as my writing. Then Vietnam was finished. America's first draft, anyway. *Saloon* was in galleys. Without war or writing, life faced head-on seemed unendurable. Neither of us was primed for a peacetime resolve.

We headed West: She to Honolulu, then a Vietnamese relocation center at San Jose. I to Montana. Where I'd been working to reach Tom McGuane by telephone these past two days.

My call was expected. I stood in the New Atlas saloon, Columbus, Montana, waiting to be put through. Last night Tom's line had stayed busy for hours, then strangely was vacant. I'd holed up in a trailer motel at Kaycee, Wyoming, drinking beer with locals and commiserating with a young woman who'd fixed me sandwiches and told when she'd radiophoned her husband in Vietnam every time she said "I love you" she'd had to add "over." Columbus was eighty miles from McGuane's. I'd researched New Atlas for *Saloon*. Sipping cold draft at its mahogany bar, I noted how much less romantic the spot was minus the imperatives of art. A frightening realism inked fixtures lately perceived as quaint. Its old bars were darkly grotesque; its stuffed animals sandbagged cadavers flecked with dusty hair. My call came through.

"Oh, God," McGuane moaned. "Well, you're here. I've just spent three days with no sleep behind a weekend of partying. Today's my day with the kids. But come ahead."

He offered directions. "Why do we do it?" he said, cataloguing his weekend's indiscretions. I mumbled something about amalgamating the neuroses and rang off.

Art had not been kind to Thomas McGuane this past year. The film version of his novel *Ninety-Two in the Shade* had been panned by film critics, then buried by United Artists, its distributor. Wounding deeper because McGuane not only had written book and screenplay, but had directed. A contemporary Western, *Rancho Deluxe,* directed by Frank Perry from a McGuane screenplay, had fared poorly at the box office. The heavyweight, *Missouri Breaks,* a ten million dollar extravaganza directed by Arthur Penn which starred Marlon Brando and Jack Nicholson, was likewise climbing feebly up the charts. McGuane's original screenplay of *Breaks* had been partially rewritten by Robert Towne and metamorphosed by Brando's reinterpretation of a principal character. McGuane was being blamed for all this, and critics had not been kind, adding swipes at his personal life. Interviewers had proved most vitriolic. It was a wonder McGuane had consented to see me at all.

Perhaps because we were friends. In that tenuous manner in which writers maintain association, through shared work and the occasional postcard. I'd first met McGuane in January of 1974, at his house in Key West, Florida. I'd knocked on his door. Walked through a gate which stated: BEWARE OF DOG, ignored the snarling antiquarian, and rattled McGuane's screen. I'd read *Ninety-Two* and, being in Key West, thought: There is no way I'll not risk approaching this man. The book had simply changed my perception of things. Seductive as rhythm and blues, incisive as middle Dylan, mindwarped as Hunter Thompson, literate as who could say—the work was mind candy in a sour season. It isolated certain confusions of seventies apostasy precisely. And it was lonely. I held this mental picture of a man, its creator, lonely, slight, shy. McGuane answered the door and he was huge. His face was tan as old saddle leather, roughed up but friendly. I fumbled through an introduction, said a complimentary word about *Ninety-Two* while we shuffled around the doorstep. McGuane wore a Hawaiian sport shirt, Levis, and was barefoot. His sun-streaked hair hung in a ponytail below his shoulder blades.

"There's this book I wish you'd help me with," I said, setting him up.

His face sagged.

"It's called *Saloon* and it's about my search for the Great American Bar."

A grin broke across McGuane's features. "You look like a man who could stand a drink," he said. And invited me in.

We shared dinner that night at a Cuban restaurant where McGuane was known. Complimentary sangria; cold beers to follow. Conversation revolved around fishing, music, writing and movies. Both of us knew Key West, had fished the Keys. But McGuane had not been fishing much lately. He was embroiled in a screenplay, *Rancho Deluxe.* That corraled his energy. At one point, circa 1968, McGuane had worked toward being a fishing guide, figuring he could make seventy-five dollars a day, guide one day a week, write the remaining six. He lived higher in the Keys then where one could still survive on seventy-five a week. To that end he once fished sixty-eight consecutive days and boated one hundred four tarpon, each a hundred pounds. Beat to shit from gaffing these fish, skin blistered nearly cancerous from the sun, McGuane entertained second thoughts. Yet he'd seen wondrous things. McGuane sketched these adventure stories avidly. Irony crinkled his smile, but it was slight, obligatory. You could laugh all you wanted but the universe stymied. He'd written a book about it.

Ninety-Two in the Shade had received top reviews, remarkable praise, most notably in a front-page *New York Times* rave which compared its author to a gallery of greats. McGuane seemed unswerved by this attention. He was eager to talk books, talk literature, talk the sort of whacked-out experimental journalism I'd been practicing. At evening's end he'd said, "Why don't you sort of consider my house your base of operations?" and invited me for dinner the following night.

Becky Crockett McGuane was everyman's paradigm of the perfect writer's wife, that fact impressed itself up front. You could substitute "perfect wife" without shattering your demographics. She was small, blonde, cheerful, with an unthreatening sensuality and a steady diligence any man could work behind. She was charming; magically so. She had a way of listening to what you said which overstepped politeness. And she knew men, how to mother untamed herds of them. Descended from Davy Crockett, you'd never have guessed frontier lineage until you'd seen her defuse various Alamos of masculine unrest. She and Tom had been married since 1962. They had a son, Thomas IV, aged six. Everyone was in love with Becky McGuane.

She fried yellowtails caught that afternoon with Dink Bruce—son of Hemingway's good friend in Key West—the fish served prettily on attractive china, domestic wine poured into beveled crystal, five or six of us seated about an antique dining table in Victorian side chairs, Cuban artifacts around, paintings by friends, McGuane's house itself settled amongst subtropical foliage in a yard cluttered with large-boy's toys: a sailboat, dinghy, ten-speed Peugeot, nautical miscellania. In truth, the yard was immaculate. As was the house.

The evening unfolded not unlike half a dozen others I enjoyed over the next ten days: food, drink, conversation, joking, hilarity, jitterbugging to the stereo, and a warming to newcomers which approached the familial. That familiarity was peculiarly small-town. Its warmth was the McGuane's near-perfect life together, one which hesitated to travel. "Let's stay here," it seemed to say. "We don't need outside. The party's us."

Tom was working hard on *Rancho Deluxe* and reveled in these hearthside gatherings. Becky ran the house, cooked meals, screened calls, took care of Thomas IV, entertained guests, to the benefit of McGuane. Who, up at dawn, wrote eight to twelve hours a day in a converted outbuilding behind the house. At supper his mood was even-tempered and sleepy. "When Tom's writing he's no problem," Becky said. "It's between things that the tension rises."

Even in the face of work, a mild tension percolated. It had been six months since the publication of *Ninety-Two,* a year and a half since its completion. Though McGuane had produced scattered journalism and two screenplays, he had no novel in the fire. Movies intrigued him—he had taken an MFA in drama at Yale, and saw his work with screenplays as an extension of that training—but the novel remained his metier. "I really need to get up to my elbows in prose," he'd say wistfully. Then head back for another stretch with *Rancho Deluxe.* "Writing screenplays is fun," he'd blurt, letting the thought drift. Movie rights had been sold to *Ninety-Two* and there was speculation as to who might direct. Robert Altman was first choice; apparently he'd bowed out. McGuane was not speaking of directing himself, yet his fascination with movie-making at every level intruded upon conversation. While he wrote, however, contradictions leveled themselves off.

It cannot be overemphasized the degree to which McGuane had captured what later would be maligned as "every English major's wettest dream." Prizes for his novels—a Rosenthal for *Bushwhacked Piano,* National Book Award nomination for *Ninety-Two*—contracts for screenplays which had downpaid a house in Key West and a ranch in Montana; time for fishing, hunting, sailing; a compact family, a broad circle of friends which included the most energetic of sport, screen, rock and literary figures . . . he was soon to become the first novelist to direct a film of his own book. He'd expanded a seventies version of the prototypical writer's life to have eclipsed Ernest Hemingway. He wintered in Key West, spent summer and fall in Montana. He had talent to back it up.

My last day in Key West, Becky invited me for lunch. Tom looked distracted. He had stuck *Rancho Deluxe* in the mail that morning. His screenplay was finished. "I woke up at six without an idea in my head and slumped out here to the typewriter," Tom said. "Nothing." Withdrawal had set in.

We ate at a little seafood restaurant beside the shrimp docks. Tom stayed nervous, preoccupied. "I feel *awful,"* he complained. "I can't think of *what* to do." Driving home McGuane's Cortina ran out of gas. We shuffled idly through verdant streets, along sidewalks contoured like jungle paths, suffering writer's unease. A family dilemma.

McGuane's discomfort in the face of leisure did little to dissuade me from emulating his perfect writer's life. Single, I sought companionship and found a smallish blonde, delicate, attractive—though substantially less tolerant than Becky. How much consciously I was imitating McGuane is difficult to gauge. I remember driving north through the Keys, however, and thinking: Tom's domestic situation seems an effective way to counteract the loneliness of writing, the chaos of existence away from one's typewriter. Corinne and I were married about the time McGuane's marriage tore apart at the seams.

"Just checking in," a postcard read, April, 1974. *"We're going to Montana this week to make the movie. Hope to see you some-*

where ... er ... along the way. —Tom." That film was *Rancho Deluxe,* shot around McGuane's Livingston and starring Elizabeth Ashley, Jeff Bridges, Harry Dean Stanton, Sam Waterston, Slim Pickens, with a soundtrack by Jimmy Buffett. The ruckus of partying could be heard in Kansas City. Tom spent that spring studying moviemaking in his back yard, with a cantilevered eye toward directing. By fall he had convinced Elliot Kastner, *Rancho*'s producer, to pass him the throttle on *Ninety-Two.* Tom would direct. A shooting schedule was set for October–November. That film would star Margot Kidder and Peter Fonda, among others. Within a year Tom would be living with Kidder, Becky married to Fonda.

Articles came out in *People, New Times* and the Village *Voice* exploiting these new relationships. *Rancho* appeared. "Don't know that I *like* that film," Tom admitted in a telephone conversation. *Ninety-Two* appeared and disappeared. A long silence from McGuane. Then, the following fall from Montana, on Beverly Hills Hotel notepaper (*"Big Snazz. A Real Hot Spot."*):

"Dear Toby. Here's some stationery from when I was in movies. —Had a baby girl, hard at a novel; been hunting in the mountains off my house. Having a good old time. Yeah, that guy from the Voice. I guess that's what they do there though. I sent off a letter enumerating the lies but I don't figure they'll print it. That stuff just makes me tired. Stay on that saloon book now 'til you get it. Hope to see you. —Tom."

He'd see me, all right. But it would take a year, the dissolution of my marriage, and the intention to collate another book—some sort of guide to the pitfalls of the generation, concentrating on writers—before we got together.

"I want to be Writer-Hyphenated," Tom had said. "I tend to transgress categories."

My plan, in that book, was to profile a novelist, poet, journalist, songwriter, scenarist, dramatist and technical writer, with side trips into the world of writers' psychiatrists, grade school teachers and parents. To try and establish why certain people were drawn toward language as art, why some people used it as offense, some defense, and why some hid behind it as if it were a mother's skirts. I wondered why in this age of TV and film anyone should want to *be* a writer. Endure the seclusion, rejection, endless wait. In short I wanted to learn about myself while studying others. McGuane was first on my list.

"NO HUNTING," a sign read at the edge of McGuane's property. "CHILDREN, PETS AND LIVESTOCK. THANK YOU." That sign itself intimated a ducking behind language. I bumped my jeep across a cattle guard and swayed down the short drive. Another sign, RAW DEAL RANCH, hung from a log outbuilding. Three or four outbuildings crowded McGuane's ranchyard. A white clapboard house faced them contrastively. The effect was frontier and rugged.

A pale blue pickup sledded across the cattle guard, coughing to a halt before McGuane's front door. Tom stepped out. An exhausted grin. His hair was redneck short. He was dressed in boots, jeans, a James Dean jacket and high-crowned summer straw; he carried a beer. He looked roughed-up as his ranchyard. We tossed arms about each other's shoulders and headed for the house.

That night I slept in Margot Kidder's studio—Margot was in L.A. filming a series. She'd return by week's end. Tom was sitting Thomas IV and Justin Fonda. But only the night. Becky slept across several hay fields at the ranch house she shared with Peter Fonda. That was part of the McGuanes' agreement, to live close by so that Thomas could ramble. Still, hayfields were hayfields. With a marriage in between. Tom was more alone than had seemed possible a year and a half previous. His compact family had split, he'd halfway constructed another, his father and sister had died, and art was treating him most unkind.

That art was the art of the Western movie, I could not help thinking; a difficult taskmaster, one which had done its damnedest to rifle the consciousness of our generation; and which continued to shuffle archetypes through choreographed violence and bloodied romance. Redneck Chic had evolved in the nineteen-seventies from clodhoppers and bib overalls to stovepiped Tony Lamas and sateen cowboy shirts. One could not help but credit the movies. The cowpoke ethos to redneck culture was the ethos of hip—it actuated silence, reserve, physical grace, competence in the face of danger, primitive ardor, and above all an inimitable style. That style had encouraged our first emulations of art as children . . . through costume and an appreciation of Wild West as theater: horse opera. Thank Hollywood, thank Saturday TV, the fact was established as Roy Rogers, Hopalong Cassidy, the Lone Ranger, Lash LaRue, Matt Dillon or Palladin; it was as current as *Missouri Breaks,* inescapable as the entire Outlaw notion in seventies culture. From Richard Nixon to Waylon Jennings.

That Peter Fonda—who, with Dennis Hopper in 1969, had released one film, *Easy Rider,* which would do more to perpetuate divisionism in a mindless youth culture than any other work of sixties art—lived in rural Montana, hay ranched, drove a four-wheel-drive pickup and kept horses, surprised. That he had used rock 'n' roll, the Western ethos (cowpokes on motorcycles) and sixties technology (endless jump cuts) in the orchestration of *Rider* made perfect sense. That was hip. *Rider* was an essay on hip for sixties' deviationists, perhaps the final word. It had made Fonda millions and established him as box office. Hollywood movies were as serviceable a conduit of hip as had been rhythm and blues, hot cars, fast sex and an absurd war. That *Rider* exploited an ethos, capitalized upon deep-seated fears, is hardly worth mentioning. Somewhere, on Merv Griffin I believe, Fonda had said: "I worked hard during the sixties so that I could enjoy myself during the seventies." He was explaining an eighty-foot sailboat.

Fonda's character in *Rider* had represented the apotheosis of outlaw America . . . longhaired, dope-smoking, coke-pushing, hip-talking, motorcycle-riding freakdom . . . an antithesis to Redneck Chic. A pickup load of Florida crackers had blown him away. In *Ninety-Two,* McGuane had cast Fonda as a Florida fishing guide and had put him on a bicycle. The opening scene of *Ninety-Two* showed Fonda riding in circles, round and round, on a totally unhip Schwinn. That was vision.

Tom's vision was mightily blurred when he roused from the sack at one P.M. next day. By three we'd piled into his pickup and were rattling along Deep Creek to Old Hoffman Route east of the Yellowstone River, heading for Livingston. Tom was frenetic, tensed up. He had a novel in progress but had not worked on it for five months. He'd been collaborating on a "redneck screenplay" with Jimmy Buffett about a gang of Florida low-lifers who take over an abandoned jet strip in the Everglades and run cocaine. He had another screenplay under way titled *Dry Run,* about a pair of Confederate blockade runners in Texas who never make it to the coast. But conversation tended to de-emphasize art: "This summer has been the happiest of my life," Tom said. "I broke two horses and planted a garden. My hay crop should pay off my hired man's wages. I don't care if I ever put another word on paper." Yet he did not cease ranting about movies, about New York critics and that literary establishment which he felt certain would "shit all over" his next book for dalliance with the film industry. "Like I told that woman from *New Times,*" Tom said, "If I had spent the past two years shooting heroin rather than making movies, critics would have seen that as supportive of my art."

We had lunch at the Sandarosa motel, Tom drinking margaritas and joking with the waitress. He rambled on about art, about writers such as Harry Crews, Larry McMurtry, Ken Kesey, himself, who "never would be taken seriously" by the *New York Review of Books.* "Art's just no longer important to me as living," Tom reiterated. Then we were on into Livingston for a round of chores. As if to show what he meant.

We stopped at a hardware store to buy nails for a corral Tom was building; at Sport Saloon to pay a bill and to joke with its owner about dally roping—a craft Tom was learning; and at Colmey's Pet and Grooming to purchase deworming medicine for his horses, five of which had distemper. At each spot Tom had spoken with authority about ranching topics. He held each proprietor's interest, if not his respect. I marveled again at how much tougher Tom's demeanor was in Montana; it showed through the roughness of his dress, but most notably in the shortness of his hair, so recently shoulder-length. "I don't want to look like Baba Ram Dass," Tom laughed. Once we'd climbed into the pickup, conversation ricocheted back toward art. "I'm dying to learn the secret of a film like *Texas Chainsaw Massacre.*" Or, "there's this guitarist around town, Ron Taylor, who's played with the Rolling Stones—I'm hot to write rock lyrics with him." Back home, Tom's freneticism quickly eased to torpor. Retiring early, he would clock another twelve hours in the sack. A pattern which continued five days, until Margot's return from Hollywood.

During that time I did not come close to a formal interview but engaged myself thoroughly in the diversions of Paradise Valley. I had my own psychic havoc to weather, a storm system I held in check with long hikes into the Absarokas, drinking at cowpoke saloons, dancing to hokey bands, and the ingestion of central nervous system depressants unobtrusively packaged in pharmaceutical vials. A community of artists had gathered outside Livingston, Montana—a band of refugees drawn by the charisma of McGuane and held in thrall by the awesomely beautiful countryside. There was William Hjortsberg, the experimental novelist, who had known Tom at Yale; Russell Chatham, a painter, writer and fisherman who had met Tom in Key West; Dan Gerber, the writer, publisher and Grand Prix aficionado; Peter Fonda, Warren Oates, both of whom had acted in *Ninety-Two;* Margot Kidder, whose credits* besides *Ninety-Two* included *Sisters, The Great Waldo Pepper, The Reincarnation of Peter Proud;* and Richard Brautigan, world-famous as a poet, novelist and literary pied-piper to half a generation.

I saw Becky in town and at McGuane's. Where she'd appeared cute in Key West, if a trifle drawn, here she radiated a kind of frontier elegance—something fancy, a deeper, more relaxed physical beauty. I took Thomas IV and Justin Fonda fishing, letting them show me favorite spots, accepting hand-tied flies as gifts, remarkably well-wrought from the hands of eight-year-olds. They were bright, interested kids; if over an evening their natural restlessness got out of hand, McGuane would suggest: "Why don't you guys head back to the bedroom and read a little science?" I drove down near Emigrant Peak and met Warren Oates. Searching for a trail Tom had recommended, I startled Oates fishing the creek back of his house. "H'lo, I'm Warren Oates," he'd said. Then, "See this cutthroat I caught?" with childlike enthusiasm. Oates, an outlaw archetype of the Peckin-

* Pre-*Superman.*

pah genre, terrifying in his onscreen depravity, was here a mountain-struck Cub Scout.

The notion of a band of refugees dogged me as I hiked each day outside Livingston. If Vietnam represented the violent extreme of that journey to the East inaugurated by Columbus in 1492 and intensified through westward expansionism, a war with Japan, a war with Korea . . . then Cowboy Chic implied a step back to the frontier, physically and metaphysically. Since armistice, embarkation port San Francisco had received a thick stream of refugees, both Asian and American G.I. These people were filtering into the countryside, asserting their independence where practicable, more commonly settling in relocation camps. Livingston seemed a relocation camp of sorts. None of the McGuane clan had been born in Montana. Their migration to the Rockies was a seventies deal. And symptomatic of a shift in values collectively perceived by the public at large.

If the Green Beret had been an American hipster pushed to a nethermost extreme of America's hegira to the East, the American cowboy—or outlaw, more precisely—was his nineteenth-century counterpart. By meeting the Asian primitive on his turf and confronting certain ambiguities—that firepower would not douse shamanism, that technology could not suppress animism, that homeland was inviolate and inescapably spook-ridden—the Green Beret had conceded defeat. Conventionally. But his mission had been far from conventional, one could argue its design as military. It had been the tail end of Columbus's search for the East, and in that sense may have proved successful. One hesitates to say victorious. Both Lyndon Johnson's and Columbus's treks eastward were business ventures which had failed, but which, arguably, opened broader vistas. America knew the resignation of defeat from Vietnam; there was one lesson which could be catalogued as victory. That Cowboy Chic had surfaced during the seventies, that Rocky Mountain High had become a way of life, that McGuane's Livingston—an intentional community of sixties malcontents albeit highly successful ones—existed, that both Corinne and I post-armistice had felt an irresistible pull toward the West, suggested paradoxes worth considering.

Outlaw Chic was a concept that had been toyed with by popular artists for nearly ten years. Bob Dylan had broken from the circularities of a limitless recording technology with the primitivist production of *John Wesley Harding* in 1968. Hardin had been a notorious Western outlaw and Dylan's album proved as much of a renegade, shifting rock toward its Country Western roots. Sam Peckinpah filed the notion sharper in *The Wild Bunch* (of which Oates was a member), but laid open the wound with *Pat Garrett and Billy the Kid,* a post-combat, Wild West swan song in which he cast rock stars as outlaws . . . Bob Dylan, Kris Kristofferson, Rita Coolidge . . . hiring Dylan to compose a score. *Billy* was an affirmation of the theatricality of all combat, ritual, hunting, and a railing against its imperatives. Discouraging, *Billy* nevertheless hinted America had instigated a retreat, and was winding its way home through a cast of psychic archetypes.

Street theater had worked as psychodrama for millions during the nineteen-sixties; street demonstrations, street riots, street collectivizations of rage inexpressible but for frenzies of rock, fast cars, easy sex and technologies of approved warfare. Cowboy Chic was just another role; its dedication to the rigors of hip, even Western Hip, was no more serious than the pretentiousness of a hundred million hippies to alternative consciousness.

The irony of mass attraction to Cowpoke Chic was that, again, "rebels" were assimilating an ethos more conservative than their intellects were equipped to fathom. Just as hippies had embraced urban hip, with no bow to implied psychopathy, these new cowpokes adopted accoutrements of a lifestyle few had thought to assess. Dylan had turned away from the conformity of sixties culture with *John Wesley Harding,* all those hippies and communalized beatniks who'd been gumming up the life, and now things were coming full circle. Cowboys *hated* hippies, hated that concept of self-indulgence and dependence. Cowboys wore their hair long and smoked a little dope, but their ethos remained firm. You were your own man out here under a peopleless sky who took gaff from no boss. An ironic bit of horse opera on its face, but never mind.

"The Cowboy was an instrument of the cattle industry," it had been written: "His job was to protect and move an investment in cattle for ranch owners and their backers."* Eleanor Aveling, daughter of Karl Marx, had painted the cowboy as slave to economic forces in her book, *The Working-Class Movement in America.* The romantic era of the cowboy (1866–90), such as it was, had been short-shrifted by the railroad to haul and by the introduction of barbed wire to fence what was left of the open range. During that time your average cowpoke was just another footling for a faceless corporation, moving the product from point A to point B. His concept of himself as romantic emerged from art: popular song, theater, the dime novel, penny journalism, Hollywood. When Buffalo Bill couldn't make it any longer on the tent show circuit, he packed the first Hollywood crew on location to Wounded Knee, South Dakota, for a "real-life re-enactment" of that massacre. He hired General Nelson A. Miles to play himself plus real Indians, many of whom had lost real relatives at the battle. Nelson's shenanigans so enraged Indian actors that Wild Bill nearly had another massacre on his hands. Cinema vérité. Indians had never felt much affection for horse opera, but like most Americans they'd face anything for a buck.

The West had suffered businessmen grudgingly, from its earliest trappers, who systematically depleted wildlife, to miners who created boomtowns while wrecking the countryside, to cattlemen who fenced with barbed wire or criss-crossed with railroads land which had provided graze for migrational herbivores and hunting ground for nomadic tribes for eons. Tourism had been big business since Theodore Roosevelt opened Yellowstone Park as America's first Western playground in 1903; but until recently one could not say the Northern Rockies had been threatened by art. McGuane, Fonda, *et al.* posed problems— particularly McGuane, who had set a book and two movies in the region. Yet location scouts for Hollywood film crews had advertised in neighborhood yellow pages some years now. The art which threatened Big Sky most thoroughly was the theatricality of style. Everyone, stepping back, sought a revamped ethos. For most, commitment skated the surface. But ice was thin. No one

* Peter Snell. *Preservation News,* January, 1978. "Home on the Range: Interpreting the American West."

wanted Paradise Valley desecrated to another Aspen. Hip attracted unhip (the falsely committed), and unhip encouraged speculation. Business had done its best to unhinge the West, cowboys were both first and last perpetrators.

You could argue trappers; many had worked independently but most had been agents of the great fur companies, even legendary frontiersmen like Mike Fink, Jedediah Smith and Jim Bridger. You trapped your pelts and traded to the corporation. A similar spiel could be coaxed for the miner. Many had toiled independently, but sooner or later most encountered corporation, government or national currency. True Western primitives were its Indians. Model for black and white hipsters alike: the holy aborigine.

Like Cochise or Al Jolson? I'd speculated, while contemplating Green Berets painting up for night raids in Vietnam. *Like Billy the Kid or Burt Reynolds?* I conjectured, assaying their counterparts here in Fantasia land.

Hollywood had made the down payment on Tom's ranch, he freely admitted, and screenplays were the chores which kept it from the bank. Margot Kidder helped with the odd TV series, but care of her infant daughter had forced a sabbatical from films stretching toward a year and a half. Margot was the least *Hollywood* actress I'd met. Unkempt, loosely organized, beautiful. She was beginning to pick up her career. She returned home Friday after being stranded overnight in Salt Lake City with the baby; something about a lost wallet, missed connections. McGuane had hired a plane to fly her back. "What could I do?" he said. "Leave them forever at that airport?"

By then I'd moved into Livingston. I'd located a four-dollar-a-night room in an old railroad hotel which boasted saloon, restaurant and lobbyful of oldtimers who vied for impermanence with aged buffalo heads and stuffed trout encumbering the walls. Across from Burlington Northern's tracks and at the center of town, the Murray Hotel was a timeless caravansary of Western disorder. I slept on the fourth floor, but I had mountains within view plus a scenic diorama of the town. I had three excellent saloons on my block. There were old-fashioned luncheonettes nearby, general stores and a dusty pharmacy. There was a pint-sized movie theater. A railroad cafe open twenty-four hours where strangers broke off the Amtrak for coffee and homemade pie. There were softball games in Sacajawea Park, trout fishing at the center of town. Rows of quiet houses. There was roller skating at the roller rink. An objectless circling of pickups on Saturday night, whooping, hooping, horseshit in the street, kids leaving bicycles unlocked, friendly teenagers and old men who would bend your ear. A sensible town.

One week passed. Then two. I didn't mind. I was familiar with Montana and knew how to amuse myself. I unwound. I made friends, kept McGuane's troupe to visit, but most often struck out on my own. I met three fellows living in tepees west of Emigrant. They were logging the summer season. Their tepees were kinetic art, sculptural folds of skeletalized canvas. White men, their shelter suggested a step back from cowpokes. But their work was current: Chainsaws promising early deafness, a stench of blue smoke, ravaged tree trunks. They offered summer elk hospitably and a sweat lodge banked with volcanic rock. Grouse browsed in the sage behind their tepees like Rhode Island Reds. Fridley Creek ran a constant forty degrees.

I'd set a date with McGuane and showed up on time at the ranch. He came busting out saying he had to get a blood test, why didn't I ride along. He and Margot were getting married. Our interview was postponed. Once again life had intruded upon art. We stopped at the Tastee Freeze, then drove straight to Livingston Memorial. Tom disappeared, reemerging with a bandage inside his elbow. The sole conversation revolved around why not just go ahead and do it. Tom had other errands. We walked into Sax and Fryer's, a combination sporting goods, stationery, artist's supply, photo, hardware, book and souvenir store, where Tom greeted John Fryer, pulled back his sleeve and said: "This is how close I am to getting married." Fryer kept a collection of antique saddles in his basement; we admired them, as if to celebrate. I was impressed again at the *convenience* of Livingston. Everything was right there. If the frontier represented Step Two back from Vietnam, a small town or neighborhood such as Livingston approached One.

Over lunch, we discussed hay ranching, dally roping, quarter-horse breeding: crafts of the white man's West much on Tom's mind. "I'm just going to do it," he said of horse breeding. "It's very complicated. It has a tremendous amount to do with blood lines and other stuff that has to be learned. People say: You don't know anything about it, which is true. I know a lot about using horses but I don't know anything about breeding them, in terms of what blood lines cross with other blood lines and how to get results genetically. But I'm going to do it, that's all." He said the same for dally roping. Hay ranching he had a handle on. These were chores of the Old West which had a firmer hold on sanity than producing screenplays or jackpot journalism. They were crafts whose mastery paralleled the disciplines of art.

Driving home along East River Road, Tom talked about drugs as occasional escape from his Natty Bumppo existence. He'd toughed out a cocaine jag in the early seventies which lasted approximately a year. At one extreme he'd snorted a dime-sized hole in his throat doctors thought would have to be closed with sutures. "I'd get incredibly violent," Tom said of this period. "I had this huge capacity for drugs. I can take more drugs than most people ever dreamed of. Drinking with Marlon Brando one afternoon I downed two fifths of Jack Daniels while he sat nursing a beer. The adrenalin kept me sober. Concentrating on something I'm really interested in will do that."

We set a later date for our interview. That date was broken. Another week passed. I hardly minded. Livingston was balm. The simplicity of small-town life with a proximity to wilderness was healing me. I awoke each morning by ten, boiled water for coffee and munched granola, studying rooftops and the crewcut ochre of Mount Baldy. I glassed mountains which encircled the town, for snow, game or tractor-trailers which slid along I-90. I read. By eleven I was mobile. I kept forest service maps for a hundred-mile radius, depicting trails. I chose between Ramshorn Lake, Passage Falls, Emigrant Gulch, Palace Butte, Coffin Mountain, Snowbank Camp, Bear Creek Meadow, Fairy Lake, Flathead Pass, Battle Ridge, Soda Butte as objectives—their names were enough. I walked through the Crazy Mountains, hitting Big Timber for a rodeo. I drove up to Ringling, a semi-ghost applauded by Jimmy Buffett in song. I parked back of

McGuane's ranch and hiked into wilderness which ran sixty miles to the Wyoming border. I saw a bear. I saw a moose. I saw innumerable wildflowers, birds and small mammals. What's more, I communed. I fished spring creeks, glacial lakes. I soaked in hot springs. I ran seven, eight miles round the high school track daily. A track ringed by snow-tipped Absarokas where footballers trotted alongside wondering at my Southern accent, trading regionalisms. I caroused with Richard Brautigan, supped at William Hjortsberg's, partied at McGuane's. I hung out at Peter Fonda's—his housekeeper ranch-sitting while he and Becky sailed off Maui—Fonda's mountain view unsurpassed, house simply Western, primitively furnished, spooky in Fonda's absence, redolent of an archetype. I drank in Livingston's saloons, danced until closing. One evening a lady trucker said, "You ever ride in a semi?" and off we went circling town, before eighteen thousand pounds of plywood bound for Rapid City, South Dakota. Another midnight I stepped through the Wrangler's swinging doors in time to hear a hometown girl stand and sing "I Want to Be a Cowboy's Sweetheart," the yodeling of which brought Wrangler's eight stupefied patrons to their feet. By the time a week was done I had forgotten art, reassessed fear, worried only slightly over McGuane's interview.

Tom and Margot got married. That was Monday. We set an interview for Wednesday, two mornings later.

The phone rang. "I'll do it," Tom said wearily. " 'Cause I've put you off. But I am exhausted."

I drove to the ranch astride a mood of confidence that approached exultation.

"Let's walk out to my study," Tom said.

This was one of the several log outbuildings in Tom's ranch-yard; part of it comprised an implement shed, part of it a tack room. Tom slumped to a ragged couch with Hudson Bay and Indian blankets spread across its length. I had visited this study to pick up mail but never had taken a serious look. Tom's desk fronted a picture window, affording an unobstructed view of trees, outbuildings, a vegetable garden, corrals, stable, Deep Creek, a dirt road and mountains beyond. I touched his desk top—laminated butcherboard—and his typewriter, a venerable

Olympia upon which Tom said he'd produced all his major work. Tom observed my perusals tolerantly, answering questions, flipping out information. The room was indelibly McGuane. A pair of saddle bags with T.M. tooled into their leather dangled from its rafters. I'd owned such a pair when I was seven. A stuffed hawk adorned a wall; two identical five-pound trout ("caught on consecutive casts") hung to the left of Tom's desk, above several rifles: a Hawken's gun, a Bedford-style Kentucky flintlock, and a 1903 Springfield 30.06, with Lyman scope. Minus esoterica, this was like my bedroom as a child. Both flintlock and Springfield were custom made for Tom by Montanan Don King.

Book shelves lined three walls and contained editions on hunting and fishing, a leather set of Dickens, editions of *The Bushwhacked Piano*—one leather, a gift of Simon and Schuster—other McGuane publications in other printings, some foreign; and a small stereo tape machine with assorted rock and Country Western tapes. There were books on film and film editing, a veterinary handbook, books about the Confederacy for his *Dry Run* film project, a leatherbound *Pepy's Diary*, and perhaps a hundred novels.

Crowding study walls were a needlepoint of the cover to *Ninety-Two*, a rattlesnake hide, drawings by Thomas IV, photos of daughter Maggie, of Margot, novelist Jim Harrison and Elizabeth Ashley. On a far wall was the casting-call bulletin for *Missouri Breaks*, welcoming the "physically eccentric—those with permanent physical injuries such as scars, missing teeth, broken limbs, broken noses, missing limbs, etc."

To the right of Tom's desk was a cartridge loader for his 30.06. A tree-stump table faced the couch where Tom lay, the tack room off to its side containing saddles, bridles, pack gear, fishing equipment, waders, an Orvis creel, rucksacks. A framed ad for *Ninety-Two*, novel, hung near the tack room door. To its left was a raised topographical map of the immediate countryside. Books on quarter horses and calf roping shared space on Tom's desk with several pages of his novel-in-progress. A Confederate cavalry pistol, used as paperweight, rested at what would be Tom's right hand. A .22 rifle and Browning over-and-under leaned against one corner. An Estate wood-burning stove provided the room's heat. Gun-cleaning emollients soiled its shelves, one a homemade mixture resembling pea soup, which Tom insisted "did the job." I studied this junk like a kid at the Museum of Natural History. This was where the work got done. What a wonderful place to hide.

Tom looked shaky. He'd had scant sleep in the two days since his marriage. Propped up by pillows, he watched me with resignation. I'd not seen him so accessible since Key West. All the toughness had flown.

I began with some remarks about sanity and art, their interrelation, particularly concerning language. Tom shifted to his side.

"I have no theory of language essentially. But I have this— there's a thing that's fascinated me for years, a notion in Zen philosophy, which is that to name a thing is to kill it. And I've often used that as an excuse not to learn the names of plants and birds. But the Japanese—Chinese poets, too—felt often very relaxed about having no idea what the name of a thing was. And they would try to surround it with a kind of envelope of language rather than try to catalogue or tag it. But I do think the interesting thing about the use of words as a way of killing or holding reality in essentially a death grip is: It is a key or an index to the way in which extreme language-oriented people like myself are people who are or have been fear-ridden."

What was this?

"I know that when I go back to the part of my life when I became fascinated with language—and this applies especially to comic language, and for a Catholic like myself, to the wonderful sonorities of Latinate language with the kind of comic echo that Joyce made a science of—within that kind of English language, it's a way of saving yourself. I mean, as a kid, I was afraid of absolutely everything, and now that I've grown up, I'm only afraid of most things."

"You want to elaborate on that?"

"Yeah. It's like breaking the butterfly on the wheel, though. I don't think there's a lot to be made of the point. Except that we know how you remove fear from things by getting some kind of grip on them. Say you're afraid of snakes, even garter snakes. If you can get to the point that you can pick up the snake, you're going to cancel the fear. Language is a handhold on things more universally applicable than, say, physical contact. If you can name things, ridicule, surround or conceptualize them within language, you can detoxify them for yourself to a great extent."

Born in 1939 to Irish Catholic parents who'd raised him on Grosse Ile, Michigan, near Detroit, Tom said, he'd attended a "crappy little parochial grade school" with eight kids in his graduating class, where he'd first become intimate with fear.

"I never went on any of those playground things, for instance. I mean I never had the nerve to go on the monkey bars or a swing. I was just totally afraid of other children. As a young kid I was a terrible student. I remember that I was so uninterested in reading that my parents tried to bribe me to read books."

"When did language come in as defense or escape?"

"I think that I began to escape from this world of terror—of other children and everything else—by becoming known as sort of a wit, as being a funny person. People began to like me for that. It was an excoriating sort of humor that was actually a kind of humor based on hostility . . . but it was so carefully funny that there wasn't much recourse for the victim. It was sort of a black humor, but people liked it, and they valued me for it. You know how all young boys want to be tough guys. Well I was a tough guy because I said a lot of outrageous, unrepliable things."

The genesis of a hipster. "Can you remember when you started doing that? The actual point? Of using language as a club?"

Tom smiled. "It isn't anything much more profound than discovering the ability to talk your way out of things."

An artist conceived.

"My earliest memory is of being in some kind of terrible trouble in school. And the monsignor came over to deal with me. He took me off into this little room. Instead of just attacking me he decided to come in from an unusual angle. And his angle was: Exactly what is it you want to do with yourself, McGuane? We don't know what to do with you. You're a problem to everybody, and—what do you plan to do? Because we don't have any idea how to cope with you. So . . . I told him that I was in some distress at that time because my conduct, my sociopathic side, seemed to be at odds with my desire to become a Jesuit. Well, this was a complete lie. But what I knew was that he would say to himself: My God, here's my chance to reform a real stinker and turn him into a really energetic priest. I remember watching him swallow this whole thing hook, line and sinker. And to me it was like cracking the atom."

Tom had spent childhood summers in Fall River, Massachusetts, at his grandmother's house, where crazy uncles pitchforked malarkey around the kitchen and a story of more than two lines was met with open derision. "My concept of paradise for a long time was to be in my grandmother's kitchen. I had one uncle who would come to the door, after not having seen me for ten months, look at me very solemnly and say: Tommy, remember, you're among friends and this is no clambake. Then he'd turn on his heel. He just knew how exciting the absolutely ludicrous or absurd was. You'd stand there dismayed, and by that time he'd be on the second floor. He might hang out the window and say: Remember that. Then he'd vanish and you might not see him for a day. That used to absolutely fascinate me. So language, playing around with it, became a happy place to live, almost. Just in the sense that now, when I'm writing a novel, however grim, I'm absolutely happy. For me there's no suffering associated with writing. Except touching pain centers, stuff like that."

Tom shifted uncomfortably.

"What's happening now?"

"I haven't been writing for a while, and I just barely have a kind of grip on my existence, you know, from not having written for about five months. But I feel confident of kind of pulling it out of the fire. In fact, this week, for this first time in five months, I've written fiction. And it's just, it's absolutely, it's . . . it's . . . for me, writing is literally a matter of mental survival. If I were unable to write for two years, I'd definitely be a psychopath."

"What happens in your head when you're not writing?"

"I'm trying to write, very often. Or I must say, recently, like in the last couple of years, I've tried quite a lot *not* to write, because writing can become kind of an emotional panacea for me. Not necessarily directed toward good writing. It's a way of staying happy. So as I get into the middle of my life I find that one of the tough things about this era is that I now have to make real choices about that. I can't simply write because I need or want to write. I really have to constrain myself to writing when there's something to be said. The easiest, the laziest, most self-placating thing I could do would be to just hit the machine all day every day."

"What's the new novel like?"*

"Well . . . it's in the first person . . . and about somebody really having trouble with his mind. This guy seems to be unable to get into specifics on anything. For instance, he has a dog who's dying of old age in this book, and he's not named it yet. And he has this relationship with this lady that's gone on for years and years, and he's had a period of taking too many drugs. He's talking to her, and she makes some sort of remark about their marriage. And it absolutely baffles him. He says: What marriage? And she says: Panama in 1967, and I can prove it. Then he goes on, the whole point's dropped. Sort of later in the novel, she brings the papers over, you know, and he looks and he puzzles over his signature, and he says: You're absolutely right. But he notices things on another level. And I associate mental health in myself with the noticing of all those things."

"Noticing what?"

"What people do. How birds move. What trees birds pick, around here, when the wind changes angles, so they can keep turned into the wind and keep feeding. Why they stand on one leg. I'll pick up that stuff all the time when I'm in a good mood and I'm working and my energy's going well. When I'm not, I don't notice anything. The car runs out of gas all the time. I forget to look at the gas gauge. And I guess I associate a kind of solidity with intense observation."

"Even when you're writing? If you get up from your desk and go out, do you still notice those things?"

"Well sometimes I carry that thing around all the time. But a typical observation in this novel would be, from this character's point of view, would be: Something shot by, a car—or some-

---

* *Panama,* published in the fall of 1978.

thing. Like he's at a place where he really wouldn't make that much of a distinction between a car and a pancake."

I mulled that one over. "Right. That's where I am now."

"In your own life?"

"In my own life."

"That's a tough place to be. I'm a little bit in that, because I've been just slopping around and not taking pains."

"Do you have a working title for the new novel?"

"Oh, my God, I've had a bunch. *Eleven Ways to Nigger Rig Your Life* is the present one. It was called *Fuck All That* for a while. It was called *Third Mourner from the Left.*"

"What's this character do?"

"This character—one of the things I'm going to do all the way through the novel is, you absolutely never really know what he does. What you know—the main thing—is that he has been some kind of stupendous success. I mean the kind of person who was literally almost killed by mobs in places like Tokyo and Ankara. You just don't have any idea why. And what's happened is he's in his home town, you know, where he was the creepiest person in town before this happened to him. I mean, there's a kind of life that can be led in our time because of our communications and the number of people on our planet, the kinds of lives in which you can essentially nova in your mid-twenties, and then you have this incredible task of reconstituting yourself. And that's kind of what it's about. Say Fitzgerald or Faulkner or Hemingway or Ford Madox Ford might open a novel, in the way in which they intended to exemplify the age, by having a man coming back from war. And World War I was apparently a war that had an enormous force for horrifying people at a very, very fundamental level. I have a feeling, with the perceptions that these people grew up with, and came to war with, that the horror was unbelievable—the First World War. I think it was probably much worse than Vietnam. Not because it was a worse war. Vietnam was a worse war. But I think the kind of novocain factor in our era is such that you're just not set up to be really horrified the way they were."

"Right."

"But I think—we have another thing going on. We have this kind of ambient war of souls and spirits and minds that exists in a kind of zone, like the war zone that Mailer proposes be set up as a permanent part of planetary society. I think there's a war zone, and I don't really know very much about it. But I know that it's out there, and I know that I've been in and out of it, and I know to enough of an extent—that I want to write for a couple of years about it. I know that I've had a kind of shell shock, and received a kind of damage."

"You talking about movies and the success of your books?"

"No. I was never in a place where success was going to do anything except produce a check. I've never lived in a place where I got a lot of adulation. I remember walking into Elaine's and getting a lot one time. I remember how startled and shocked I was. Being buddied-up to by older novelists, things like that. And I remember thinking: Jesus, if you were living in New York and you had a successful book come out, you probably could get yourself all fucked around by this. Because you'd get into it if you were at all flatterable, or liked people and wanted to be liked. And then it's like coke or something. It's one of those things where you keep snorting it up—and you find that you can't get off."

"Tell more about this war zone. That fascinates me."

"The war zone I think is really this. I mean—war is kind of an effluent from a cultural uproar. And increasingly, we will manage to civilize ourselves to the place where we won't have wars anymore. But what we do have right now is cultural uproar. And we have another kind of effluent. We're living in a kind of regressive period right now. But I think in this strange kind of symmetrical way, turning twenty in nineteen-sixty and thirty in nineteen-seventy as I did, I can sort of see the grand scale running up through those ten years. And I know that the center did not hold in the sixties. And what happened is the culture went apart like a frag grenade. I mean it just literally did. And I think what happens is that you begin parceling yourself out, your spirit or whoever you are, into the gambles you are taking on what the cutting edge of the best life you could lead was. And you took terrible risks with yourself, and you paid terrible prices. I'm not—I mean, drugs is one of the least impactful aspects of that. I went into the sixties a fairly ordinary Midwesterner wanting to be an old-fashioned American novelist. I had an absolute model nuclear marriage and compact family, with no sense of missing anything. And by the time it was over, my wife, my family, my sense of myself, my belief in a set of standards in anything that anybody did in the world, et cetera, had all completely fallen apart."

"Due to—"

"I don't know. I'm trying to find out. That's really why I'm writing the book. And that's why I have to rewrite it and rewrite it and rewrite it. Because I'll only start to find out in that first draft. The reason I think I can write the book now is that I feel I'm on the other side. And the reconstruction is beginning. And it's going to be successful. What's peculiar is that I have the feeling I might just reconstruct what I was doing fifteen years ago."

"In terms of writing?"

"Writing and my life. And everything."

Twenty-five years ago Tom had been a radically skinny kid growing up in Grosse Ile, Michigan, where his father was a salesman. In the ten years or so before he decided to become a writer, Tom would suffer various metamorphoses. The most notable his slipping from a fear-ridden grade schooler toward a more aggressive, nearly sociopathic teenager.

"The house I lived in was one hundred thirty-five years old. A very beautiful place. Grosse Ile Jim Harrison defined perfectly as sort of the Midwest's equivalent of Tidewater. It was a resort before the Civil War, and an extremely Protestant kind of place. Not upper-middle-class Protestant, but Joe Midwest Protestant. And we were Catholics, and I think all us Catholic kids felt funny about being Catholic. We'd get a lot of riding, you know, and that kind of ridicule."

Tom had brothers and sisters, but didn't feel terribly close to them.

"Until I was in about the fourth or fifth grade, I lived in total terror. I mean I couldn't ask to go to the bathroom. So for like the first three or four years in school, I just wet my pants every single day in school, which made me sort of famous. And I had a collection of turtles which were my friends. I used to bring them to school in a box, and I had them all named. I had about five different kinds of turtles I brought everywhere, and the safety patrol—when I was in the third grade—the two safety patrol guys, the kids with the white bands, took my turtles away from me and at forty-five miles an hour splatted them one after another on the highway. Which is—and I'll never escape this—the beginning, middle and end of my impression of authority. That's absolutely the way I feel about authority at all levels. And I'll never escape it, even if I reason my way around it."

Tom nearly flunked his first year of high school. He got into trouble; went to jail, for drunk and disorderly, concealed weapons. "I was hanging out with hoodlums, had a ducktail haircut, and you know, we used to get beer and go out in the swamps and spear pike at night. And break into boarded-up houses, steal copper tubing and sell it to the junkyards and buy camshafts for our hotrods. And, I mean, something had changed by then."

Tom's parents, alarmed, got it together to send him to an okay boarding school: Cranbrook, thirty miles from their house. "I arrived right in the middle of the Ivy League era. Everybody had crew-neck shirts, and they had J. Press and Brooks Brothers outfits, and I arrived in blue suede Flag Flyer shoes, you know—I had the kind you flipped open instead of laced. I had my ducktail haircut, a James Dean red nylon jacket, flyer's glasses, and believe me, was I ever out of place. I was in immediate trouble at the end of my first term. From then on I spent virtually half or three-quarters of the rest of my time on what they called probation. What that meant was that the few privileges you had as a boarding school student were cut by about two-thirds. I was also on what they called the Unsat List, 'unsatisfactory.' Which meant you sat in—year round—study hall on Saturday. Then Sunday, because I was Catholic, I had all these numbers I had to do with the Catholics. We had this priest who came to school; it was an Episcopal school, and he was very keen to make sure that the Catholics really stood up against these Protestant dogs. So I had a week of school, you know, classes. Saturday I sat in study hall for being an unsatisfactory student. And then I had this shit-heel priest who'd come around, and we'd go to mass, and have special meetings about what it meant to be a Catholic."

Nevertheless, Tom's interests were beginning to shift.

"All I had succeeded in doing before I went to boarding school was becoming a hoodlum. And getting into trouble. I mean, I wasn't even popular. I was an unpleasant kid, essentially. Somehow or other with that radical change of moving away to school, I got a kind of fresh start. On a *social* level, between me and my contemporaries. It was a boys' school. I had been quite unsuccessful as a young Lothario. I just wasn't good at that. I was essentially afraid of girls and didn't have the nerve for the dating game. Then suddenly I was thrown into a boys' boarding school. And that contact, that kind of male contesting in the presence of women in a public school, was something I was a failure at. That game was suddenly removed from the atmosphere. It was an all-male world for the next three years and I was sort of successful in that world. I was considered funny, and as kind of a hood I quickly reformed and adopted some coloration. But people were fascinated by me, you know, because they hadn't stolen cars and stuff like that."

"You were still telling stories. Sort of leaning on language?"

"Yeah. My room was where everybody hung out and bullshitted about how much they'd get off chicks. Like: 'What'd you get off her?'—'Uh, I got a little covered tit, I dunno'—things like that. 'Well how'd you do last week?'—'Well, shit, that's what pissed me off. Last week I got covered box and covered titties, and fuck, this week I spent twice as much time and I only got covered tit.'—'Well could you French kiss her?'—'Yeah, she went for everything. It's just the whole thing about the snatch really put her off. I don't know what it was.'—'Well I heard Al Smith was out with her Wednesday, and he finger fucked her, and it wasn't even *dark.'* And: 'Are you serious? He finger fucked her and it wasn't dark?' So anyway at that point I would get to say something like: 'Oh shit, I wouldn't fuck her with your dick.' And we'd talk dirty a lot. Also, I met two or three guys who wanted to be writers and who'd read a lot of books, and I got put onto kind of a reading list."

Boarding schools during the nineteen-fifties were such stultifying places that anyone interested in language turned instinctively toward two most immediate escapes: bullshitting and reading. Hip language as art derived from the bull session; in prep school those sessions were dormitory equivalent to street-corner jive, primers in expressing oneself with brevity and wit. Reading followed, for one could not bullshit forever, one would deplete energies, short-circuit any will to survive. Reading was the principal escape, nearly one's sole entertainment. There was no television at boarding school, there were few movies. One had the radio with its lifeblood of rock 'n' roll, one had reading, and one had bullshit. If one was hip one also had Style—a sense of presence which broached theatricality, presence itself an artistic mode of expression. What the budding hipster carried to boarding school, from years of home TV and access to movies, were role-models of mythic cowboys, silent, graceful, World War II soldiers barking a language closer to that our fathers spoke, and actors such as James Dean, Marlon Brando and Montgomery Clift, whose outrageous mumblings and defiant garb were tantalizingly contemporary. Throw in a Carl Perkins or an Elvis Presley, you had the stew. Prep school was prison, a limbo between infantilism and the adult gratification of infantile goals. The hipster could do little but fantasize. He could express himself through bullshit or he could lose himself in books. Mostly he groped through a fantasy-theater of unrealized opportunities, thwarted drives. That was prep school; that was the nineteen-fifties. Sixties culture (and college) would explode fantasized theatricality into the street. But this was 1955 and no clambake. McGuane sniffed around the books.

It is notably ironic that Tom's first exposure to "serious" reading was the decadent tradition in European literature: Huysmans, Oscar Wilde, Proust, Lautreamont. McGuane the hood. Tom had found a mentor, a bookish kid—now a successful author—who was "blatantly queer." He was impressed with Tom's bullshit and thought he possessed some kind of verbal brilliance. "This guy was absolutely, incredibly precocious, and he'd read everything. I mean, by ninth and tenth grade he'd read all of Dostoyevsky, Proust, Tolstoy, which was pretty remarkable for a sixteen-year-old." Tom at this time nursed a kind of secret life as a writer—he kept a notebook. "I wanted to be a writer by then. I think because it struck me as a very romantic life. It wasn't so much that I wanted to write. It was because I wanted to *be* a writer." Prep school theatricality. "I'd gradually begun to see the life of the writer as being the ultimate kind of free life. I had this thing about authority—which I am not jacking up for autobiographical interest. I am almost totally incapable of dealing with authority. Teachers, police officers, political figures, everything. It's been a huge force in my life. So I began at a very primordial level to try to figure out a way of never having to have a boss of any kind. Also, at that time, I was smoking dope. Now that was nineteen fifty-six, fifty-seven. I didn't know anybody else who was smoking dope, and therefore I concluded that I was a junkie."

Tom had become tremendously interested in jazz. When free, he would drive any distance to hear it. He was playing drums, taking lessons from a jazz drummer who would supply marijuana. "I used to go to Toledo. And in those days it was great, because you could go to, you know, very dense black neighborhoods and hang out in the bars and listen to bluesmen and stuff like that. I did that a lot. Also, all my sexual beginnings lie in that world. All the women I hung out with in any sexual sense, until I was maybe twenty, were black whores. I knew a lot of black whores, and they were like friends of mine. And—I look back on those years, the academic part was no fun, and I came away pretty unhappy about schooling—but I must say I had good friends in school, and I felt liked. I'd really started to come out of whatever my shadow had been before then. I felt kind of strong and ambitious about trying to do some of the things that I wanted to do and had kept secret."

"What sort of writing did you crank out in prep school?"

"Mostly melancholy stories about lost youth. They were just awful. I had two awful periods. My first was that, when I also wrote this lachrymose poetry about autumnal themes. Then when I went to college I became a beatnik."

Tom enrolled in the University of Michigan, where he flunked out with a 0.6 on the four-point system. He managed to con himself into Olivet, a country college which financially was so poor nearly anyone could get in, but academically was rather good. There Tom received his first adult encouragement to be a writer. He received certain privileges for spending time writing. He was experimenting with plays then. He transferred back to Michigan, flunked out again, and returned to Olivet. Then he attended Harvard summer school, taking a heavy load of courses centered about writing, and got spectacular grades. He took Harvard's advanced writing course: "I was young and scared, and all these other people were older and very sophisticated kind of East Coast people. And I got a lot of encouragement. At that time I was very much under the influence of beat writers, primarily Jack Kerouac. Which was a very unconstipating way of getting at writing. I probably wrote three hundred pages that summer. I mean I wrote continuously. I was also very heavily into Southern lady writers: Carson McCullers, Katherine Anne Porter, Flannery O'Connor, Shirley Jackson, Eudora Welty. They were the best grotesque writers around, and I was very interested in grotesque writing in all forms. Nathanael West was a guy I liked a lot."

That was 1960. Tom had plans to be a writer. Planning to do anything was a scarifying notion, and even though Tom kept his writing self-consciously grotesque, hid behind a beat facade, he'd come to think being a writer "was the most splendid thing you could be in the world—it's still true—to me being a writer is the way some people feel about making the New York Yankees. I just wanted to be one so badly, it was a literal, absolute burning, consuming thing with me. At Harvard I explicitly asked my teacher with terrible fear: Do you think I could ever become a writer? And his reply was something to the effect that: Absolutely no question about it. If you can endure the waiting and keep writing. That literally blew my mind."

The University of Michigan, from which Tom had flunked out, then was considered the only Midwestern school with Ivy League standards. Its literary prize offered more than the Pulitzer. It had a large, self-conscious literary community, many poets, with a very stuffy literary scene. McGuane hadn't managed any cachet with that crowd. He went off to Michigan State, the cow college, and it had an okay English department. There he met other writers, so different from the pipe-smoking literati, that Tom sat back and took notice.

"They were these really *crude* sort of characters. Outrageous. And my impression was that they were much better writers than the ones at the University of Michigan. These characters were always shooting pool and getting thrown out of bars or throwing things through plate glass windows. I couldn't believe it, because we'd talk about writing and we'd get very excited, talk like maniacs about Apollinaire and we'd be gobbling these cheap steaks— we used to get these rotten steaks and marinate them in vinegar until you could get a knife through them, and we'd eat these things and shoot pool and buy Pfeiffer beer in what they called GIQs—Giant Imperial Quarts—and chug 'em, puke in our cars, and . . . it was the first time I was ever in a literary scene where I felt really happy with the kind of combination of the life and literature. We'd go to rallies of right-wing politicians and harass them by calling them fuckheads at the top of our lungs. It was pretty exhilarating. It was pretty exciting. It wasn't a bohemian literary scene. It was just characters."

Tom's ambition was some day to write a novel good enough to deserve that blurb he had observed on Dos Passos' *U.S.A.:* "An explosion in a cesspool." He was still being influenced by Southern women writers and Nathanael West, he was slogging through his Jack Kerouac period, with a "phony Midwestern regional" period to follow, but the romance of simply being a writer had slipped toward the commitment of working a craft. Tom's stages are worth repeating: Fear-ridden child discovering language as defense; hoodlum developing the patois of hip; beat dissolving into stream of consciousness, bop prosody of Kerouac, salted with Westian grotesque; convoluted hipster discovering pleasures of redneck unchic in agricultural literary milieu. By 1962, Tom had graduated from Michigan State and was accepted at the Yale School of Drama. Professionalism had set up shop.

"Somewhere along there the beginnings of the first really good influence on my particular needs as a writer came in—which were the classical European novelists. Those writers were Flaubert and Turgenev, mostly. They taught me that it was not enough simply to report that you had felt things. The conflict there was turning that line where you're trying to keep a kind of shapeliness in a novel and still keep that whole kind of kinetic energy driving into it at the same time, without one killing the other off. That seemed to be the important feat. It ws the power-to-weight ratio in the novel that was its most important feature. That made me really concentrate on getting energy and strength into the most carefully made shape you could."

McGuane might have been speaking of building a race car. Or designing a rocket. Or otherwise delineating that early sixties fascination with mechanical construct which fell under the heading: Technology.

For subhead, read: Theater. Aristotle defined drama as "imitated human action," not a bad classification of that lull before the storm which affected American artists during the early sixties. For a young novelist, whose aesthetics were energy and compaction, playwriting was apt technical training. Tom's shift in interest from the self-consciously grotesque to the finer lines of classical European literature, paralleled, in painting, what would be the leap from abstract expressionism to pop art; in music, the leap from rhythm and blues to rock; in fashion, the leap from blue suede shoes to Pierre Cardin; and in cars, the leap from '57 Chevies to Volkswagen Super Beetles. For the literary world, as with every layer of American culture, the early sixties provided a respite. Theater during the nineteen-fifties had enjoyed a remarkable resurgence; off-Broadway boomed with success after success, the controversial writings of Williams, Genet, Weiss, Beckett, Ionesco, Pinter, Arrabal, Albee, Frisch and Duerrenmatt. During New York's '61–'62 season, the *Times* counted one hundred off-Broadway productions, thirty-four more than on Broadway. A decline had begun by '62–'63. Theater would remain the most powerful dramatic medium for exorcising cultural frustrations until those frustrations were primed to hit the street. But in between was that lull.

"I arrived at the Yale School of Drama just as the theater that interested me in America was dying. It was dying simultaneously with my education as a playwright. That was between 1962 and 1965. Plays—I still love them, I'd write them if there were a theater—to me, movies are plays. I consider my work in movies as the result of that part of me which wishes to be a playwright. By my second year at Yale, though, I had really lost interest in the

theater. I was writing novels and just enough theater stuff to satisfy the academic requirements. The Yale School of Drama was
really a dull place to be. It was that or the army."

Tom had simultaneously applied for fighter's school as he had
applied to Yale. The power-to-weight ratio of the navy's monster
Phantoms held that much fascination. But Yale came through
and the technicalities of literature overrode those of bom-
badiering.

"The nature of things was that I stayed in school a long time. I
used school in two ways. Once was to get a deferment from the
draft, which was very important. There was no way I could have
written novels in the army. Also, my father never gave me any
money in a direct way, but he believed very strongly in education. He was a poor kid who went to Harvard on an athletic
scholarship, and he saw education as being the panacea to
everything. He had a deal with me, which was I think a very generous one. I could go to school anywhere I wanted, I could study
anything I wanted, for as long as I wanted on a no-questions-
asked basis, and he'd cover it. He'd open me a charge account at
a bookstore, wherever I was in school, and provided I read
everything that I bought, I could buy as many books as I wanted.
Comparing that to going to Schenectady and writing the obituaries and doing your novel at night, it was ideal. There were a
lot of kind of experiential things that beat novelists used to list on
the backs of their books, you know; dishwasher, blocklayer, that
kind of thing. Well, I didn't do any of that stuff. I worked on
ranches, farted around a little bit. But mostly I was just an
American idler. As soon as I got any kind of directed energy, it
was toward preparing myself as a writer—and I would modestly
say that I don't think I've met another novelist who knew as
much about novels as I do. At one point I *technically knew* the
novel metier. I knew it backwards and forwards. I had just read
every bloody novel there was. It had become systematic. I was
reading a novel a day, for I guess close to three years.

And in honing that technique, Tom found his life inverted. "I
turned from a sociopath into a bookworm." He was exploiting
the lull. Instead of laying back like most of the culture, he was
laying into literature. "So my life as a writer was curiously re-

versed. Most writers would have, at twenty-six, suddenly decided to educate themselves, after having been oil-riggers or something. You know how that goes. What happened to me at twenty-six was I started to become a complete illiterate, and a barfly, and a junkie. I spent all my time fishing, getting drunk, hanging out, chasing women, just messing around. I've had periods in recent years where I literally can't even read a newspaper. Just absolute, almost pure illiteracy. Now things are starting to balance back."

Tom and Becky were married in 1962, the year Tom disappeared into literature at Yale. He quickly learned what a valuable tool was marriage in the technical kit of a writer.

"You know that line of Flaubert's: 'I live like a bourgeois so that I can write with passion.' That's very true. We didn't have any money, but I had a really good little bourgeois life, in the sense that I had three absolutely regular, well-cooked meals a day, and enough clothes, and enough room to get away from the noise to write. I'm in a very different situation right now. Margot has enormous ambitions of her own . . . she'll soon be going back to work. I'll kind of be cooking for myself. I no longer have the sense of that kind of perfect household for writing, and I have to find a little bit different way of doing it."

While at school—an extended foray which would lead Tom from Yale to the Scuola per Stranieri in Florence to Stanford, and which would not culminate until 1968 when *The Sporting Club* was sold—Tom exploited every technical aid accessible. He exploited his marriage, but most thoroughly, he exploited himself. His earlier "sociopathic" side, his hooliganism, hipsterism, his propensity toward the overtly theatrical, became sublimated in the systematic study of literature. By removing himself from "life" he believed he could master "art," and in doing so proved not much different from millions of white middle-class males who had been suckered into the cure-all of formal education. And who were dodging the draft. The paradox here was wicked. They were being encouraged to remain in school because school was the ticket to perpetuation of that postwar wealth their parents enjoyed; simultaneously they were being denied the experi-

ence of war, thereby frustrating all horse-opera dreams of heroism. One might endure prep school if one played the hipster,
college if one professed the beat, but grad school was a stymie.
Especially during the mid-sixties. All one's psychic energy lay
sublimated in technique. The mastery of "life" through technology, during those years, saturated the culture at large. Illicit passions lurked between the pages of typescript as surely as monster
engines lay hidden beneath the hoods of family automobiles,
blue jeans hung in closets behind three-piece suits, Richie Valens
discs inserted themselves under insipid Ahmad Jamals, sex
boiled, and legitimate theater sagged. Yet theater was impossible
to kick. It was after all ritual, formalized expression of unspeakable practice. For the literary artist to abandon it would be to
admit defeat. Or start dancing in the street.

The development of Tom's art throughout the sixties and early
seventies was a case in point. Tom would write three novels before *The Sporting Club* was published in 1968, but parts of *Club*
were written at Yale and theorizing on its construct was
fomenting.

"I had been thinking back about plays. I was thinking about
three-act plays, a form that really fascinated me. Because the
proportions are something like sixty-forty-thirty in the acts, and
there's a thing where you come out of the chaos of the original
material with new information for the audience that culminates
in this interesting way at the first-act curtain. Then there's a mysterious thing in the second act, which is this very strange zone in
the play, and then a third act, which is the conclusion of the
piece. And I was thinking in those terms. I was looking for a kind
of novel, I mean a setup for a novel, in which you could isolate
the usual inputs of the modern realistic novel. In other words I
wanted an almost *theatrical* situation—to write a novel. I was
going through my own experience, trying to think what I knew
about in actuality that had that quality, and I suddenly thought
of hunting and fishing clubs, which were these peculiar enclaves
in the middle of forests, with people who don't belong there. And
it's really theater. In life it's theater. It seemed to be absolutely
perfect. Fundamentally there was something inescapably comic

about it, and I didn't see how to write *The Sporting Club* except as a comedy, as a kind of savage comedy. It's the shapeliest of my novels, really."

The Sporting Club, though published in 1968, reflects sublimated conflicts of early to mid-sixties America precisely. The tone is a mixture of sixties jockishness and redneck vulgarity, cased in a Victorian preciosity which lends the drama shape. Two young men, one a conscientious businessman, the other an irascible idler, joust about a gossamer female character and, in their fumbling, manage to hurry the collapse of a hundred-year-old sporting club ... the republic, symbolically ... with assist from a bizarre outlaw hero: a post-cowpoke, pre-redneck, seller of bait. There are Harley-Davidson motorcycles and expensive fly rods all gone up in smoke. The scenery is quintessentially McGuane. As in most of his work, two principal characters represent the split in Tom's nature between pragmatist and sociopath. Or businessman and dreamer. Or realist and artist. In no later work, however, is the split so neat. And it fits sixties culture to a T.

"The kind of fiction I write is one in which the line between autobiography and pure fiction is laminated. Those two panels are laminated in a way which is the secret of the author. One of the things people wonder about my books is whether or not they're autobiographical. And the answer is: yes and no. They're autobiographical where it suits my purposes, and they're not where it doesn't.... Our best writers have always done that. We live in a fast-forming civilization, and artists are always going to be people who are telling you about their lives to some extent. We're not really situated to produce an art-for-art's-sake type of novel culturally."

Tom's life had begun to change by 1971 when *The Bushwhacked Piano* appeared. He had forsaken school, had been shuttling semi-annually between Livingston and Key West—and the road burn showed. *Bushwhacked* is nearly Rabelaisian in tone, if one can imagine that monk suited up in Kerouac denims with a side order of sixties roiling in his gut. "One book for me is always a reaction to the previous. I got very interested in picaresque novels, all the way from Lazarillo de Tormes and *Don*

Quixote to Gogol. And I got fascinated by the *idea* of picaresque novels. I was reading Fielding all the time, *Tom Jones* ... I got interested in English sloppiness in fiction. *Tristram Shandy* was a book I liked very much at the time. And instead of trying to plan a novel—as I had done in *The Sporting Club,* on a three-act play—instead of trying to get a projectile shape for a novel, I began to be interested in a paste-up kind of book."

The late sixties was nothing if not paste-up, and by 1970 when Tom was adding final touches to *Bushwhacked* the culture was certainly picaresque. The long-sublimated drives toward sex, speed, violent sport, war and unfettered art had split America like an overripe melon. Everyone had his role. Theater had gushed into the street, either through formalized demonstrations, costumes, unshakable positions, or Dionysian revel. The tone of *Bushwhacked* is late sixties, but its themes and time frame are set back. *Bushwhacked*'s characters struggle against an impending chaos by hanging on to earlier conceptions of rebellion. Notably, sociopathic prep-school hipsterism and a dilettantish indulgence in art. Art is attacked most desperately in *Bushwhacked.* The piano symbolizes America, bushwhacked since Columbus with unfair assaults on its potential. Most contemptuously by business and art. The drygulchery of art here is vivisected by McGuane as thoroughly as that of business. One encounters the usual socio- pathic protagonist, railing against these extremes. There is his artistic foil. But a curious amalgamation occurs in the form of a third character, a pest control magnate bent on "curing" America with a prophylactic chain of coast-to-coast bat towers. His target is mosquitoes but his intention is bloodsuckers. C. J. Clovis is an entrepreneur and something of a charlatan, but he is foremost a romantic, an American businessman with an artistic dreaminess about him which McGuane applauds. At *Bush- whacked*'s conclusion, art, in its popular guise, remains escape from reality, and experience for experience's sake remains un- moored sociopathy. There is no resolve. Clovis, the pest-control magnate, dies consummating a fraud, his heart "on the fritz."

About this time, Tom had started to make money. He had sold *Sporting Club* to the movies and was writing screenplays himself. For ten years he had stuck with fiction; he had stayed broke. A certain uneasiness was attendant to receiving those large checks. "The vanity of literary poverty is pervasive," Tom said. "But making money's fun. Especially the first couple of times it happens. I'm a pretty good businessman, which is something that I guess until recently I felt fairly embarrassed about as a writer."

Tom's father was a businessman, a tycoon in fact; in the larger sense all our fathers had been businessmen, bricking up the postwar economy to stifling heights—so far as we were concerned. To be an artist during the late fifties–early sixties and lust after Mammon was less than despicable. It was Eisenhoweresque. Yet those artists who came to maturity in the mid-sixties toiled under a more complex imperative. Just as World War II had produced hip—a post-Holocaust aura of doom, war heroes to emulate and a war ethos to protest, so had it engendered in the sixties artist a powerful drive to pull in the cash. If our dads had proved heroic in their mission to save us from fascism, they had been equally heroic in their rescue of a prewar economy from postwar depression. But to make money was so *unhip* for the fifties artist. His sixties counterpart felt the same negative ions but was jostled in contradictory spheres.

To be a success at art, outside cultism, one had best have the business acumen of a Colonel Tom Parker and the presumption of an Elvis Presley to back it up. One had to sell one's product even as one need sell oneself, and this was the great lesson of Pop. Born of fifties adsmanship, Pop Art said, "See me, I'm simple, I'm ironic; buy me, I'm expensive but I'm hip—you're in on the joke." It's not insignificant that Bob Dylan's association with Andy Warhol led to his embracement of Pop, its aesthetics and munificence. Dylan's father, like McGuane's, had been a harddriving businessman. Dylan's business sense during the sixties separated him from a dozen other talented songwriters, propelling him to the top of the heap. As Dylan, Warhol, and later McGuane lampooned the business ethos, they profited from it. It was hip to rip off a stooge. Take the money and run. It was all part of the carnival, sideshow atmosphere of the nineteen-sixties. That was it on the surface. But running deeper was that fiercer imperative: beat dad at his game by flinging it in his face. The outlaw notion in popular culture thereby was born, where artists like Dylan and Peckinpah were literally "knocking over the stage," then hightailing it to the badlands.

All this of course was contrary to any notion of serious literature. It smacked of best sellerdom. Tom was not ready to compromise there, but he was willing to reevaluate theater, his notions thereof, and opportunities for recompense. Hollywood beckoned, as did Key West and its more immediate avenue of street theater. Key West during the early seventies was a microcosm of American culture. At land's end, it attracted a special breed of zany ... cloaking any style of specious behavior in a gauziness that decried pretension. Tom reverted to "sociopathy," became a "junkie" and a "barfly," fished the live-long day and consorted with loose women. This phantasmagoria he intensified with work in movies—a medium phantasmagorical itself, less real than theater, more fantastic, but closer somehow to the street. You made movies in the street and people walked in off the street to view them. "There are these great physical excitements about moviemaking," Tom said. "It's thrilling." You were taking theater to the streets, yet maintaining control, through a phantasmagorical medium. Movies' manufacture, direction, editing and photography were highly technical. To say nothing of their marketing. You needed the vision but you likewise needed the business sense. Making movies was like waging war, Tom would say. There was something Napoleonic about the adventure.

McGuane undertook that adventure in its totality only after *Ninety-Two in the Shade* had appeared as literature. Published in 1973, the novel proved an apex of Tom's technical approach to fiction—yet it was hazy, jump-cut, like a movie. It was not unlike TV. Its passages were brief, as if to accommodate commercials—there were regular spaces in the narrative—and the prose shimmied with the opacity of television, colorful as Cousteau, caustic as Johnny Carson. Though that comparison is unfair: *confident* as Johnny Carson, with his chilled irony and technical expertise. Tom's drive into fiction had remained technical throughout the nineteen-sixties. As had other sixties technocrats, he'd applied technology to his work like a hot shot. The emphasis was on technical description, lyrical prose, little obvious emotion, everything technically funny and bright. Hemingway, of course, was the godfather in American letters of technical precision. He showed how much could be hidden, emotionally, with a paucity of words. There was no paucity to McGuane's prose, it was flat out, full bore, technological overload. Tom was masking demons in his personal life: tensions of marriage, art, art's seclusion. His novels emerged as subliminally supercharged and loaded for bear as sixties cars, sport, sex, rockets and Airborne Rangers. McGuane's technologizing would never approach that of more academic novelists—John Barth, say, whose *Lost in the Funhouse* he'd subtitled *Fiction for Print, Tape, Live Voice*—but it would remain aloof.

Ninety-Two in the Shade is simultaneously a monument to aloofness and precision, in life as well as art. It is about commitment. "What I tried out in *Ninety-Two* was the idea of commitment at an abstract level. Instead of taking the position that one's commitments will be a continually negotiated and continually supple approach to eventualities, what if one were to take one's commitments as being final and make that a basis for a kind of comfort and sanity, knowing that you were not always negotiating? This, I suppose, is not really all that far from Hemingway's idea of honor being that you would do what you said you would do, or something like that. But it's not the same thing."

For a novel set in Key West which concerns fishing and violence, an intentional piece of neglect is the omission of so much as Ernest Hemingway's name. Two fishing guides, one pragmatic, the other a dreamer, fumble to shape the destiny of a third younger guide, who looks to encroach upon their trade. This younger guide, Tom Skelton, seeks some mooring in his life above which he might anchor contradictory tendencies toward sociopathy and responsibility. Or dreaminess and precision, or imagination and conscious "reality." Or ocean and dry land. One of these guides, Nichol Dance, is a murderer and redneck sociopath, "an incessant addict of long shots," whose style of guiding Skelton favors. The other, Faron Carter, is a model of civic virtue, emblematic of Key West's business world. Due to a complication in plot and the vile scheming of Carter, Skelton and Dance are faced off—with the upshot that Dance forbids Skelton to guide. Skelton, whose family oddly mirrors conflicts of that business world he hopes to join, sticks by his guns. So does Nichol Dance. Skelton guides and Dance blows him away, is in turn blown away by Skelton's client. Both men die for "doing what they said they would do," and the business world profits. Skelton, the McGuane character if such can be named, is notably tragic. His maturity has been marked by a comprehension of extremes—between his father, the helpless dreamer, and his grandfather, the tyrannical tycoon, and between Carter and Dance. He is nearly a happy compromise, a harbinger of the seventies, yet he dies as the decade begins. His murderer should have been his pal.

"The novel was not so much pessimistic as it was critical," Tom said. "It was critical of a cultural situation in which we exist in this country, a cultural situation which puts people who should be friends on homicidal courses." Skelton, the prescient ex-freak, and Dance, the redneck dreamer, should have come together. In Tom's life, and perhaps the culture's, they had. That was the deeper meaning to Redneck Chic. Its layer of sincerity. It shadowboxed around commitment.

"I still believe—and I'm working this out in the novel I'm writing now—that you have to have some fundamental known things in your life that sometimes exist in the form of personal assertions that are the donnees of your going on, and that if you're always in the position of negotiating those things, then you'll never be sane.

"So if somebody says, How do you feel about killing people—you're about to go to war—and you say, I'll figure that out when I get into that situation, I consider that an absolutely insane position. I believe unless you bank that idea, or you bank that conviction, or you bank that commitment, you're continually in a kind of quicksand. I think it's better to be wrong, and then if necessary have circumstances demonstrate with their absolutely peculiar brutality that you are wrong—at which point you may have to make some kind of reassembly of your posture.

"As time goes by, I become more extremely interested in the idea of a *subject* in writing. I think the most interesting subject in fiction is the attempt to assert a code of life, a kind of personal metaphysic, that you can try out in the form of a novel. And one of the most dramatic things about a novel to me is very often watching that thing arise and succeed or fail. Right now, that's mainly what interests me in the idea of writing fiction. I mean that notion that Camus had that it takes a man ten years to develop a single idea with which he's comfortable. That's a very salubrious notion to me. I'm not looking for a very complicated, systematic world view. I'm looking for some fairly simple tools of survival that can be demonstrated, not only to a reader who matters, but to oneself, in the forms of fiction—which is a real test track for that kind of thing, in terms of your own thinking."

In the film version of *Ninety-Two,* Tom changed his ending. Dance fails to kill Skelton and the two men emerge from their jousting as friends. It was 1974—the culture might have changed. Tom filmed his ending both ways, backing up the reconciliation with Skelton's and Dance's deaths. It would be 1975 and a winter of editing before Tom finally decided.

"Ninety-Two in the Shade is just a wonderful example of book-into-movie for me, because I wanted to try out a different set of conclusions with the same evidence and see if I could make them plausible. Whether or not I succeeded at that is another question."

Tom's conclusions may have succeeded, but, it is generally agreed, his movie did not. Tom had the vision but he lacked the technical expertise. He technically could not pull off, on film, what he had on paper. He would spend a week in Livingston Memorial with a bleeding ulcer for his pains. Yet he learned.

"A movie, like a book, has its own gestalt, which in some sense is immutable. It rolls forward and has a way of finding its own shape, as a book does, when you're writing it. Moviemaking is very much less intense, emotionally; when you're writing a novel the excitement of creation is much hotter and clearer. As for changing *Ninety-Two*'s ending—my novels I consider as being very non-monumental. They're checkpoints on a kind of developmental curve. The conclusions are tentative, and because my life is changing at a very fast rate, I don't see why I should pretend to be speaking ex cathedra when I sit down and write a novel. It's very important for me to make it clear that I'm not sure about anything, but here's what I think. I have absolutely no fear or regret about contradicting myself."

The business of literature, combined with the business of running a ranch, seemed to have eclipsed the allure of film making. For McGuane, the artist, fiction survived as the more attractive medium. He'd set certain aesthetics: his new novel would be in the first person, employ fewer technological ruses, and prove more heartfelt.

"I think the part of me that is sensible, the part that's most on the nose about making decisions about how and what to write, is the part which wants to continue working toward the Turgenev model in fiction. Which is simply based on the idea that novels have to be extremely efficient to survive. Also I think that one has no right to waste other people's time. That's really my main aesthetic conviction right now.

"I want to write a novel that contains important information which I can conceivably represent as *being* important. I want to write a novel that will represent whatever it is I've learned about living. And I want to write a novel which will be hyperspecific, and which will have some utility, you know. I'm not interested in writing a novel to dazzle or entertain right now. Reading Jim Harrison's novel, *Farmer*—was like a glass of ice water being thrown in my face. It had the pleasant quality of cleansing my eyes about literature at a time when it seemed like everything I picked up was sort of anticipatable or dull. Also, the fact that I had really not been getting anything done that I cared about for a while—to read something, a piece of work written straight from the heart, without any cheating, by my best friend, had not a little of the quality of reproach about it. There are books that remind me immediately of the extreme importance and dignity of the profession of writing. To me that novel improved the world. It's like if I go out here in a field where horses or deer are running around and I pull up a lot of rusty wire which will eventually catch the animal's leg and kill it, that *improves the world*. That's the way I feel about Harrison's novel. That's the way I feel about some things in some of my books that I've written. I feel that they've opened eyes, or they've opened perceptions. And that's kind of what I want to do. But I don't want to be Baba Ram Dass. I want to do it in those terms that I know."

Tom shifted on the couch, sat up, rubbed his eyes.

"I have absolutely one major theme, which is: Why go on? It's been rephrased by lots of people. I almost think it's the master theme of literature. It's the thing that Camus said: There's only one serious philosophical question, and that's the question of suicide."

"Will what you've learned in these past years alter your life as an artist—how you go about getting things done—in any significant fashion?"

"The only thing is—here's one thing I know: that the perfect situation for a writer to work in is one that's tremendously diminishing to the people that he lives with. And I find it so hard to approve of any kind of a life situation in which there is a support team of two or three human beings for the prince." Tom laughed. "I mean I haven't got the conscience to do that any more—especially now that I see it for what it is."

Fall descended upon Paradise Valley. Snow powdered the Absarokas, cottonwoods yellowed, cowboy's hats molted from straw to felt, pillowy vests sprung from their vertebrae like winter fur, and fishing rods transmogrified to firearms as window dressing for pick-up trucks. Tourists vacated Livingston's motels. Except for a few hunters and old men who lived at the Murray, I was alone there. Livingston's bars stayed lively, but the wind had frost in it and on hikes outside town one made certain he carried extra clothing. The high school football team played every Saturday, supplanting rodeo as Livingston's sporting concern. I shot grouse with Gatz Hjortsberg, fished mindlessly, and wondered why I didn't move along. In response to the season a slew of onetime Key Westers—McGuane's retinue—arrived, invading Brautigan's and McGuane's spare bedrooms like tide.

Tom brightened the moment Jimmy Buffett hit town. The two enjoyed a week of private frolicking before communalized festivities began. Tom and Jimmy had shared Key West in those years before they or the town came to symbolize excesses in seventies sharecropping. Key West had been a town where sixties lingered through early seventies, and where, unobtrusively and without camp, anything went. McGuane and Buffett had produced their best work there; in fiction and in song they had done more to mythologize the island than any artist since Ernest Hemingway.

I met Buffett one afternoon stooped beside a sawhorse near Tom's study, Lexoling an antique saddle. "You're the last decent reviewer I've got," Jimmy said, laughing over something I'd written for the *Washington Post.* Jimmy's recent album had not received favorable reviews, and though his career was progressing his creativity back-pedalled in limbo. He looked healthy. He was tan, his blond hair was sun-bleached, and he affected a gold earring. He looked a trifle fancy for Montana. But I'd been away from the world awhile, certainly any world so fancy as Aspen.

Buffett was in Montana for a breather, to visit Tom, to shop for esoterica such as that forty-year-old saddle, a reliable Winchester, antique Indian rug for a house he was buying in Snowmass . . . but also for a conference on that screenplay envisioned, *Mangrove Opera,* about redneck smugglers in the Everglades. I did not hear them discuss that movie. They were saddling up for a ride when a hailstorm broke, spooking horses and dropping a curtain of translucent hailstones between ourselves and the setting sun. The spectrum was revealed; even a rainbow. "Spectacular," Tom said. I plucked iced beers from my cooler and we four, Margot included, hoofed it to the stable. Ankle deep in manure, seated on troughs and hay bales, we waited out the lightning— bullshitted about sailboats, pack equipment, and laughed about the significance of it all. The horses trembled.

Over supper that night was familial small talk—Jimmy seemed to relax Tom while simultaneously revitalizing him. Tom and Margot likewise had new saddles and the three spent hours after dinner oiling them, as I strummed a guitar. Next day there'd be a party at McGuane's with venison picadillo and jitterbugging to the stereo, everything innocent and non-excessive. Then some tendril would snap, and Saturday in Livingston would turn into all night at Gardiner, sixty miles south, with an overindulgence in chemicals above an old-fashioned sloshing of tangleleg. There would be nude swimming in hot pots along the Yellowstone, tagged by a fierce dawn illuminating Gardiner's Two Bit Saloon where we sat slackjawed and comatose. Somewhere during the night Buffett would pick up a guitar and sing a song whose lyrics were strikingly apropos:

> *Wastin' away again in Margaritaville*
> *Searchin' for my last shaker of salt*
> *Some people claim there's a woman to blame*
> *But I know it's nobody's fault.* *

It was an unrecorded tune which, within a year, would escalate Buffett from the obscurity of crossover cultism to the heights of pop superstardom. It was a song about Key West.

Jimmy Buffett was the grandson of a sailing-ship captain and son of a naval architect who'd raised him in French Catholic circumstances, with a smidgeon of antebellum decadence tossed into that salad of gulf port extremes which was Mobile, Alabama. Musically, he was a sixties folkie who had hopscotched rock for country, and whose style was a weird amalgam of Latin rhythm, pop cliché and Texas sentimentality. He'd released one failed album when he first saw Key West in November, 1970, and he was running from a busted marriage. He and Jerry Jeff Walker had driven down for the Hennessy Ocean Races, they did that carnival right, but when it was over, Buffett more or less stayed. He was working Key West bars for a hundred twenty bucks a week, it was warm, he'd found a place to stay, he'd bought a little Boston Whaler, had excess time to explore Key West's day and night life . . . so that when McGuane wandered into Crazy Ophelia's one evening "it was like no need for introductions, we were off on the streets going crazy."

---

* *"Margaritaville."* Words and music by Jimmy Buffett. Used by permission of Coral Reefer Music/Outer Banks Music.

Buffett and McGuane, career-wise, were in comparable straits. Tom had not settled yet into *Ninety-Two,* the book which would secure his reputation, and his work with movies had been limited to one screenplay. Buffett's first album, *Down to Earth,* did not receive enough attention to raise an eyebrow, and he would not release his second album, *A White Sport Coat and a Pink Crustacean*—which would solidify the Key West sound in popular music—for three years.

"We were both sort of on the edges there, still having a good time," Jimmy said. "And the town was right, you know. It was pretty free. So we spent a lot of time just raising a whole bunch of hell. That's the way I got to know Tom. He started getting serious about his work about the same time I did—I mean things started happening that took us out of the streets and into the studio and back to the typewriter."

What inspired pause in this debauch was some sense, in each man, of the passing of one era and the debut of another. McGuane would explore the notion of commitment above reasonable excess as a seventies alternative, while Buffett would vitiate the despair of post-sixties tristesse with a total exploitation of physicality. His lyrics would become anthem to the seventies good life: sun, sailing, sex, righteous dope and tropical libations in quantity.

The irony of Buffett as papa-san to this Key West version of Outlaw Chic, was that he, like McGuane, had suffered a harsh Roman Catholic upbringing where any notion of physical pleasure induced nightmares of perdition. Buffett had attended McGill Institute, a Catholic boys' school in Mobile, where, like McGuane and prep school hipsters everywhere, he turned to bullshit as release. "It was the only way to let your imagination go. Because everything else was pretty well cut off. You were taught if you jerked off that you'd go blind, and if you died with mortal sin you'd go straight to Hell and be roasted like a goddamned piece of pork on a skewer. So any kind of physical pleasure was eliminated through religious training. Lying was the only outlet. I used to make incredible bullshit stories. I loved to do it and would risk punishment to see how far I could get. That's terrible to admit—"

But bullshit was excellent practice for the type of story telling Buffett would incorporate into his music; songs which celebrated escape, fantasy gratification and evocation of place, Key West, an island Xanadu which miniatured chaos and lent dreams focus.

Key West had remained a haven for writers since Ernest Hemingway stepped ashore there in 1928, taking the next ten years to inculcate in our parents that special brand of tough-guy hipsterism which was his forte. McGuane once had replied to a comparison between his life and Hemingway's: "I can only agree that they appear to be very similar. . . . What might be more pertinent is to think how my father was influenced by Hemingway. Places like the Keys and northern Michigan, those were places I was taken by my father."* Romantic hipsters of every stripe invaded Key West during the seventies, seeking to weave loose threads of sixties illumination into the ancestral fabric of that Hemingway myth. Though few seventies Key Westers might have articulated it. They responded more to post-World War conditioning in another guise—the lure of small-town life with a tough guy, outlaw overlay, an attraction disconcerting to pinpoint. Of course no one could miss Ernest Hemingway. His face was pasted all over town.

Buffett rejoiced in the literariness of Key West. "I was writing a ton of stuff. Key West has always been a good place to write. But it took me out of the mainstream of music for a while. There were no other songwriters. They were all literary, you know, novelists. There was no music scene in Key West. There were local bands and I'd go in and jam, but there was nobody on a contemporary level."

Removed from Nashville and L. A., Buffett allowed island music to launder his psyche; pulsating Latin rhythms adored since childhood underscore a Carribean sense of *carpe diem,* above a down-home addiction to rock 'n' roll. Buffett's music developed in counterpoint to that late sixties cerebralism and obsession with technology which proved the bane of rock, as it

* Portrait of the Artist as a Young Director," John Dorschner. *The Miami Herald,* October 13, 1974.

lingered in most manifestations of sixties art throughout the early seventies. Buffett hid in Key West and let it all slip by. The music he produced was nearly prophetic in its concern for delicate ecologies of neighborhood and wilderness; or Key West and the sea. But he may have written too well. Key West would change more quickly for the precision of his art. Like Hemingway, Buffett was inculcating a fresh myth of salvation.

"You had to have the realization in the back of your mind that places like Key West were rapidly disappearing from terra firma. I feel no responsibility for hastening Key West's demise. To me, at the time, it was paradise."

Real estate people, greedy politicians, legions of the unhip capitalizing upon a once hip enclave—that is what befell Key West by the late seventies. Buffett had seen it happen before. He had lived in New Orleans ('66–'69) during its post-bohemian, pre-hippie phase, and had watched a beloved cityscape deteriorate. He had worked to capture that fragile period in song before it blew away. Much of his early composition struggled with Montana, its ghost towns; Livingston, the changing relationship of contemporaries to wilderness, and small towns which punctuated it. Buffett lived outside Aspen, Colorado now, a town which could not better typify the conflicts of hip and environment. Were mythographers such as Hemingway, Buffett, McGuane justifiable celebrants of magical landscape, or were they business speculators mining a product guiltlessly as the most rapacious building contractors?

"Come on down to Colorado," Jimmy said, after we'd slurred goodbyes late Sunday morning. "I'm giving a concert Friday, then I'll take you on the road with Bonnie Raitt."

Buffett was off in a private plane he'd hired to fly himself plus acquired gear low over Yellowstone Park, back along the Rockies to home.

I took the next few days to say goodbye to Montana, so long to mountains, trails, saloons, back roads, cheap cafes and good friends I'd consorted with for two and one half months. I saved heartiest goodbyes for Livingston. After a party Wednesday night at Hjortsberg's, I grabbed my gear at the Murray, slugged down a double dose of speed and hit Yellowstone Park by dawn

... not a camper in sight, but a zoo's worth of deer, elk, antelope and bear clumped together in herds as I brodied through cramped turns, mist clouding the valley, tape deck up high, the sadness of a chapter closed tugging at my heart as I powered through Wyoming, seventeen hours to Colorado and the prospect of something new.

I raised the Hotel Jerome, Aspen, at eight that night and before I had time to register Buffett called "Toby!" from the bar. He was drinking in a barroom which enveloped the most glamorous women I'd seen—certainly in recent months. Expensive cars out front should have warned me; Jerome was an 1889 hotel left over from Aspen's silver mining days, a different boomtown era, one no less exploitive than Aspen's current incarnation as "Hollywood of the Rockies." I'd parked my Jeep out front and sauntered through Jerome's polished Victoriana attired in soiled Levis, Justin roughouts and a leather flyer's jacket, Randall hunting knife at my belt. Everywhere people were in silk or tailored denim. I'd last visited Aspen in 1972, had thought it fancy. What I encountered now zapped me into culture shock more intimidating than coma. Within hours Buffett had ensconced me in a two-story condominium at Snowmass Village, fireplace warming each bedroom, fireplace downstairs, fireplace warming the fucking kitchen, costing God knows how many hundreds a day. I was to share it with Buffett's bus driver. Other Buffett functionaries inhabited condominiums about the Village. It became instantly clear that Buffett's and McGuane's turns on the road leaving Key West had charted startlingly divergent courses.

Buffett's bus was a 1976 Silver Eagle, Greyhound-size, customized to a cross between a psychedelic van and a sailing ship. It had six mag wheels, chromed, a mural on its flank of a sailboat with tropical sunset, portholes aft and a mock-teak interior. It was parked before our condominium where vacationers in yellow jogging suits ogled it suspiciously. I took a look myself, then hiked through a forest of townhouses, past swimming pools, paddle tennis courts, calisthenic and outdoor ballet classes, hunting coffee and a bite to eat. I was fighting to regroup. The transition from a four-dollar-a-night room in a railroad hotel in Livingston, Montana to a condo in Snowmass Village I found precarious to bridge. Last evening had been long. Buffett had rehearsed with his band, then retired to Aspen's Holiday Inn lounge, where he jammed with Vassar Clements. It had gotten drunk out. I was exhausted. Artificial stimulants could not perk me up. All around was an army of functionaries—Buffett's band, sound men and road crew—which confused me further. I felt overexposed to the twentieth century. Suddenly I was back East, consorting with Easterners in an Eastern-style resort. Aspen seemed some Key West of the Rockies, stultifying in its pretensions toward chic, hopelessly opportunistic and dangerously bourgeois.

I'd first seen Aspen during the summer of 1969 and catalogued it, with Key West, as one of two small towns in the United States I could consider inhabiting. It was—simply beautiful. Like Key West, Aspen was a nineteenth-century community with a hip overlay, offering easy access to wilderness with enough "urban" culture to keep one from flying back East every other month. Aspen had been founded on silver mining, but since the 1940s relied economically on sport and art. Specifically, skiing and music: the Aspen Skiing Corporation and Aspen Music Festival instituted concomitantly to attract athlete and aesthete. In recent years, sport and art about Aspen had spread to epidemic proportions. Backpacker and four-wheel-drive chic vied with skiing for top stakes in the tourist derby; rock and a stunted version of Outlaw Chic had supplanted "serious" music as cultural draw. On the tide of both swam speculators in real estate, housing, and art.

By 1970, enough sixties refugees and conservatives of unconventional bent had settled in Aspen to encourage Hunter S. Thompson to run for sheriff of Pitkin County—on an antigrowth ticket. Thompson, who then had one published book to his credit, *Hell's Angels,* campaigned with shaved head and the untempered promise to sod Aspen's streets, minimalizing vehicular traffic, and to more or less legitimize drugs. He wanted to change Aspen's name to Fat City, thereby discouraging commercial exploitation. Thompson lost, but not by much. He was ahead of his time. Between 1970 and 1973—when an antigrowth candidate was elected mayor—condominiumism hit its stride. Speculators did their damnedest to cash in. Pitkin County suffered. By 1976, the tide was said to have turned, but Aspen had become synonymous with Rocky Mountain High and legions of the hip unhip maintained influx. A Detroit automobile had lifted the town's name, as had a best-selling novel, plus countless fashion lines. Thompson himself, through his writing and lifestyle, had done much to celebrate Aspen. The fact that he *lived* nearby was enough. Superstars attracted by Aspen's microcosmic cultural life, plus its various chics, had transformed the town into a suburb of Los Angeles. Aspen threatened to supplant Palm Springs as Hollywood's favorite resort. Mercedes and lush four-wheel-drives jammed Aspen's streets at nearly any hour. The traffic was horrendous. To think, I had been attracted in 1969 to this small Rocky Mountain hideaway for its simplicity and quiet.

News that Cher had bequeathed herself "a condo in Aspen" as signification of her marriage to Greg Allman, was, for me, the final word. I got on the phone to McGuane.

"Head back up here if you're freaked," Tom said. "We've got antelope chili for supper and I've just been firing my flintlock."

But I wanted the whole dose. Wanted specifically to ascertain Buffett's part in this cultural morass; how he might be exploiting Aspen through art, how he lived as an artist, and how he amalgamated business and art through the machinations of a seventies rock star.

The afternoon of Buffett's concert we met at the Jerome bar; Jimmy was intense but not tense. I tracked his borrowed Mercedes eighteen miles out Highway 82 to Snowmass proper, where he was living—in a friend's house, it should be noted, in a spare bedroom. We parked by a river where Buffett showed me property he had bought: a weathered ranch house connected to the road by a covered bridge. Eighteen miles was close enough to Aspen for Buffett. "I'd live in Montana except that I like to get a good meal—and a little excitement," he said. "I'm not ready to cash it all in for Friday night parties at the ranch." The house where Buffett stayed was less pretentious and, spacewise, less comfortable than the condominium I occupied. It was a suburban-style ranch house in a cluster of mates, no different for their mountain setting than a thousand others circumscribing Cleveland. The antique saddle Buffett had purchased jockied for space in a utility room with a matching washer-dryer. We settled onto a couch before that Indian rug with cans of beer.

"Artists are the most discriminated-against people," Buffett said, as if that idea had recently occurred to him. "Writers, musicians, painters ... I'm buying this piece of property here and my business credentials are as clean and good ... but like the realtor told me, he said: If this was anybody else's financial situation, any other occupation, there'd be no doubt at this moment we'd have the money. But for you, they want to check you out. So you learn to live with it. Because it's easier to play the game and beat them, than to try from the start to antagonize them. You just hope you'll reach the point where you won't have to pay more for a fucking phone deposit than a normal citizen does."

I thought about that. "There are so many artists in the world who are broke," I said. "You and I know a million of them. They feel guilty about making too little money. Have you felt guilty about making too much?"

"No," Buffett said.

"I guess that would be like, if you're a Catholic, getting to heaven and feeling guilty about that."

Buffett laughed. "It's—just the fact that I didn't sacrifice my integrity to become wealthy. The norm for a successful singer or songwriter, the way most people think, would be to live in L. A. or Nashville on a huge ranch, drive a Mercedes and hang out at the rock scene. You're supposed to be cast in these molds. I don't feel guilty about making that much money because I have worked hard for it. Long, hard hours. It's a fact that I'm generous with anybody who needs anything. I'm not sitting there trying to hoard it and spitting blue flames from my mouth to draw six bucks a head. It's obvious that people wouldn't come to the shows if they thought they were getting ripped off. We've had one commercial hit, *Come Monday,* and our albums sell a hundred to two hundred thousand copies. We don't have this huge following."

I had to admit, there seemed little of the rip-off in Buffett's attitude toward Aspen. Maybe he had learned from Key West. He'd written no hip "Rocky Mountain High"s, sang no songs directly related to Aspen, and did no business there except for the occasional concert. He'd lived with the same woman for years. Buffett's business sense appeared slicker on its surface than, say, McGuane's—Jimmy wasn't breeding quarter horses. Perhaps that was the shiniest new tool of Outlaw Chic. Buffett consorted with musicians, accredited outlaws such as Hunter Thompson and politicos. He fit no precise mold.

Thanks to his background, I thought, which remained stolidly middle class. For all his frolicking, Buffett had taken a journalism-history degree from the University of Southern Mississippi, and had worked a year for *Billboard,* the music industry's principal trade sheet, as a staff editorial writer. There was something startlingly practical about having taken that job. Buffett quit the day his first album came out, but he'd packed in a year of learning Nashville's business side—a conservative move any post-WW II father would have applauded. Buffett's roots in sixties folk music, with its literary pretensions, plus the narrative focus of his songs in an era of technological overkill, likewise separated him from the norm. Buffett had been a reader from childhood; he'd disappeared into Mobile's public library afternoons on end with volumes of Coleridge, A. E. Housman, Rudyard Kipling. His push toward the theatricality of rock 'n' roll had been tempered by a real interest in literature. His songs were literary, some nearly Kiplingesque. Musically, he was original. Culturally (despite trappings of rock and pretensions toward Outlaw Chic) Buffett fit no category except middle class. He was like some disaffected grad student with a split major in Business and Art who'd decided to pursue both paths.

"You're trying from the start to be successful, and you're lying to yourself if you don't admit that. I don't go out for aesthetic value alone, you know. I want to live comfortably."

Buffett's secondary ambitions remained literary: to write screenplays, poetry, journalism, a novel about pre-seventies New Orleans, and nonfiction about rock stars—"a book which will probably tell the opposite of what everybody thinks. I mean, we don't get laid every night by beautiful women. Most of the time it's backgammon and getting stoned on the bus with people on the road."

I thought to ask what Buffett's earliest recollection of literary success might have been. Something far away as childhood.

"In Catholic school we had to write an autobiography. I don't remember what year. I was still an altar boy. Probably sixth grade. You were supposed to write it from the vantage point of when you were thirty. I was going to be a priest of course. So I wrote it from that viewpoint. It was entitled: *My Compass Points to Heaven.* I remember the cover. It was blue with a compass seal I'd designed showing north-south-east-west. It was one of the top five autobiographies and it got read in class."

Twenty years later that compass seal would reappear on the cover to *Changes in Latitudes, Changes in Attitudes*—an album which would top *Billboard*'s charts and, with the popularity of "Margaritaville," establish Buffett as the most successful new product in Rock.

> *Nibblin' on sponge cake*
> *Watchin' the sun bake*
> *All of those tourists*
> *Covered with oil.*
> *Strummin' my six string*
> *On the front porch swing*
> *Smell those shrimp they're beginning to boil . . .**

Wastin' away again in Margaritaville. Tonight, Snowmass Village chapter, where Buffett's music ricocheted about the interior of an overlarge circus tent, the tent itself rippling nautically in a valley of ski lifts, condominiums, chic brasseries, boutiques, hot therapy pools . . . in short, that barrier reef of monied excess which was Aspen in exurbia. Everywhere were battalions of the unhip costumed in predictable down vests, Western shirts and leather Topsiders, hooting like frat kids at Homecoming and stomping along to every favorite Buffett lyric. Jimmy onstage was energetic, vital, but reminiscent of something antediluvian in popular culture, something prewar, nearly surfer in its noncha-

* *"Margaritaville."* Words and music by Jimmy Buffett. Used by permission of Coral Reefer Music/Outer Banks Music.

lance. Buffett wore T-shirt, jeans and jogging shoes—physical embodiment of the relaxed life. His blond hair shimmered under the lights, perspiration dripped from the tip of his nose. His audience fell off their chairs, drunk, drugged and giving not a damn. Their unself-conscious enthusiasm was pre-seventies, but their inebriation was current. Not an unwarped brain in the bunch.

I'd been speaking with Hunter Thompson, himself cranked up with contradictions of this scene, enjoying Buffett's music but abashed at the surroundings, what had befallen his beloved Colorado. "This is as strange to me as it is to you," Hunter said, shuddering beneath the weight of Snowmass' condominiums. We stood on a wooden deck outside that circus tent where Buffett was well into his second show. The crowd had not ceased screaming. We were hard by the bar, a relief. The chic unchic pressed close. Hunter was dressed in a red and white golf cap, red windbreaker and doubleknit slacks. He wore white basketball shoes. He looked like some Andy Warhol of Aspen's bohemia, dressed like what he most despised. His hair was professionally trimmed. In years past, when hip had been ethos rather than fashion, Hunter had flaunted black turtlenecks, Levis and a shaved head. He had run with Hell's Angels and taken solace from a magical San Francisco underground. What transpired here, ten short years later, seemed beyond irony. Hunter himself had become culture hero to the sort of fraternity goons he regularly crucified in *Rolling Stone*. King Contradiction kept a drink in his hand, his right knee pumping.

The sixties had proved devastating to impractical romantics such as Hunter Thompson . . . to any artist who cringed at a capitalization upon his individuality, but who'd seen that first mass movement toward hip as the coming of a new order—one which might appease loneliness, particularly of the writer-hipster's life, by the wiring of community. Or communalization of the wired. Whenever fashion encountered business, however, compromises were effected which blunted the corners of hip. The ethos of hip was beyond compromise, it was too infantile, too grounded in individual gratification. Still, there had been a moment. The sixties were a time when anything had seemed possible, even the communalization of hip. Hunter and other fiction-oriented writers had turned from fantasy to street life as subject matter; now that street again was one way, and they were finding it difficult to reverse. Hunter was having real trouble producing contracted journalism for *Rolling Stone.* He was a novelist who'd been seduced toward journalism by the promise of the sixties. With that promise shattered, no wonder he and myriad artists were working poorly. How could one comfortably retreat to fantasy when the future fantasized was bleak?

We'd been discussing the writer's predicament when I hazarded this observation: "Everything you publish these days seethes with a contempt you bring to journalism."

Hunter stared at me. "There are not many people who get that," he said. "You're the first who's said it." I figured he was pulling my leg. But his expression was grave. What kind of sycophants had Hunter been privy to these past years that such a comment could upset?

All I need do was glance around. They were everywhere, drunk as their fathers on aged bourbon, loaded on expensive dope, raucous, conformist, more rightist in their leftist posture than a hundred ad execs on Madison Avenue. Buffett riled them onstage, working all the favorite Key West numbers, nostalgic canapés, the Montana hucklebucks, booze, dope and get-drunk-and-screw songs, like the Beach Boys in concert at a college weekend. There was innocence to the infectiousness of his music; half of that was comforting. But the nether half was dark. Distant from reality, lobotomized to lessons of the sixties—of war, race relations, corruption in government, exploitation of resources—to a point where it sounded like the sixties never happened. We had regressed to the morning of that decade suffering a lately departed president, discord in the streets, and "Let's Go Surfin' " on the jukebox. I looked about this Snowmass audience and spotted not one black face, not one Indian. It was the American suburbs at Rocky Mountain High. That suburbia removed from Vietnam and Watergate as fish in the sea.

Thompson felt this, I thought, and it amused me to watch the old hipster fidget. Buffett in some aggravated posture epitomized the seventies unhipster in that he synthesized divergent tendencies toward business, art (the business of selling oneself), rock and theater, with its horse opera fantasies of Outlaw Chic. But something was terribly wrong. Aspen's return to theatricality was precise: If Vietnam had been the farthest reach of Westward Expansionism, tupping the Oriental mind, a retreat to horse opera delusionisms which had promulgated Vietnam was, pathologically, a healthful step. But without some recollection of lessons learned there, some obeisance to that primitivism first engendered by rhythm and blues, later apotheosized by My Lai and countless slittings of countless Oriental throats—the culture seemed doomed. Most especially what survived of hip. The logical step back from theater was to street—not street theater of the late sixties with its middle-class solidarity in numbers—but to sidewalks of the inner city, a retreat to hipsterism, to urban life, and a reassessment of primitive beneath the scar tissue of the decade. These Aspenites were so far removed from street-corner hipsters who had godfathered their chic, they'd likely never make it home.

Aspen, once an end-of-the-road town sanctified as Key West, blew rank with their putrescence. Aspen appealed to the worst instincts of the white middle class, and was itself an environmental My Lai. What once had been primitive, the countryside, had been machine-gunned by speculators in real estate, sport and art.

I looked round for Hunter, but he had fled. Buffett was slowing things down; he was singing softly now.

> *Years grow shorter not longer*
> *The more you've been on your own*
> *Feelings for movin' grow stronger*
> *So you wonder why you ever go home.**

There was a despair at the center of Buffett's frivolity which rescued him as an artist. Speaking of Key West, and tangentially Aspen, Buffett had remarked:

"It's melodrama, you know. It's a lot of comedy heaped on a lot of tragedy. The despair comes from the fact that it's the end of

---

* "Wonder Why We Ever Go Home." Words and music by Jimmy Buffett. Copyright © 1977. Used by permission of Coral Reefer Music.

the road. I mean you can't go any further without leaving your car, which would be too un-American for most people. Consequently you pile up this menagerie of people. Most of them have seen better times. They flipped out or they drank too much booze or their lady left them or they shot somebody. And they slid. If I couldn't get another date, another contract, it was done, I was broke, my car ran off the road, I didn't have a dime ... what would I do? I'd go back to the islands. Because there'd be a terrible shock to my system. A terrible blow to my ego. But I know I'd survive, because I could go back there, and I could be living that life."

I wondered if it wasn't too late.

POSTCRIPT: In September of 1977, McGuane and Buffett's sister, Laurie, were married. Buffett had been married in August to Jane Slagsvol, his long-time companion. A daughter, Savannah Jane, was born to the Buffetts in June, 1979. *Changes in Latitudes, Changes in Attitudes* went platinum, selling one million three hundred thousand copies. By June, 1979, Buffett's subsequent album, *Son of a Son of a Sailor,* had sold one million five. Buffett was composing sound tracks and had written an impressive cover story for *Outside* magazine, on Antigua Sailing Week. Hunter Thompson was holed up in Buffett's apartment in Key West, writing a screenplay. A movie was being made of his life. McGuane's novel *Panama* had appeared to mixed reviews, the New York press proving most vitriolic—a signed rave in *The New Yorker,* New York's most noteworthy exception. The following letter arrived from Tom in June:

"Dear Toby,

"Had a lariat break last night, nylon rope, came back and hit me right in the middle of my head and gave me a concussion. Percodan currently courses through my veins and consequently I'm a leetle goofy. ...

"A lot of the stuff I was saying came true, and some anyway didn't. My disenchantment with the word passed. Writing prose is again the ballast for everything. I'm at work on a long Montana

book, hopefully a final outlaw volume, meant to take that disagreeable stance once and for all as far as I can. I want to: look deep into the eyes of Jesse James, try to figure out why democracy makes you trigger happy; and burn some churches.

"The ranch is a great passion with us. We are raising cutting horses, running yearling cattle and raising dry land hay on our place up the Boulder, on Poison Creek, where the eagle traps the Indians made are still in the rimrocks. I'm growing my own serrano peppers to dry and give my friends; and to make antelope chili when it gets cold again.

"It's grand to be able to report to you that I am absolutely happy, have one of those marriages twenty lifetimes might never produce. We're expecting a baby in December, a special thing because Laurie had major surgery last winter that left childbearing a little in doubt. Laurie's daughter Heather; Thomas and Maggie make this a frequently noisy madhouse but I think everyone knows where home is. The ranch is over 1000 acres now and I am sneakily pleased when people call me Big Daddy: I don't know whether it's Amin or Varner; or that I weigh 200 lbs: I just like it.

"I've been in this house longer than any house in my life. I feel an inchoate devotion to the idea of 'Montana' as a society of government-hating nesters. As forty approaches, I want to write thirty indelible American novels, a shithouseload of original movies, have an unconscionable number of kids, train a world champion cutting horse, run a big cattle ranch that has no farmland on it, addict myself to opium at eighty and die five years later when increased tolerance makes it too tiresome for us to refill the pipes and fetch the scrapbook one more time.

"Fond regards,

"Tom"

Futures

Home in Washington the act of survival became the art of collating attitudes.

In less than a month I sought out and consulted: the commander of the National Socialist White People's Party; a futurist, formerly a Mississippi civil rights worker and founder of Earth Day; a born-again Christian, formerly a sixties computer person; a gentleman fox hunter, formerly a radical ordinary-language philosopher; a cabinet maker, formerly a business student, now building manager of the Freer Gallery; a black feminist, formerly a Black Panther, civil rights worker, member of SNCC, SDS and NAACP, for two years chairperson of the National Women's Political Caucus, currently in the Human Resources department of the Corporation for Public Broadcasting; an English teacher-fictionist, formerly disc jockey during Vietnam for the Far East Network, later a screenwriter for Otto Preminger; a communard at Woodstock since 1969; a Jehovah's Witness, formerly hip musician and painter; a disaffected CIA agent, cofounder of *Counterspy,* the Mailer-funded journal dedicated to exposing CIA activity abroad; a radical Indian; a male psychiatric nurse, "Queen of the Queens" around Washington during the sixties, a black who had struggled against racial and sexual oppression; a black guitarist, a hipster during the fifties, a reformed alcoholic, now a fruitarian and night club owner.

There was a pattern to these peregrinations, though often it eluded me.

Over lunch one afternoon, I listened while a friend interviewed an ex-Special Forces captain for *Rolling Stone.* "The proudest thing in my life," this veteran said, "was having been commander of a Special Forces A-team in combat." Lean, manic, with stringy red hair, the fellow was articulate about veterans' problems on every level. He was bitter. An ex-Viet Vet Against the War, he held no empathy for draft evaders or deserters. "It's much easier to make war than love," he smirked. He'd served in Vietnam's Central Highlands between '68 and '70, having extended for a second tour. He'd come home to find his wife reconciled to his death, suffering "anticipatory grief." They'd divorced. Max Cleland (head of the Veterans Administration) was an establishment Ron Kovics, he said. VA hospitals were the biggest drunk tanks in the country. He'd witnessed combat atrocities but felt he'd served his country honorably. Though he detested America's involvement in Vietnam, he was "ready to go" if a legitimate conflict arose. He talked for an hour about veterans' problems—medical, economic and psychological. I thought of Corinne.

"What about female Viet vets?"

"Only two percent of the problem," he said. "They weren't combat vets so they don't really count. Most WACS were unattractive women following a war to get laid."

I paid my tab and hit the street.

A week earlier, Corinne had left for Nepal. She'd landed a job with the Tom Dooley Foundation; would trek from village to Himalayan village, inoculating natives, teaching health care, spouting Nepali. She would be gone two years. Our marriage was finished. Having pushed back the boundaries of Westward Expansionism to central Asia, she somehow transcended Vietnam, transfiguring her experience there to a more personal quest. She needed the company of primitives, to feel needed in primitive communities. Two years in the bush might suffice. She'd strapped on her boots.

Likewise ambulatory, I parked my automobile whenever practicable and hiked throughout the inner city. For a month I'd not crossed the Capital Beltway, felt drawn the more powerfully toward city-center, avoiding circumferentials and suburbs like Armageddon. Washington blew cold with the onset of winter, black as the future, but not mandatorily bleak. Black could be bright. Assuredly brighter than that fate allowed white suburbia. An article caught my eye in *Historic Preservation,* tracing the development of suburbia to a Victorian fascination with rural cemeteries. That amused. The suburbs had inherited even the Victorians' preoccupation with death. Their hanging out in landscaped graveyards had led to our hanging in. Now the cities were decaying and suburbia lunged back. Its necrophilia was appalling. Rehab was revitalization, but at what cost? Poor blacks were pushed out, unequivocally, toward the suburbs. Would that be their final ignominy?

Washington was the town to ponder such injustices, for it was black, seventy-five percent black, overseen by a white Congress and Metropolitan Board of Trade ... a black colony some sneered, with no vote in Congress, a black mayor and city council with little political power, and a constituency surrounded by the richest-per-capita suburbs in America. After '68's riots, Washington four blocks from the White House and east had been no man's land. White suburbanites hesitated to drive through the inner city, let alone live there. Now they infiltrated in battalions, purchasing Victorian townhouses gutted since Martin Luther King's death ... refurbishing them, moving into black neighborhoods or selling their investments for triple profit. White middle-class liberals who fifteen years previous might have marched at Selma or sat in at Birmingham today displaced black families from ancestral neighborhoods with skyrocketed rents and the developers' frenzy to restore. Blacks were forced east to overcrowded Anacostia or suburban Prince George's County. The irony of this being that inner-city blacks the white liberal displaced were those who had rescued him from doldrums of mid-century suburbia ... through rhythm and blues, expressive sexuality, civil rights, and the ethos of hip.

It seemed no accident that heaviest white influx had begun post-Vietnam. America's first integrated war, it had stacked whites in close proximity to blacks, to black patois, black style, inner-city hip and attendant garnishments. Not the least of which was exposure to marijuana. Blacks had comprised perhaps ten percent of Vietnam's armed forces, but they'd held fifty percent of the combat roles. White Americans freshly confronted with absurdity—an absurd war, America's absurd commitment there—took comfort from those who'd been living with absurdity for centuries. Little wonder they might wish to further the association post-armistice. Urban life, not suburban, had fostered that grace under pressure. Life in the city was a war of sorts. Its attrition held revenues only guessed at genetically, in some presuburban collective unconscious.

Vietnamese discos rocked Fourteenth Street, where Kevin Walsh had operated his black night club in 1960. To see Vietnamese women dance was to comprehend an added element of the complexities of our involvement. The Vietnamese were coolness and grace. America's newest immigrants, they were her newest niggers; they would accept wages even the black would spit at. Too fresh in-country to have become streetwise, they were wary to test a spanking new culture with chiseling and petty graft. America assimilated Vietnamese the way she'd assimilated Germans and Japanese—exploiting postwar desperation with overlong hours and the "opportunity" to excel. Vietnamese had snatched most jobs available to domestics and were sparring with Hispanics for restaurant work—busing, waiting tables. A few had opened restaurants of their own, the pungency of *nuoc mam* contesting oddly with burger stench in the American night, over a sour reek of beer. Fourteenth Street, traditional boundary between black and white Washingtons, boiled like Tu Do Street, Saigon. White prostitutes—kids from the suburbs, barely fifteen—joined blacks in platoons at every corner. The neon of sex shops hawked pornography, prosthetic devices, "marital" aids, massages, rank hand jobs and lip service toe to pate. It was the old-fashioned, Wild West of American nightlife. But with a moroseness to its glittering. Unemployed veterans, black and white, congregated in empty lots, swilling wine and bitching about the future. More prosperous veterans paid their money and took a best shot. Nobody appeared happy with his alternatives. The war seemed to have wrought some elemental change.

If there was a religion of hipsterism left, it was of the dead hipster such as Elvis, who one year post-mortem had become an industry for producing memorabilia; or the re-created hipster such as Bruce Springsteen, who via theatricality summoned the magic of a long-lost summer of rock 'n' roll. Street hip was a flourish, so unrealistic as to approach camp. Hipster infantilism was archaic now. Vietnam and a post-armistice economy had made everyone old. It was like the nineteen-thirties downtown, a new sophistication distinguishing those who held jobs from those who shuffled raggedly on the dole. Have discarded World War II imperatives in Vietnam, America had stepped back to Depression. You could see it in the contradictions. Middle-class whites might have retreated from Vietnam through Outlaw Chic to an urban experimentation reminiscent of "going up to Harlem," but the urban black had a darker Harlem to rediscover. The end of the road for him was less likely to be Aspen, Key West or some pre-World War II cityscape than unemployment, jail and the rapid emasculation of poverty.

A most startling post-Vietnam contradiction was the renewed proliferation of racism. Perhaps twelve years in the maw of Asian culture entitled Americans to an isolationism of sorts. Hate groups such as the Ku Klux Klan and American Nazi Party were enjoying a banner season. Black, Jewish, Chicano, Indian and Chinese American activists responded with promulgations of tribalism. It all seemed part of the new conservatism, a dipping back to pre-sixties ethics in search of stability. America had been racist so long; there were those who conjectured America's rage against Hitler had been but response to an unbearable vision of self. Certainly civil rights had been a liberal bloodletting, a resettling of the White Man's Burden. Hip had been racist from its inception—assuming primitivism as racial characteristic rather than by-product of social deprivation. All blacks were hip no more than all possessed rhythm. That fact was driven home with the rise of a black middle-class which wanted nothing of inner-city contradictions but preferred hightailing it to the suburbs. Those whites who accommodated with an intracultural musical chairs encroached upon urban blacks as thoroughly as they'd transgressed psychic boundaries of hip. It had taken white musicians only half a decade to wipe blacks off the sixties hit parade, exterminating r&b and rock 'n' roll with the technologies of rock. Would they do the same for urban life in the eighties? Not likely. Economics would not permit. Racism was at least openly expressed, personally encountered; gone were the days of suburban isolationism. We were immigrants again. Both inner city and suburbia resembled New York's Lower East Side, circa 1900: diverse ethnic groups bubbling amid the slumgullion of America.

You could rehab your Victorian townhouse in the ghetto, flee to suburbia, strap on a $150,000 mortgage at either remove—or you could come in from a different angle. A group of white middle-class Catholics, the Community for Creative Non-Violence, had done just that. Creative non-violence was a term coined by Martin Luther King; since 1970, CCNV had been pursuing that ideal in the heart of black Washington. Dedicated to a redistribution of the middle class's "ill-gotten goods" among the poor, they were thirty full-time volunteers, living communally, who'd established a free medical clinic, a pre-trial house with free legal aid, a soup kitchen feeding six hundred people daily, a hospice where the destitute might sleep, a print shop where the unskilled might learn a trade, and a program of policing winter sidewalks, with a van that transported homeless from heating grates to night shelters. Of the thousand or so intentional communities which had collapsed in downtown Washington since the sixties, CCNV was a noteworthy survivor. Like the National Socialist White People's Party (George Lincoln Rockwell's American Nazis) in suburban Arlington, CCNV was one of a handful of politically oriented communes which had weathered the seventies.

Committed to divergent solutions of America's racial problems, the two collectives afforded striking comparisons. Both lived communally on subsistence wages, both proselytized politically, both demonstrated in the street, both saw the black's economic future as central to domestic tranquility—each was involved emotionally with that issue. One sought excoriation through hatred, the other exorcism through love. The Nazis wished to ship blacks back to Africa, CCNV to shelter and clothe. The Nazis sought a revamped nationalism, CCNV a reintegrated neighborhoodism. Both were socialists of sorts.

At Nazi Party headquarters in Arlington I'd knocked on a plain wooden door beneath a black swastika and was admitted—to an antechamber where an armed storm trooper presided over desk and blinking telephone, distributing hate literature to Party visitors and channeling calls deep within the organization. Visible through an interior door was an arsenal of weapons. Ushered to a conference room adjacent to the commander's quarters, I was confronted with the commanding officer seated at a long table before a red and black nazi flag, flanked by portraits of Rockwell and Adolf Hitler. An armed trooper stood at parade rest.

At the Community for Creative Non-Violence I'd knocked on a glass door beneath a hand-painted sign and watched as keys sailed from the sky to a child who'd scampered up behind. I'd met the child's mother, Kathleen Guinan, wife of CCNV's founder, and followed her up a rickety flight of stairs, listened as she matter-of-factly recounted her Connecticut middle-class upbringing and subsequent affiliation with CCNV, laughed as she joked about a sixties infatuation with San Francisco and a flirtation with the Haight—particularly to a drawn-out tale of Owsley the acid king, who'd escorted her one night to dinner, stopping by a large apartment building of perhaps fifty units, bicycles out front, obviously family occupied, but actually housing an LSD factory, nary a family about, the interior a vast acid works hiding chemists in laboratory gear. I'd sat before a bay window at CCNV headquarters watching traffic on Fourteenth Street, the hookers, the pimps, as Kathleen reminisced about Kansas towns she'd loved as a traveler and downplayed romance of that inner city she'd occupied five years, saying that anyone who could escape the ghetto should. She spoke of poor black men, their egos shattered by an inability to support families, beaten by a terrible cycle of failing to find jobs, drinking, seeing their children starve, living on sidewalks, in warehouses. . . . Within fifty square blocks, seven to ten thousand Washingtonians were destitute. CCNV helped welfare mothers with eight children sleeping on a single bedroom floor, in squalor, their families crumbled, by assuring one solid meal a day and adequate medical care. But there were limits to what a private, unfunded organization could accomplish. Over one hundred doctors and lawyers offered services to the clinic, D.C. markets were generous with spare food . . . but the system was diseased, wanted major surgery. Ed Guinan was whom I should speak to: CCNV's founder, a forty-two-year-old ex-stockbroker, priest, cohort of King in the sixties, the Berrigans in the seventies, who was devoting his life to this work.

There was a chilled, nearly winter feel to the afternoon this Sunday before Columbus Day. Whores were active at Fourteenth and N, alongside CCNV's headquarters, working a block as rife with prostitution as any in America. They shivered in satin shorts and abbreviated halters. It was a beautiful, windy-cold day after a rainy night and morning. I transgressed the ghetto in a psychic squadcar. Outside Zacchaeus House, a sandwich line of eighty derelicts stretched toward the corner past CCNV's Hospitality House, where staff members and homeless cheered the Redskins on TV and shared a supper of chicken wings, stewed vegetables and chocolate flan. Ed Guinan expected me at Community headquarters—itself reworked Victoriana, a former brothel leased by the Community and alchemized to an impecunious temple of love.

Guinan was reading in a corner of CCNV's common room, oblivious to commotion as only one well-accustomed to communal life can be. He wore a brown gingham shirt, tan corduroys and desert boots. He had an Irish face with a pronounced nose beneath a full head of blondish gray hair. Kathleen introduced us. Ed was cordial, but street-wary of hype or any inroad to the cheap shot. Within ten minutes we were communicating. Children banged about, two of them Ed and Kathleen's. CCNV members sauntered through on errands or in search of company. The racket of light carpentry offered counterpoint to kitchen noises and a scuttle of traffic. Fourteenth Street was not quite dark.

"Let's make it simple," I said. "Where were you in 1960?"

Guinan's stare was a challenge. "In San Francisco. Entering

the financial market, training as a securities trader. I'd just left the University of Colorado."

I nodded. He eased into it.

Like Henry Di Giacinto, whose hegira had led him from Green Berets to securities, Guinan had a background in recon, having served in a naval air group on top-secret missions against China. He'd been a radioman. Born in Denver, to a blue-collar family who'd hustled during the Depression, Guinan had joined the navy out of the high school, "not then being older and wiser." That was the tail-end of Korea. He'd completed college on the G. I. Bill, taking a degree in international finance. San Francisco, between 1960 and 1964, provided Guinan with the opportunity to experience a higher end of that consumer chain he'd rattled as a child. It was party-time for the future priest: trips to Acapulco, a Victorian townhouse in San Francisco, an apartment across the bay in Sausalito, fat salary, Jaguar in the garage, steaks in the freezer .... "You finally have some bucks, so you throw it around a little." But disaffection set in early.

"Radical shifts in my life have always followed any introduction to human suffering. In San Francisco it was the Chinese ghetto, behind Nob Hill. I was working several nights a week there with a young priest, and came to the conclusion that I'd rather respond directly to human suffering than perpetuate the wealth of the already wealthy around the world. I preferred to spend my life and energies working with people who were being crushed in a lot of ways."

Guinan quit San Francisco's financial market in 1964 and came East to prepare for the priesthood. The sixties from '60 to '64 had touched him strangely.

"Immediately I had a deep suspicion about the assassination of Malcolm X—probably was more affected by it than the assassination of John Kennedy. I'm not sure why. Maybe that was some of the civil rights effort coming home. I'd read a lot of Malcolm. But I wasn't really involved politically or radically. Maybe it was a first awakening that something was brutally wrong with the racial lineup of the United States. I don't think that reaction to Malcolm's killing was the common American experience."

"You seem to evince particular sympathy," I interrupted, "for the downtrodden of other races—"

"I've worked with many Caucasian poor," Guinan countered. "But the reality is that in any urban center the unemployment, the poverty, the destitution becomes so much higher as racial lines are crossed."

After a year's novitiate, Guinan moved to Washington to study philosophy and theology at St. Paul's College. His first three years with the Paulists included extracurricular ghetto work—time filched dangerously from the books. Guinan fixed on Anacostia, Washington's highest-crime neighborhood and a "significant ghetto, upon which the great urban renewal plan has focused to shift the poor, mainly black." A radical basis to Guinan's philosophy was fomenting. He'd spent the summer of '65 at Berkeley as assistant chaplain, "a great introduction to a more radically political view of dissent just starting to evolve." Thanks to Mario Savio, the Free Speech movement . . . Guinan began counseling conscientous objectors against the contradictions of Vietnam. Nineteen-sixty-eight tipped the emotional balance. "An explosive year for everyone: Tet, Biafra, Chicago, Johnson refusing to run, my working with King, his assassination, Kennedy's death, my traveling to New Hampshire with Eugene McCarthy, Thomas Merton dying—I'd been completing my thesis on Merton's theology of non-violence. That radical non-violence and critical way of looking at socio-economic-theological issues proved helpful in pulling my thoughts together. I came to feel things were much too symptomatic. You were chasing hunger and chasing war and chasing poverty and it was rooted somewhere. In the way economic and social orders evolve."

Guinan decided in his ministry he could not be satisfied with parish or university work. "We had to get radically beyond that, into basic community, basic poverty, basic judicial configurations." In 1969, he presented the Church with a plan stating that upon ordination he would not accept a traditional assignment but wished to be free to establish the Community for Creative Non-Violence. Surprisingly, he received unanimous support.

On August 25, 1967, George Lincoln Rockwell joined the

ranks of the sixties assassinated, and Matt Koehl was thrust into prominence as commander of the American Nazi Party. Rockwell had been murdered by a disgruntled Party member; Koehl had been loyal to the Party since 1960. Koehl sat before a red Nazi banner at Party headquarters in Arlington and reminisced about his life. He wore a tan sports jacket, black slacks, black military shoes, white shirt, black tie, sabre tie clasp, and a swastika in his lapel. His black hair was clipped militarily on the sides but combed full on top, in a rakish pompadour. He affected a small mustache. He spoke quietly, sincerely, winningly. He bared his teeth when excited, exposing yellowed incisors. Koehl was a revolutionary. His Nazis perhaps the last openly militaristic revolutionaries of the sixties. Koehl pursed his fingers as he talked. He was anti-black, anti-Jewish, anti-intellectual, anti-hippie. Like Ed Guinan, he came from a religious background and was forty-two years old.

Within a year and one half, Ed Guinan had moved CCNV's six members from their first address on Washington Circle to Fourteenth Street, where the community expanded to a corps of thirty regulars. Guinan had been immersed in communal life since 1964, so he had a handle on how best to proceed: "What isolated us from most communal groups of the sixties was that we were task-oriented. Our living together was a better way of facilitating that task. Doing political work, judicial work, poverty work, whatever. We weren't hit with people who wanted to sit around and find out who they were, or I-Thou for eighteen hours a day. The average life expectancy of a commune during the nineteen-sixties was thirty days. As soon as too many dishes piled up on the table they split. People jumped into community life without having done a lot of homework. It's like marriage, vocational calling, anything—takes effort to make it great. We were blessed in that we didn't start the other way, saying: Let's get together and live in a community, see what that means, find out who we are, how we interrelate, how we relate to a bigger structure. We had our tasks somewhat defined. Which is the historic way in which all religious communities got going. They didn't necessarily want to live together. Some couldn't stand each other. They opted for that arrangement because it made sense with the task they were doing. It was consistent with their vision. We ended up with a rich community life that came from being in a crunch with other people, over issues, not living-room dialogues."

The first crunch Matt Koehl squeezed through with his Chicago-based Nazi compatriots was in 1960 at a premiere of *Exodus.* That proved Koehl's "coming out party." There was shouting, shoving and not a little fisticuffs. Before that, in a Milwaukee high school, Koehl had carried *Mein Kampf* to irk Jewish classmates and had been summoned before his principal for distributing anti-Semitic, anti-Red literature. He was told he'd best not read *Mein Kampf* and that he could not preach his beliefs. This was 1949 to 1952. Koehl's First Amendment rights were being stepped on. By the time he graduated from high school, his thinking already was "proto-N.S." It would be 1960 before Koehl met with Rockwell to found a Chicago branch of the American Nazis, 1961 before Koehl headed that faction. In the interim he sold encyclopedias.

CCNV had its soup kitchen, its medical clinic, its hospices, its pre-trial house, its political activism, so there were numerous tasks to be accomplished. The age-spread of Community members ranged from two to sixty-five. An average commitment was two and one half years. Most members were college educated, holding at least a B.A. Some were taking time off from college to be educated by the poor. Although families such as Ed and Kathleen's participated, CCNV relied on single volunteers. Guinan saw exposure to poverty as schooling and hoped Community members would go elsewhere and continue work among the poor.

Matt Koehl grew up poor. A second-generation American of German and Rumanian descent, Koehl's father had been a skilled laborer, a machinist and landscape gardener. He had believed in the American dream. There'd been homesteading in the West when he immigrated in 1908—tracts in the Dakotas, mustangs to corral, gold for the mining. "Horatio Alger," Koehl smirked. The upshot had been compromise-life in Milwaukee where Koehl's family was hard hit by the Depression. He'd known meager food, patched clothing. But a "beautiful society," Koehl reflected, white, Aryan, and "truly integrated—not in an interracial sense, but a racial sense." Milwaukee sheltered a sizeable German-American population. Koehl's parents were apolitical despite the presence of a German-American Bund. But they were sensitive to propaganda. "Our party is accused of hate," Koehl said, "but we couldn't ever hate like they hated back then—hatred that was preached for all peoples of the Axis nations." German-Americans were treated suspiciously during World War II and their reaction was often super-patriotism. Koehl recalled a wartime propaganda effort where school children were encouraged to buy war stamps—so many producing a bullet, so many a machine gun, so many a fighter plane. Koehl read newspaper accounts of a "forty-mile road of human ash" constructed by Nazis, and smelled a rat. "I was being lied to. I don't *like* being lied to." Koehl had grown up pro-Jewish. His fundamentalist Protestant training had portrayed Jews as the chosen people, patriarchs in flowing beards and overlong robes. This view was changed once contemporaries were encountered. Koehl's Jewish classmates bothered him tremendously. They seemed "pushy, obnoxious, show-offy." He banded against them. Soon he was distributing anti-Semitic leaflets. Koehl was not worried by blacks until high school. Their numbers had increased in Milwaukee, postwar, as in most American cities. Koehl's Aryan society stood besmirched. Though he'd encountered few blacks, by sixth grade he'd received racist conditioning in a one-room schoolhouse overseen by a white-haired schoolmarm. Koehl was taught that discrepancies in technological development between Aryan and non-Aryan countries were caused by racial configuration. Norway, for example, had fewer natural resources than Uganda, yet Norway was more technologically advanced. Therefore: "The difference must be found in the human resources, in the quality of the people." Koehl spent two years at the University of Wisconsin, Milwaukee, but dropped out. He'd always had difficulty with mathematics; adding things up. An accounting course offered particular trouble. Koehl quit to work construction. His formal education was finished. Koehl's father had not completed eighth grade. He'd wished his son to earn a college degree. That too was part of the American dream.

Ed Guinan stepped up CCNV's political activities throughout the early seventies—encounters in which sixty-odd people were arrested at a shot, pray-ins at the Nixon White House in protest of the Indochina war, blocking entrance lanes to the Pentagon—physically symbolic manifestations of civil disobedience which Guinan saw as linked to his work with community. A majority of CCNV's members were exposed to multiple-arrest situations, and many served time in jail or prison. Yet Guinan began to focus more on economics as panacea, economics and a restructuring of the political order.

"There are soup kitchens and there are medical clinics and there are people who're suffering *because* of an economic-political order that has to be fundamentally changed. When a person can freeze to death three blocks from the White House, and you can see, from the Executive Mansion, people sleeping on hot air grates at ten below zero, it reminds you of Czarist Russia. There, people came begging for crumbs and were gunned down. Here, they're not gunned down, they're ignored. That's less merciful, in a way. And not just a scandal, but an incredible crime. Two blocks from the White House exists terrible poverty. Serious malnutrition. Sickness. Last winter within five weeks eight people froze to death on Washington's streets. Because they had nowhere to go. I don't think a healthy society tramples its sick, its children, its old, its cripples. This one does. Ours is a society which is incredibly sick. We've acted out that sickness in more exaggerated forms, such as Vietnam ... but it's not just those people down at the soup kitchen, they're sick enough. It's the society that's pushed them off the end. Poor people have no rights. To food, shelter, medicine, anything. There are limits to what groups like CCNV can do. We're always distributing scarcity. That's the political situation we're put in by a government which is pathologically disordered, and an economic system where the human being is not considered ... where property is sacred and human beings are way down the list of priorities. If you're part of the GNP, fine. If not, you're a bag of garbage. We have a system which is the most technologically advanced in the world. But as it functions has no sense of justice or compassion for people. It's geared to production. There's no qualitative distinction between what we produce, whether it's Barbie Dolls or MIRV warheads. It's what sells. That's how people are elevated. We reward belligerence, both military and corporate, and real human tenderness we demean. I think that's a fairly good definition of insanity."

Matt Koehl took an aptitude test, out of college, which indicated he might pursue careers in public administration, law, advertising, or the social sciences. Koehl looked hard at these alternatives. Considering his beliefs, where might he go? "All traditional channels were cut off," Koehl said. "In a way my path was laid out for me: I *had* to be a revolutionary." Koehl joined a Marine Corps reserve unit in Milwaukee, went on active duty, then moved to Chicago. There he worked for Compton's Pictorial Encyclopedias, while perusing right-wing organizations and studying National Socialism. Reactionary groups such as We the People proved unacceptable by Koehl's standards. "Their only excuse for political action was to preserve wealth and privilege, they were economic conservatives who were afraid to touch the racial question." George Lincoln Rockwell wasn't. Koehl met him in 1957 at a Knoxville rally of racist dissidents and immediately was impressed. There Rockwell outlined his plan for repatriation of American blacks to Africa, the meeting's most effective presentation. A United White Party emerged from that convention, later to become the National States' Rights Party. Koehl worked with them briefly. Rockwell abstained, however, having already set his mind on an out-front National Socialist organization. In early 1959 he hung a Nazi banner in the window of his Arlington home, floodlighted it, and began taking brickbats.

Rockwell was an ex-navy pilot, the son of a vaudeville comic, who would spin a mesmeric net over his racist colleagues. Koehl, in his reminiscences, painted Rockwell as a poverty-stricken revolutionary, ostracized for his beliefs, hounded from his neighborhood, but relentless in his goals as a National Socialist. He would retreat to the hills like Castro, suffer incarceration in mental institutions, endless harassment by the FBI, and confrontations in the streets before his ideas gained national attention. Koehl became infatuated with Rockwell. He organized the Chicago party in 1960, under Rockwell's supervision, and headed it until 1963 when transferred to Arlington as National Party Secretary. In the meantime, he'd lost his position at Compton's Pictorial Encyclopedias for political activism, discovered corporate racism in hypocritical guise—blacks were "Number Two" customers at Compton's, as were black salesmen—and encountered FBI harassment. Corporate hypocrisy most enraged Koehl. And amused him. "When blacks complain that this is a racist society, they have a point. We're one of the few groups who are honest enough to admit it. Blacks were poor credit risks to Compton's and the company should have been allowed to say: we don't want to sell to blacks. But institutionalized racial hypocrisy is pervasive. Here I was the big bad Nazi and there they were playing games—while condemning me for my openness. That's American business." Koehl accepted the small allowance offered by Rockwell and began working for the Party full-time.

Kathleen had been living at CCNV two years when she and Ed Guinan got married. She'd been there since the soup kitchen's opening, she was as committed to CCNV as Guinan and to the lifestyle that commitment insured—so that their marriage was a union of individuals already fixed upon a life's work. Guinan's position had grown crazier in a community where families loved and he remained celibate, so that his marriage to Kathleen evolved "naturally and organically" as adjunct to the greater family of CCNV. Still, he entertained reservations. He was the sole active priest in Washington working full-time with the poor. He would revert to lay status once married, and felt that a symbolism would be compromised. He would forsake the privileges of parish work and of saying mass; having violated Church law he thus would be disciplined. A priest is ordained forever so he need not forfeit more than his priestly faculties. All Guinan's active ministry had been within the Community, living downtown, working in the soup kitchen; he wasn't affiliated with rectory or parish, he received no direct support from the Church, so his life would hardly change. The support of a family within CCNV made more sense to Guinan than the abstract approval of a distant bureaucracy. He and Kathleen exchanged vows in July, 1974, continuing much as before.

"When I arrived in Arlington," Koehl reflected in *White Power,* the Party publication, "there was no heat in our barracks. Party income was little more than a trickle, and we couldn't afford heating oil. To get warm, we would take turns huddling over a small kitchen toaster. It was all very primitive. We had constant problems with the plumbing. The cook was allotted only three or four dollars a day to feed beans, oatmeal, instant mashed potatoes, powdered eggs, day-old bread and watery soup to a crew of ten to fifteen."

Currently, Matt Koehl received housing, meals and twenty-five dollars a week for his services as commander. In 1963, cash was distributed on a draw system and few provisions existed for regular allowance. Members slept stacked up in bunks at a barracks affectionately known as Hatemonger Hill. Above ruins of a Civil War fort, the Nazis drilled, trained physically and prepped for political rallies. Party mission then, and until 1967, was "publicity at any cost." Good, bad or indifferent. "How do you break through a Jewish-controlled media?" Rockwell mused. "Be newsworthy. If I thought it would do good to run across the White House lawn naked, I'd do it."

"Commander Rockwell would have been a great entertainer," Matt Koehl said. "He had Doc Rockwell's blood in his veins and it served him invaluably." Rockwell hijinks included sneaking a Nazi, costumed in blackface, loincloth, stove-pipe hat and carrying a spear onto the House floor, where he screamed, "I'se the Mississippi delegation and I demands to be seated." Rockwell followed that Nazi with another, who distributed "Back to Africa" boat tickets. Anti-Vietnam demonstrators were doused with red paint, Communist Front speakers were heckled at college assemblies, CORE and NAACP picketers were picketed at a segregated amusement park, Fair Play for Cuba hearings were disrupted, New Left headquarters were stormed at late-sixties moratoriums ... ad infinitum. A lid had been placed on the media, Nazis believed, concerning publicity for extremist groups—white or black. Rockwell did his damnedest to blow it. His life was threatened, he was shot at, beaten; with his cohorts

suffered police brutality, FBI surveillance and anti-racist harassment. Rockwell sent his family abroad to escape harm. Whatever
desires Matt Koehl nurtured for a family of his own were being
subverted by increased Party responsibility. He'd been promoted
to deputy commander, was Rockwell's number two man. In
1967, however, Koehl became engaged to be married. Rockwell's
assassination shelved that option indefinitely. Koehl took over as
Party head. "Hitler was single. Rockwell became single. Neither
could have made it as a married man, not with the top responsibility of a movement on his shoulders. So it is today."

As Ed Guinan lamented the status quo: "We have an en-
chantment with death, mental patients wouldn't take the risks we
do . . . what's more, we have the power to eradicate poverty tomorrow yet we consciously refuse to do that . . . Sadly people,
and systems especially, *need* their slavery, need people below
them so they can know who they are." I thought how different
the communalism of CCNV and the National Socialist White
People's Party was from the Woodstock generation's, whose tribalism had been learned from a three-day mudbath, or the film of
that mudbath, where they'd been manipulated by rock entrepre-
neurs who'd helicoptered from motel to dry stage with no
thought but for theatricality of the event . . . a Woodstock generation whose communalism assumed suburban ideals, remained
suburban in its homogeneity and ignored the inner-city black
who culturally was their founding father. Their commitment, in
most cases, had been to the fulfillment of suburban needs: infantile gratification, free food, dope, the readiest appeasement of
loneliness. Nothing worth spending a life for. Both CCNV and
the Nazis put their asses on the line daily. Their commitment
skirted theatricality and honed in on the disparities at ritual's
base: love and hatred.

In *The White Negro,* Mailer's seminal discourse on hip, published 1957, he'd noted that "since the hipster lives with his hatred . . . many of them are the material for an elite of storm
troopers ready to follow the first truly magnetic leader whose
view of mass murder is phrased in a language which reaches
their emotions . . . the hipster is equally a candidate for the most
reactionary and most radical of movements. . . ." In a sense, the

primitivism of Rockwell's Nazis, their reliance on tribalism and racial purity, was a sixties posture. It smacked of hipsterism. Hitler had founded National Socialism on the atavistic propensity of Aryan peoples, but he might have been a chieftain in equatorial Africa for the shamanism he employed. He had his scapegoats—the Jews, Communists, and Capitalists—he had his swastika as totem, and he had his taboos. He used blood sacrifice. To this animism he added the theatricality of staged rallies in Nuremberg, a medieval town, and World War II technology.* Technology, primitivism, theatricality, rage . . . it was a recipe for the nineteen-sixties. One tasted as hungrily by George Lincoln Rockwell as other sixties revolutionaries.

But how could white primitivism be categorized as hip? In the larger arena, its contradictions explained Vietnam. Sartre had noted in his "Portrait of an Anti-Semite" that a principal component of hatred was a deep sexual attraction to that which one hated. The emotional state an anti-Semite loved *was* hatred. Furthermore, he embraced Manicheanism, a view of existence as the struggle between good and evil. Manicheanism itself masked a profound attraction to evil. Both tenets added up to an intense desire to possess what one most despised. Was the American Nazi, like the Green Beret, a secret white Negro?

Much sixties tension had centered around conflicts between hip and beat, it was nearly as if the decade had been composed by Jack Kerouac and exemplified with his casting of Neal Cassady as eternal hipster and Allen Ginsberg as long-suffering beat. Cassady, a Westerner, a loner, Protestant, spontaneous, physical, remained manic, violent and constantly striving, while Ginsberg, Jewish, a New Yorker, intellectual, religious, pacifistic, mystical and attracted to community was quieter, able to experience peace. The decade seemed to break down into those who would follow Cassady and those who gathered around Ginsberg. At a farther remove it simplified to whether you fought in Vietnam with an A-team of eleven compatriots, isolated on some unspeakable recon, or with half a million communards in the streets of Washington, D.C.

* Louis L. Snyder, *Hitler and Nazism* (1967) Bantam, pp. 74–75.

For seventies revolutionaries such as Koehl and Guinan, the crux had less to do with numbers than means to an end. Both were communards from necessity. CCNV with a proclivity toward beat, the Nazis with a proclivity toward hip. Each had his cross to bear.

That cross was not an insignificant symbol. CCNV as a Christian organization was despised by the Nazis, for they saw its teaching grounded in Judaism, subverted by the Old Testament, a Jewish book, and rendered ridiculous by the teachings of Christ, himself a Jew, who would cloak the indigent, the sick, the criminal, the inferior, in a halo of mercy and love. The Nazis preferred their swastika, a primitive sun symbol reinterpreted as a wheel-like pronouncement of the succession of generations. Post-holocaust, one spelled love, the other hate. Both read: commitment.

For years a swastika adorned the pavement outside an Econowash in Arlington where George Lincoln Rockwell was slain. The Nazis had not painted it. It appeared without explanation, as John Patler had appeared on the Laundromat's roof, expecting Commander Rockwell, extinguishing him with a Party-issue, broom-handled Mauser. Patler had been apprehended within hours, and though convicted, never offered an explanation, never admitted the deed. Matt Koehl's conjecturing ran thusly: Patler was a malcontent, a disenchanted Party member who had been disciplined often, dismissed from the Party twice, and who bore an inestimable grudge against Rockwell. Moreover, Patler had been studying Maoist tracts and "consorting with a Jewess," Koehl believed, "possibly working with the ADL." Patler was of Greek descent, dark-haired, dark-skinned. He resented the Party's blue-eyed members and rebelled against concepts of an "ideal Nordic type." Rockwell tolerated Patler's eccentricities for his talents as an illustrator, badly needed by the Party. He had forgiven Patler on several occasions. It was thought he might have talked with Patler the day of his death. How else, but through conspiracy, might Patler have known Rockwell's whereabouts? It was a question lost to time, as obfuscated by contradictory inquiry as Malcolm's, King's or the Kennedys' deaths.

Ten years later, in the powder keg of Party headquarters, Matt

Koehl—recalling Rockwell's murder—became visibly shaken. "It was like the bottom of the world had fallen out," he said. Then paused, staring the length of the conference table. "That's one time I'd never like to go through again." Koehl touched his forehead. "It was an utter feeling of loss. Before I'd have faced a moment like that I'd sooner been shot myself. And dropped into a grave."

Koehl faltered only an instant that day. He had but to imagine his adversaries' glee at Rockwell's passing and his mood shifted to one of defiance. The press already was composing obituaries of the Party. "I didn't know how or in what manner we'd proceed, but I was determined we would."

George Lincoln Rockwell had intended to be President of the United States by 1973. That ambition had been cancelled by John Patler—who received a twenty-year sentence, who'd be paroled after seven. There was little else but to follow another Rockwell guideline, that of moving the Party from Phase One of its operations—publicity at any cost—to Phase Two—disabusing the public of stereotypic notions concerning American Nazism.

"I don't think there's been a more hated idea than National Socialism in two thousand years," Koehl said. "The subject of a real campaign of hate."

How did Guinan's and Koehl's visions of an ideal future, their divergent commitments toward love and hate, differ or interrelate? Along racial lines, they of course split asunder. But economically, their forecasts were not dissimilar. Both felt a period of chaos was desirable, perhaps imminent, in which the system would totter. The eighties seemed a likely time for this occurrence, as the hiatus of seventies recidivism most certainly would have imbued political lapsarians with renewed vigor. Reactionary groups would not be caught with their pants down this decade. Old hands like the Nazis were ready to orchestrate and direct legions of right-wing neophytes. "We have excellent chances for coming to power in the conditions which will prevail," Koehl predicted.

"The cancer is total," Ed Guinan said. "There's no possibility of this society as fundamentally constructed surviving. It's going to be very messy, *is* very messy, and is in its death throes. I don't see it dying very peacefully. I'm speaking principally of an economic system which went out of date a hundred years ago."

Guinan would like to see "a swift and immediate transition to socialism, where we develop economic rights in this country, on a personal basis—to food, shelter, clothing, medicine—rather than a corporate basis, which starts from the premise that only property holders have economic rights." Koehl's National Socialism would follow similar guidelines, smashing agribusiness, Wall Street, inherited wealth, independent banking, the GNP, corporations, unions, but encouraging private initiative in small businesses and a return to the family farm. A modern update of the medieval guild would be an ideal. Koehl would empty the jails and set up work camps. Guinan already was implementing that, with his pre-trial house and print shop. But where Guinan would wait, proselytizing demonstratively along pacifistic lines, Koehl was prepared to act violently to hasten the system's demise. As a last resort.

First, Koehl would call a second Constitutional Convention where he would "secure the racial foundations of America" by granting citizenship to males of "Aryan" descent and to female Aryans who were willing to bear children. Others—blacks, Chicanos, Indians, Asians, Jews—would be dealt with disparately. "A love of race motivates all National Socialists," Koehl said, "and there is no perfect love without a corresponding hatred of those who would destroy what you love." Koehl dreamed of an America where it would be possible to travel "from California to Maine without encountering any but white people."

Native Americans would be isolated in independent geographical areas, reminiscent of the Indian nations. Blacks (and one assumed Chicanos) would be offered options of "repatriation" or sterilization. Asians proved less a problem, as they herded together. Blacks who wished to raise families could be repatriated to Africa—some region sub-Sahara where irrigation might make agriculture possible. Koehl saw this repatriation as the white man's moral obligation, a humane easing of the White Man's Burden. Blacks over childbearing age could remain in America to live out their lives. "I'd prefer to have a whole ocean between us," Koehl said. The Jewish problem would be less simple to resolve, for there Koehl would be dealing with "enemies of the state" and a worldwide matrix of Zionist malefactors which Koehl saw as the root of Aryan woes.

Judaism sat as confused in Koehl's mind as in most anti-Semites', but his blueprint for expunging Judaism from American culture was not. The National Socialist gripe against Jews held them responsible for the economic straits of world culture, through alleged proclivities toward usury and a backing of an international Communist front. Since Karl Marx was Jewish, all Jews were Marxist, went Party logic. Racially, the issue mushroomed in complexity. Koehl believed that genetics separated Aryan from Jew; not only were Jews inferior, but possibly a human parasite, literally the highest form of parasitic life, biologically geared to bloodsuck Aryan society. "There will be no room for parasites in the world of the future," Koehl said. "Liberalism will be out by the turn of the century. If the Bolsheviks don't decide that, we will."

Koehl would work within a revamped Constitution to smash American Jewry, once the "racial foundations" of the country had been established. Hitler preferred a constitutional approach, Koehl said; it was Lenin who preached violent overthrow. Koehl did not dismiss armed revolution, he would opt for it if necessary and if he thought he could effect it. But the Constitution sufficed. Koehl was not promulgating genocide, he was interpreting those "crimes against the state" which warranted "capital punishment." Jews who were capital offenders would be executed, not because they were Jews but because of offenses. Koehl hinted many Jews might fit that category; those in power, those with wealth and media influence. Such Jews would be encamped for trial and eventually deported or executed. Anyone, white or black, found guilty of treason, of "anti-white crimes," of "undermining the white race," would be executed. Koehl would use as precedent the Nuremberg laws. A TV show like *Roots,* for example, would constitute a crime against the white race. Punishable by death. Dissent could not be tolerated in National Socialist America. Racial community superseded the individual. "I'd like to see a spiritual revolution in America,"Koehl said, "where there's a real sense of community and brotherly love."

Ironically, the "spirituality" of Koehl's commitment, with attendant military hoopla, proved less realistic than Guinan's, with its dogmatic basis in Christian charity and religious community. Koehl's vision of a possible future—no doubt shared by millions of Americans—at present was inefficient and romantic, for it neglected problems at hand. Concentrating on theoretical ideals, it left immediate human suffering and the economic predicament of white and non-white Americans unchallenged. Koehl *longed* for the day when unemployment and "reverse discrimination" would so frustrate whites that they'd hasten National Socialism to power. Guinan likewise prayed for cultural Armageddon, that a new order might arise, but he was prepared to act in the interim. Guinan wanted socialism on a national level, but essentially he remained committed to neighborhoodism—that stepping back to street corners so emblematic of the culture at large, so symptomatic of hip, yet so much more hopeful for the distances traveled. We had been round the globe with World War II, Korea, Vietnam; we had weathered holocaust and were weathering a second-by-second existence of life in the atomic age. What need had we of storm troopers in jackboots, whooping up another military state? Solace and salvable amenities from that brave new world to come might emerge from community; first on a neighborhood level, later nationally. Neighborhoodism and Nationalism were feuding relatives slated for reconciliation in the nineteen-eighties. They would reconcile or America would retreat even further toward primitivism, to nomadic bands of marauding savages, constantly at war, inhabiting skyscrapers as cliff dwellings, ravaging land and cityscape alike until nothing remained but their own starving minions baying at the night.

Maybe Root Boy Slim had it right: *Boogie 'til You Puke.* "I am folk music," Root Boy had proclaimed. "Elvis is gone, the Howlin' Wolf's gone—I am the voice of the people."

Koehl's Nazis certainly had something of the punk rockers about them. Lord knows their vision of the future was stern. Koehl's conception, presently, of a hip evening was to relax with an Aryan history, a few Germanic folk tales, some ancient lore, then taper off with *Mein Kampf.* I had spent six days with Matt Koehl and never seen him outside the Nazi war room. I could at least follow Ed Guinan down the street. "You can't understand Matt Koehl exclusive of the movement," a storm trooper had said, and he might have been describing Ed Guinan. There seemed so little *fun* to each man's life. Such parsed levity. But they were revolutionaries. Who was I to judge? They collected dividends compounded quarterly I could not imagine.

I left Ed Guinan to the warmth of CCNV, to his children, his stalwarts, to the good work he was doing, and hit the sidewalk. Where was the fun? Once responsibilities were accepted, a future realized, community ionized, where was the *action*? Where was hip? Could it be mortised beneath tenons of restraint—or would proclivities toward excess, toward exclusiveness and a separation from community remain cankerous in the once-hipster's heart? The tribe needed point men, that was solace. The tribe needed shamans, lookouts, poets and seers. That was excuse enough for selfish fun. Elvis dead was more alive through his art than he'd been in bloated corpus; religions were forming to his vision of hip. Twenty-three years post-holocaust, Bob Dylan had played Nuremberg, Germany—Bobby Zimmerman from Hibbing, Minnesota, shrieking "Blowing in the Wind" before seventy-five thousand sons and daughters of Third Reichians, at Zeppelin Field, the house that Hitler built. Rock was strong, rock 'n' roll the *logos* of hip was nowhere near death. Even NASA had recognized that, launching Chuck Berry's "Johnny B. Goode" into space for the delight of future galaxies, in company with a stack of world melodies touted as *Earth's Greatest Hits*. Roll over, Beethoven.

A party the following week might impart some focus . . . a futurist's ball thrown by cultural impresario Sam Love. Love was an ex-Mississippi civil rights activist, a founder of Earthday, 1970's great environmental teach-in, a conscientious objector and consultant for energy-related groups around Washington, D.C. He now considered himself a futurist—one more concerned with "dreaming alternative futures" than patching up the old. I'd met Love the previous week. Had been charmed. "Projects I tackle now must be either high impact or *fun*," Love said. "I've fought bureaucracy long enough." Love held a twinkle in his eye. "I was a socialist until I started working for the government," he said. "Socialist, communist, capitalist futures are the same. I've been collecting socialist visions—they're all gloomy. They're raping the earth. Committed to dominating nature through technology, populations through social control. My aim is to increase the schizophrenia in America so that people will start dreaming their *own* futures. We've been controlled too long."

Love spun out a forty-year scenario intimidating for its all-inclusiveness. Love ran convinced that a "colonization of our unconsciousness" had been perpetrated since World War II, a colonization launched at the 1939 World's Fair by corporations which erected pavilions larger than those of any individual country and by merchandizers who mapped the coming generations' future more precisely than had George Orwell. Cars, architecture, interior design, conveniences— all had been programmed since 1939 via ad campaigns which promised nirvana through consumerism, a Ford in every future and more leisure the harder one labored. People must be encouraged "to start dreaming again," Love insisted, any future other than that programmed. We lived in a future conceived by the thirties, forties and fifties, Love said. An archaic and inefficient future, dreamed by dead folks. "The marketing of tomorrow" need be smashed; Love chuckled, but was dead serious.

"I want to teach people to sense the time," he said. The popularity of *Star Wars,* science fiction, spacey jazz and fantasy indicated America's hunger for new visions. The sixties had been a very "now" decade ... existentialist in its drug reveries, recidivistic in its nostalgia. Futurism would eviscerate that. People might start dreaming again. Love had prepared a slide show and lecture—"Visions of Tomorrow"—which would elucidate further, and which he'd premiere at Friday's futurist's ball.

Each guest is requested, but not required, the invitation read, *to appear in a costume exemplifying any vision of the future of humankind, nature or technology which you desire: religious/mystical cults of the future, sports of the future, biological mutations of the future. ...*

I went as an urban guerrilla, nostalgically attired in Special Forces fatigues, knee-high cowboy boots and Anzac hat. Mine was a more optimistic conception. All about were people costumed as Radiation Burns, clones (Rosemary Cloney), Dried Blood, Starving to Death, John Ehrlichman in Navajo buckskins, Opulence, Opulence in Decline, computer terminals ... people sat wired into private sound systems, private universes, anthropological visions of simultaneous barbarism and electronic power. A shaman of the future in prehistoric garb chanted fiercely, to "scare away ICBMs," jingling bells about his ankles. A hundred people were present. Not one positive future was expressed. Not one fun vision. Two cloneys in white tights and plastic affected crowd manipulation with incomprehensible mutterings. They constituted a Mind Patrol.

The setting was a private warehouse near D.C. Farmers' Market, a cold, cement-block interior reminiscent of a fallout shelter misplaced in the breadbox of inner city. A movie screen hung from the wall of a principal, elongated room. Satirical party decorations dangled from overheads, but nothing so intriguing as to deemphasize participants. They constituted a future, sipping wine in plastic glasses, giggling at each other's costumes, clowning for the press (two Washington papers were present), and reminiscing. For most seemed to know each other.

If not personally, by cause or movement. For here were suburbia's children—removed by a decade's activism in politics, art or community. White suburbia exclusively but for one musician, Gene Ashton, a black, who was to thread Love's presentation from stark media blitz to dreamy acceptance of a less theatrical future. For theater was what these costumes expressed. Another manifestation of horse opera recalcitrance or theatrical regressoblige, which dodged commitment and tap-danced about realistic concerns. If Future, like Cowpoke Chic, represented one step back from Vietnam—to theatrical imperatives which had insured that insanity—futurists had a step or so to go. It was the suburbs here, in darkest inner city, and hip had fled. Could Futurism afford much fun?

The brand of theatricality expressed by Love's crowd seemed emblematic of a renewed theatricality, transcultural in pervasiveness. It was reminiscent of that great national awakening ten years past, when *sixties* began permeating suburbia and costumes became uniform of the day. By 1968, everyone wore a costume: soldier, redneck, hippie, bureaucrat. The seventies, so far, had blurred those distinctions; you couldn't read anyone's mind by the stripes on his sleeve. But that was changing. People, post-Vietnam, were regaining identities. Personal identities. No longer anchored to a position, Americans felt free to express diversity . . . through clothing, dance, parties like this. The counterculture now was an establishment, it had some cash, despite recession, and guilt was archaic. A postwar, Depression ethos, sure as shooting.

If what Sam Love posited about thirties' world's fairs proved accurate, he was onto something. Stepping back from Vietnam, and tangentially World War II, America stood mired in a future envisioned by corporate demagogues. To shake completely free, perhaps America had to experience total collapse—not the recession to date, but a breakdown reminiscent of the '29 crash. Bread lines in the streets, mass insanity, a rescinding of hope. Maybe then we'd be free to fantasize brighter futures.

The bread lines were already extant. CCNV's soup kitchen affirmed that reality.

"An autopsy of the American Dream" was what Sam Love planned to undertake tonight. He stood before his audience in space suit and space booties. Slides of impossible futures slid across his movie screen. People yayed, booed, clapped their fists in total unhip. "It's time to reevaluate our images of the future," Love said. "We've grown up with these images planted in our brains: tailfins, flying cars, domed architecture. I think that has to change."

The autopsy had begun. Love made preliminary incisions, flicking slides across the eye, then laid the corpse open with wit, broad strokes of insight.

Most thirties visions had been based on high mobility, he said. "We'd have our own helicopters, rocket belts, robots." Convenience had been a major theme. Particularly along Madison Avenue. Convenience would sell appliances. Appliances would insulate. Nature was something to be feared in these early visions. "The natural elements would be shut out, agriculture would occur in large plastic domes." Participants groaned. Uranium-235 would provide energy for flying cities, walking cities, Love continued. Comic strips like Flash Gordon contributed many of these futuristic ideas. Walt Disney. World's fairs, of course. During shortage periods of World War II, magazines were packed with dream visions of tomorrow: what postwar prosperity might buy. "There's a Ford in your Future," was an advertising theme which ran for twenty years. World War II proved a time of intense marketing propaganda. Nature would be conquered. "The war with nature will finally come to an end in this glorious world of tomorrow." Whoopees. It would be dominated through technology, through energy provided by fusion and breeder reactors, the ultimate harnessing of nature.

This was our future to date. "But something was happening," Love barked. The price of these thirties visions had been a seventies energy crisis. Still we were fed the same old dreams by Detroit. "There's a bankruptcy of imagination among the establishment as to how to deal with the future." The army stood well-prepared, however. "They can run their whole operation at World War II levels, for two years, without having to tap into outside markets."

Agriculture futures, likewise, appeared bankrupt. Ford's tractor division bragged that the farm of tomorrow would be a million-dollar investment. "Bankers are the farmers of tomorrow." Socialist and communist visions of future agriculture were no different than capitalist's, Love smirked. Each wished to dominate nature, entertained specific ideas about cloning, weather modification and social control. Genetic engineering would be commonplace in the farms of tomorrow. The energy to effect these dreams would be nuclear, with its hair-raising proclivities for apocalypse.

Increasing amounts of social control would be necessary to maintain the cobweb economy upon which these technological dreams sprang. But a cobweb was as strong as its weakest strand, Love warned. Likely we'd be faced with major chaos, such as that which occurred during New York's power blackouts. As more people realized consequences of such a high-technology future, they would grope for alternative prospects. Some would return to the land. But most would retreat to the suburbs. "We're literally going to see the suburbanization of the habitable areas of the planet." To avoid high technology, government and corporate futures we'd have to explore new values—values that could control technology.

Efficiency would be one. We needed to revert to a "short-loop society," one which did not want to ship a tomato two thousand miles to ripen it. Solar energy could move us toward the short loop. Bicycles, cable or electric cars could eliminate gas guzzlers. We'd have to reevaluate our relationship to nature. The proper habitats for people could be greenhouses, or biotextures where people might grow their own structures. We'd begin to deal with that divorce from reality which corporate logic had planted in our heads. Solar collectors, bicycles, gardens on roofs, were not accustomed future images. Such images would prove realities only if we talked about cooperation.

Politics might be affected. We might change our conceptions of geopolitics from Rand McNally to bioregionalism, where boundaries could be dictated by plant and animal communities rather than national borders. Native Americans had lived that way. Why not us?

"As these old images of the future begin to break down," Love intoned, "many people will interpret this as a period of chaos. We are going to have to reevaluate our conceptions of chaos. What we have here," Love said, pointing, "is a supernova." Light filled the screen. "You could see this as the destruction of an orderly solar system, and chaos, or you could begin to see this as the birth of a new system. Our task is to initiate the birth of a new system. To do this, we have to liberate our dreams." He paused. "Let us celebrate the dawning of a new age."

Gene Ashton came in on electric sewer pipe. Dancers cloaked in iridescent plastic slid from warehouse shadows. The future was now. Ashton's music pulsed hypnotically. Primitive, yet electronically. Dancers reached into the crowd and coaxed participants. Soon everyone was dancing, a futuristic dirty-bop. A flautist interceded. Ashton switched to congas. Drinks were raised. People shouted, whooped and clapped. I tangoed with

Dried Blood. The flute whinnied encouragement. Sam Love gloated.

"I haven't had this much fun since a civil rights demonstration in Mississippi," he said.

Some future Future seemed assured.

"The deadness we feel is the tithe we pay to the passions of the middle," a participant whispered. It was Starving to Death. He grimaced maniacally.

I thanked him for his tip and faded into the crowd.